What people are
THE BEIGING (

MW00528804

"Race in America has been changing for a while now. Racism is far from gone—it is no less pervasive and vicious than ever it was. But in the current generation have arisen the insistent voices of people whose ancestries and identities are more complex than we ever thought possible. They are not just black, nor just white, nor just brown or yellow or red. They frequently own two or more racial identities—and one of those identities often is mixed. The contributors in THE BEIGING OF AMERICA tells us their stories, in their own voices. Every American should read this book and heed these voices. This is our racial future."

—Paul Spickard, Professor of History, Asian American
Studies, and Black Studies at UC Santa Barbara,
author of *Race in Mind: Critical Essays* (2015)

"THE BEIGING OF AMERICA points towards the next generation of first-person narratives about the "mixed race experience," including those stories that go beyond the usual hand-wringing over census boxes to consider, more pressingly, the where and when of racial justice for peoples of color, 'mixed' or not."

—Michele Elam, Professor at Stanford University,
author of *The Souls of Mixed Folk: Race, Politics, and
Aesthetics in the New Millennium* (2011)

"THE BEIGING OF AMERICA shows the country in full color. The essays successfully crumble dichotomies and reveal the shared humanity underneath."

—Shannon Luders-Manuel, writer/editor, author of
Being Biracial: Where Our Secret Worlds Collide: Educators' Guide (2016)

"THE BEIGING OF AMERICA is a wonderful addition to the canon of mixed race literature. This fine collection of personal narratives further demonstrates both the complexities of the mixed race experience and how multiplicity can be a source of pain and ridicule, as well as pride and self-acceptance. These stories remind us that the fluidity of identities and the demographic shifts that are occurring in the U.S. are not to be ignored or buried, but rather discussed openly and honestly, engaging in the uncomfortable discussions of racism, white supremacy and the power words have even in the most intimate spaces, such as family. These testimonies remind us of the importance to acknowledge and embrace our differences both within ourselves and collectively if we are to become a post-racist society. Bravo!"

—Rudy P. Guevarra Jr., author of
Becoming Mexpino: Multiethnic Identities and
Communities in San Diego (2012)

THE BEIGING OF AMERICA

THE BEIGING OF AMERICA
PERSONAL NARRATIVES ABOUT BEING
MIXED RACE IN THE 21ST CENTURY

EDITED BY
CATHY J. SCHLUND-VIALS
SEAN FREDERICK FORBES AND TARA BETTS

AFTERWORD BY HEIDI W. DURROW

2LP EXPLORATIONS IN DIVERSITY
Sean Frederick Forbes, Series Editor

NEW YORK
www.2leafpress.org

P.O. Box 4378
Grand Central Station
New York, New York 10163-4378
editor@2leafpress.org
www.2leafpress.org

2LEAF PRESS
is an imprint of the
Intercultural Alliance of Artists & Scholars, Inc. (IAAS),
a NY-based nonprofit 501(c)(3) organization that promotes
multicultural literature and literacy.
www.theiaas.org

Edited by: Cathy J. Schlund-Vials, Sean Frederick Forbes and Tara Betts
Copy edited by: Carolina Fung Feng and Gabrielle David

Cover art: Laura Kina
Reprinted with permission from artist.
Copyright © 2006 by Laura Kina. All rights reserved.

Cover design: Cathy J. Schlund-Vials
Book design and layout: Gabrielle David

2LP EXPLORATIONS IN DIVERSITY
Series Editor: Sean Frederick Forbes

Library of Congress Control Number: 2016944187
ISBN-13: 978-1-940939-54-4 (Paperback)
ISBN-13: 978-1-940939-55-1 (eBook)

10   9   8   7   6   5   4   3   2   1

Published in the United States of America

First Edition | First Printing

2LEAF PRESS print books are available for sale on most online retailers in the U.S., U.K., Canada and Australia. Books are also available to the trade through distributors Ingram and GOBI Library Solutions from EBSCO (formerly YBP Library Services). 2LEAF PRESS eBooks are available on Amazon, Barnes & Nobles, Kobo, Google Books, iTunes and other online outlets, and can be purchased direct on 2Leaf Press' website, www.2leafpress.org.. For more information, contact sales@2leafpress.org.

CONTENTS

■■■

The Bill of Rights for People of Mixed Heritage

I have the right:
- not to justify my existence in this world
- not to keep the races separate within me
- not to be responsible for people's discomfort with my physical ambiguity
- not to justify my ethnic legitimacy

I have the right:
- to identify myself differently than strangers expect me to identify
- to identify myself differently than how my parents identify me
- to identify myself differently than my brothers and sisters
- to identify myself different in different situations

I have the right:
- to create a vocabulary to communicate about being multiracial
- to change my identity over my lifetime – and more than once
- to have loyalties and identify with more than one group of people
- to freely choose whom I befriend and love

— Maria P. P. Root (1994)

SERIES EDITOR'S NOTE

■ ■ ■

THE 2LP EXPLORATIONS IN DIVERSITY SERIES encourages an open dialogue, one that poses questions about topics that have either been elided or not delved into as extensively in American society. It's a series about engaging in a novel conversation that re-examines diversity and identity politics in the twenty-first century. It's a series that questions and disrupts the status quo; that breaks long-held codes of silence; that poses uncomfortable questions that often don't have clear-cut answers or solutions. It's a series that explores ideas about the ways in which diversity and multiculturalism will shape ongoing conversations for future generations. It's a series that reaches readers from all walks of life and doesn't seek only to be academic in nature and theory.

The first volume in the series *What Does It Mean to Be White in America?: Breaking the White Code of Silence, A Collection of Personal Narratives* was published in April 2016 and co-edited by Gabrielle David and myself. This collection of eighty-two personal narratives reflects a vibrant range of stories from white Americans who speak frankly and openly about race, not only as it applies to people of color, but as it applies to themselves. In answering the question, some may offer viewpoints one may not necessarily agree with, but nevertheless, it is clear that each contributor is committed to answering it as honestly as possible. It features an introduction by racial justice educator and writer, Debby Irving, and an afterword by award-winning poet, author and scholar, Tara Betts. The purpose of *What Does It Mean to Be White in America?* is to, as Irving points out in her introduction, break the code of silence so we can engage in frank conversations about race.

The second volume, *Black Lives Have Always Mattered: A Collection of Essays, Poems, and Personal Narratives,* edited by Abiodun Oyewole, extends beyond the Black Lives Matter movement's principle concern of police brutality to acknowledge that when affronted with slavery, segregation and Jim Crow, racial injustice and inequality, black lives have always mattered. While many of the contributors in this collection are African American activists, poets, scholars, and writers, there are selections from people who identify as mixed race, from those of the Latino and African diasporas and white activists. In these seventy-nine selections divided into five sections, a classroom workshop setting is enacted on the page. It's a learning experience in which the poetic, essay, and personal narrative forms speak to one another about embracing a diversity of ideas even if one *thinks* one knows all there is to know about race in American society.

Similarly, the third volume, *The Beiging of America: Personal Narratives About Being Mixed Race in the 21st Century* seeks to extend this conversation. Its title was inspired by Hua Hsu's 2009 article in *The Atlantic* titled "The End of White America?", where he notes, "According to an August 2008 report by the U.S. Census Bureau—those groups currently categorized as racial minorities—blacks and Hispanics, East Asians and South Asians, will account for a majority of the U.S. population by the year 2042."[1] In 2003, when I was a senior in college, there was a discussion about race in one of my classes. I can't recall the text we were reading, but there was a white male student who mentioned that the white race was diminishing in the U.S. I remember his tone was elegiac and filled with deep anxiety and concern. Some three years later, I remember having a conversation with a white man who stated that as the races continue to mix in America there would be an end to racism. I soon began to be the one who was filled with anxiety and concern because this solution seemed to be antinomy and too simplistic.

Alexandros Orphanides stated on his NPR commentary titled "Why Mixed Race Americans Will Not Save the Country":

> ...but this hope that a mixed race future will result in a paradise of interracial and ethnically-ambiguous babies is misleading. It presents racism as passive—a vestigial reflex

that will fade with the presence of interracial offspring, rather than as an active system that can change with time.[2]

At the core of this argument is the refusal to admit the role that the system of white supremacy plays in racial identity politics; racial mixture does not eradicate racism and white supremacy, it makes it more complex. In a perfect world scenario, one could fervently believe that racial mixture can indeed end racism, but this scenario suggests that conversations are not necessary, or rather that they are too disruptive and don't provide meaningful solutions. There are conversations on topics that many don't like to engage in, or choose not to engage in, but they need to remain topics for open discussion, whether they are pleasant or not.

Often I have found myself in conversations about race with colleagues, friends, and relatives in which I have been told, "Why is it so important for you to always point out the differences?" In my response, I try to articulate the fact that our very differences unite us and demonstrate our diversity of beliefs, ideas, knowledge and values. As the poet and scholar Audre Lorde reminds us, "to break the silence and bridge some of those differences between us, for it is not difference which immobilizes us, but silence. And there are so many silences to be broken" (44).[3]

No one group can eradicate the harmful stings of racism. *The Beiging of America* offers first-person narratives that some readers may or may not relate to or agree with, but at the heart of this anthology are writers who have willingly engaged in reflections about the complexities of being mixed race in the twenty-first century. Conversations on complicated and uncomfortable topics such as race must and will continue. ∎

— Sean Frederick Forbes
Series Editor
Thompson, CT
May 2017

I would like to thank my father and stepmother Hermes Delano Forbes and Luisa Elberg-Urbina, my mother Teresa Mercedes Shah, and my partner Peter MacKay for all of their support, love, and guidance over the years. Special thanks to Anna Ziering for helping me with the writing process. I am forever grateful to Gabrielle David for her unwavering belief and support of the 2LP Explorations in Diversity series, and I am indebted to Cathy Schlund-Vials, a dear colleague, friend, and mentor, and to Tara Betts, a fellow poet in arms. ■

Works Cited

[1] See Hsu, Hua. "The End of White America?" https://www.theatlantic.com/magazine/archive/2009/01/the-end-of-white-america/307208/, accessed April 1, 2017.

[2] See Orphanides, Alexandros. "Why Mixed race Americans Will Not Save the Country." http://www.npr.org/sections/codeswitch/2017/03/08/519010491/why-mixed race-americans-will-not-save-the-country, accessed March 9, 2017.

[3] Lorde, Audre. "The Transformation of Silence into Language and Action." *Sister Outsider: Essays and Speeches.* (New York: The Crossing Press, 1984). p. 44

ACKNOWLEDGMENTS

■ ■ ■

THIS COLLECTION OWES an enormous debt to Gabrielle David and Sean Frederick Forbes, whose respective visions are undeniably responsible for bringing this project "into being." A true publishing force, Gabrielle's creative tutelage has been no less than extraordinary; analogously aspirational is Sean's indefatigable insistence that such a collection was necessary and urgent. It was through Gabrielle's skillful prodding with her sagacious advice that we, as willing editors, quickly moved the project from provocative idea to evocative book. As the series editor for 2Leaf Press's "2LP Explorations in Diversity" initiative, Sean provided at very key moments, reminders of the collection's scope vis-à-vis a more expansive artistic conversation about the role of difference in the making of contemporary U.S. identity. We want to also thank Ruby Perlmutter, whose technical expertise was integral to publicizing at specific stages the project's multivalent aims and multifaceted agendas.

Notwithstanding considerable diversity, and despite the uniqueness of authorial voices and perspectives, the firsthand accounts included in *The Beiging of America, Personal Narratives about Being Mixed Race in the 21st Century* are connected via each writer's willingness to engage – with unparalleled candor and unmatched honesty – the complicated topic of mixed race. We are therefore beholden to each of the contributors in *The Beiging of America*, whose willingness to both begin and be the subject of these difficult conversations renders visible an unequaled generosity of imagination and spirit. It is their stories that quite inarguably occupy this anthology's "center stage."

Last, but certainly not least, this type of work cannot happen without the support of family, friends, who to varying degrees make possible our work. Cathy would like to thank her parents–Charles and Ginko Schlund–who consistently remind her why doing such work matters; her twin brother, (also named) Charles, who similarly keeps her ground; and her husband, Chris Vials, a model partner and best friend. Tara would like to thank her parents Maureen Terrell and Bennie H. Betts Jr. ■

—February 2017
Cathy J. Schlund-Vials and Tara Betts

INTRODUCTION

■ ■ ■

Cathy J. Schlund-Vials
Sean Frederick Forbes and
Tara Betts

What We Are: Three Perspectives on Being Mixed Race in America

Almighty God created the races white, black, yellow, malay and red, and he placed them on separate continents. And but for the interference with his arrangement there would be no cause for such marriages. The fact that he separated the races shows that he did not intend for the races to mix.

— Judge Bazile, *Commonwealth v. Loving,* January 22, 1965.[1]

I believe all Americans, no matter their race, no matter their sex, no matter their sexual orientation, should have the same freedom to marry....I am still not a political person, but I am proud that Richard's and my name is on a court case that can help reinforce the love, the commitment, the fairness, and the family that so many people, black or white, young or old, gay or straight, seek in life. I support the freedom to marry for all. That's what Loving, and loving, are all about.

— Mildred Loving, June 12, 2007
(on the fortieth anniversary of *Loving v. Virginia*)[2]

Recollecting Mixed Race Childhoods

LOCATED ON THE GEORGIA/FLORIDA state line, roughly forty-five minutes from Tallahassee, in Lowndes Country, Valdosta, Georgia is in many ways a typical Southern city. Incorporated almost eight months before the start of the American Civil War on December 7, 1860, Valdosta would – over the course of the conflict—serve as a refuge for those escaping the war's ever-growing fronts; indeed, as a wartime sanctuary, Valdosta's population swelled during General Sherman's fateful "March to the Sea," a scorched earth policy which culminated in the seizure of Savannah, Georgia on December 10, 1864. During Reconstruction (1865-1877), more than one hundred newly freed African Americans emigrated from Lowndes Country to Liberia; however, many stayed, working as sharecroppers and tenant farmers in nearby plantations. As the nation bore witness to the rise of Jim Crow segregation in points west and north, Valdosta (along with close-by Brooks County) became a dangerous place for African American denizens: from 1880 to 1930, Brooks County had the highest number of lynchings in the state; more than 500 African Americans fled; and by 1922, the Ku Klux Klan was openly holding rallies in Valdosta.

In 1983, my family and I relocated to Valdosta from Suffolk, England; we had previously been stationed at Leakhenheath RFB. At age eight, I was thoroughly unaware that there was such a thing as "the American South"; admittedly, when my father told us we were moving to Georgia, my first thought was that we were going to Eurasia. I did not know at the time that this would be my father's last deployment: a career Air Force man, Charles Schlund was a CMSGT sent to Valdosta's Moody Air Force Base. My mother, a Japanese woman, was less than enthusiastic about moving so close to Alabama. Soon after she and my white father married, they made a cross-country trip that took them through the so-called "Heart of Dixie," where they attempted to eat at an off-the-highway restaurant. They waited for about one hour before leaving and they were not served; they endured what my father described as "knife-sharp looks" and, as my mother recalls, the meanest people she ever encountered. That had occurred almost twenty years prior to my parents' return to the South with us: two mixed race Cambodian American adoptees.

Of all the places I have lived—Florida, Texas, Massachusetts, Connecticut, and Pennsylvania—Valdosta, Georgia was incontrovertibly the most formative. It was here I learned what it meant to be different, unwanted, and othered: my brother and I were the only Asian Americans in our elementary school, and it often felt like we were the only ones of Asian descent in the city. This sense of "nobodiness" (to access Martin Luther King's evocative characterization) operated in stark contrast to our previous experiences "on base." On base meant having neighbors whose parents were of different races and children who were, as my mother repeatedly said, "half and half." On base meant being in classrooms filled with kids who, like me and my brother, were not white and who had moved every two years; as a childhood game of brinksmanship, we would rattle off all the places where we had been stationed. The winner was the child who had gone to what we deemed the most "exotic" locales (usually Okinawa).

By contrast, "off base" was alienating, unfamiliar, and inhospitable. The comforting sameness of military housing, wherein all houses looked alike and all lawns were manicured, gave way to homes of different sizes and unkempt yards. Residential diversity, however, was by no means replicated demographically: this was a white neighborhood. Though I knew we had neighbors, I never saw them. And, the children who lived on our block and in our vicinity were not interested in making any type of acquaintance. Such a sense was repeatedly confirmed on bus rides to and from Sallas Mahone Elementary, which happened to have a Smurf as its mascot. We were repeatedly asked if we had "peed in cokes," if we knew kung fu, if we ate dogs, and if our mother – due to our mixed race status – was a prostitute. These questions may initially strike a strange chord for those accustomed to a post-racial, post-Obama era; however, it was the 1980s, and the nation was dealing with the aftermath of the Vietnam War and the U.S.-Japan trade war. Not surprisingly, my brother and I were – out of necessity – each other's best and only friend. The single fond memory I have involves eating boiled peanuts – the saltiness of the snack seemed perfectly suited to the oppressive humidity of the place; and the depressed mushiness of the shell aptly reflected what I recall as one of the darkest times of my life.

Despite profound isolation, my parents – in hindsight – were the ones who had to y the heaviest of burdens insofar as they were, due to racist incidents, forced to tell their children that there were people out there who did not like "our family" and hated "our kind." It was July 1984. I don't remember the exact date, though I do remember what happened that day. As we ate our strawberry Pop Tarts, my father told us over breakfast that we were to stay indoors. Defiant, I ran outside and noticed a black mark on our lawn. And though I didn't realize why at the time, our orange station wagon looked different. Apparently, someone affiliated with the Klan had come during the night and poured gasoline on our lawn in the shape of a cross; that person – or group of people – also keyed our car with phrases telling us to "go back to our country," "God hates mongrels," and "the Lord hates race mixers." We relocated to Austin, Texas the following month. Though I know that my father had officially retired, and I acknowledge that he had likely found his job at Lockheed Martin prior to the discovery of such hate-filled vandalism, I still connect by way of cause and effect the attack on our interracial family, and how our family was forced to move out west.

Such displacementts – which assume the form of traumatic memory and take on the registers of homelessness – ineludibly encapsulate my earliest experiences with being "mixed race." However, as the essays in this collection make clear, the isolation of being multiracial within a still-monoracial world is by no means singular to the reflections of a biracial Cambodian American academic; nor is being mixed race something that must remain hidden. Instead, the contributors of this collection through narrative honesty bring to light a diverse yet interconnected community; they also accentuate a profound love that – when situated against a landmark Supreme Court case – ultimately speaks to the undeniable "beiging of America."

—Cathy J. Schlund-Vials
Willimantic, CT
March 3, 2017

Remembering *Loving v. Virginia*

WHAT FOLLOWS IS EQUAL PARTS love story and courtroom drama. It is a tale of interracial romance in the face of seemingly unbeatable odds. Last, but certainly not least, this is an account of Jim Crow segregation, long-standing bigotry, and unabashed U.S. racism.

In June 1958, Richard Perry Loving (white) and Mildred Delores Jeter (non-white) decided to marry. The couple traveled ninety-six miles from their home in Central Point, Virginia to Washington, D.C. At the time, interracial marriages were illegal due to the provisions of Virginia's Racial Integrity Act, which barred unions between those classified as "white" and "colored."[3] The newlyweds eventually made their way back to Central Point, where they stayed with Mildred's parents. This was a temporary arrangement.

Richard had promised his wife a house, and he was making good on that promise: the house was being built and it was only a matter of time before they would have their own home.

Or, so they thought.

On July 11, 1958, in the early hours of morning, local authorities and police came to arrest the Lovings, who had allegedly violated Sections 20-58 and 20-59 of Virginia's anti-miscegenation act. In particular, Section 20-58 prohibited interracial couples who had married out-of-state return to Virginia; Section 20-59 categorized miscegenation as a felony offense. Pregnant with their first child and facing the possibility of prison, Mildred and Richard pled guilty to "cohabitating as man and wife, against the peace and dignity of the Commonwealth." Husband and wife were both given one-year prison sentences; the sentences was suspended provided the Lovings did not return as a couple to Virginia for the next twenty-five years. The forced exile from Central Point proved unbearable for Mildred, who longed for the comfort of family, friends, and home. Defying state law, the Lovings returned to Virginia and were promptly arrested. The Lovings maintained their innocence, stressing that it was the law – not them – that was immoral and unjust.

This case would eventually make its way to the nation's highest court. When the U.S. Supreme Court heard the opening arguments for *Loving v. Virginia,* sixteen other states had similar anti-marriage, anti-miscegenation laws. Undoubtedly inspired by the inclusionary politics of the Civil Rights movement, the Supreme Court unanimously ruled in the Lovings' favor: on June 12, 1967, their conviction was overturned and the Racial Integrity Act deemed unconstitutional. And while this may appear to be a simple case of star-crossed lovers, at stake in the ruling was what Chief Justice Earl Warren characterized as "one of the 'basic civil rights of man,' fundamental to our very existence and survival." According to Warren:

> To deny this fundamental freedom on so unsupportable a basis as the racial classifications embodied in these statutes, classifications so directly subversive of the principle of equality at the heart of the Fourteenth Amendment, is surely to deprive all the State's citizens of liberty without due process of law. The Fourteenth Amendment requires that the freedom

of choice to marry not be restricted by invidious racial discrimination. Under our Constitution, the freedom to marry,
or not to marry, a person of another race resides with the
individual and cannot be infringed by the State.[4]

The "freedom to marry, or not to marry" was, as recent history makes clear,
not fully resolved. LGBT couples struggled for recognition and the right to
marry; it is perhaps not surprising that the *Loving* case figured keenly in the
Supreme Court's deliberations about same-sex marriage in *Obergefell Et Al.
v. Hodges, Director, Ohio Department of Health, Et. Al* (2015).

Echoing Warren, Justice Anthony M. Kennedy stressed in his June 25,
2015 majority opinion that "No longer may this liberty be denied. No union
is more profound than marriage, for it embodies the highest ideals of love,
fidelity, devotion, sacrifice, and family. In forming a marital union, two people
have become something greater than they once were."[5] This sense of "two
people…becom[ing] something greater than they were" is inadvertently at
the forefront of this anthology, which explores by way of personal remem-
brance the legacies of anti-miscegenation and *Loving v. Virginia*. To clarify,
the law against interracial marriage was not only about unions; it was–as
the very definition of "miscegenation" underscores–about the product of
these unions: mixed race children. Defined as "the interbreeding of people
considered to be of different racial types," "miscegenation" as derogatory noun
encompassed "aberrant" relationships which challenged white supremacist
assertions of racial inferiority.

While *Loving v. Virginia* has been celebrated as a triumph of rights over
racism, what is less remembered is the fact that Mildred Loving never identified
as African American. As Arica L. Coleman recounts in a 2004 interview, Mildred
stressed, "I'm not black. I have no black ancestry. I am Indian-Rappahannock.
I told the people so when they came to arrest me."[6] In emphasizing her Native
identity, Mildred–as Coleman makes clear–quite purposefully accessed a
"loophole" in the aforementioned Racial Integrity law. Termed the "Pocahontas
exception," the law allowed for those with 1/16th Native ancestry to assert a
"white" status due to the fact that so many "First Families of Virginia" claimed a
direct lineage to the mythic Powhatan figure. Correspondingly, Mildred would
be considered "white" and her marriage to Richard would be legal.

Despite the legal efficacy of Mildred's Native identity, she has historically been cast as black; such castings lay bare a familiar racial essentialism which fails to accommodate those of us who do not fit neatly in a world defined by enduring binaries and singular racial categories. To be "mixed" has always been linked to the nation's many race-based contradictions. Jim Crow anti-miscegenation laws insisted on the strict separation of the races. However, these acts strategically forgot the realities of slavery, a "peculiar institution" which rendered the mixed progeny of master-slave relationships enslaved people. Such state mandates failed to acknowledge those individuals who chose to "pass"; the very ability to do so is predicated on having a mixed parentage. Whereas such laws tactically disremembered very real histories of intermixture, the U.S. Census has functioned as an inconsistent site wherein mixed race people are statistically recollected: the 1850 U.S. Census contained the category "Mulatto"; "Octoroon" and "Quadroon" were added in 1890; and, most recently, the 2000 U.S. Census included the classification "Multiracial." While census categories have shifted from decade to decade, what has remained constant is the hypervisibility of race as a discernible site of difference. These "discernible sites of difference" evocatively foreground the narratives contained in *The Beiging of America,* which – in the face of different histories, varying accounts, and multifaceted perspectives – consistently touch on issues of identification, affiliation, and classification.

Writing (as) Mixed Race

SOME OF MY EARLIEST UNDERSTANDINGS of race are couched in people taking pause at my family and the fact that I exist. I was born in 1974. I still remember my mother saying that there were race riots in the small town of Kankakee, Illinois before I was born, and even today I could never picture that happening. What I did start to see were the differences between black and white neighborhoods, especially after the factories that employed most people began to close. The resources moved to the whiter neighborhoods, where people made more money and remained employed.

Most of the block where I grew up has disappeared. In fact, the entire building where my grandparents' tavern with the apartment upstairs, where I lived for the first thirteen years of my life, is gone. It is a green, grassy field now, dotted sometimes with dandelions in the spring. Some people might wonder what this has to do with mixed identity, and I think about how my mother was the only white person in that neighborhood. How I grew up in a place where blackness was the norm, until I attended private Catholic school where blackness was not. One of my friends in first grade was a young Portuguese boy named Nathan, probably because we were both markedly different from our classmates. My brothers and I left Catholic schools behind when my parents divorced.

Oddly enough, when we moved into Section 8 apartments near I-57, we saw more Mexican and white people than we ever had throughout my childhood. As this shift occurred, I think my brothers and I had our share of experiences regarding race. My brothers and I had been called niggers at least once, a word we had only joked about a little at home in private, because it was a curse word, and it was only funny when Richard Pryor said it on the albums our parents played in the living room after we were supposedly asleep. When I went to junior high school, I saw how girls wanted to criticize me and call me "white girl" because of my grades, but not typically because of how I looked. If my complexion came up at all, I was light-skinned or "high yellow." At the same time, there were girls who chased my light-skinned brothers. Since I always thought that people found love where they can luckily find it, I let it be, but part of me has always wondered if self-hatred always extends such deep-rooting tentacles. It wasn't until our parents died, and my brothers and I were talking about race as adults that the three of us realized that we saw a range of complexions as "black." Calling each other "African American" is so formal it is almost laughable, and "mixed" fell under that category of black as well. Part of the realization that we felt the same was informed by what my brothers and I saw in our hometown of Kankakee, when we saw our parents change and disappear, much like the place we knew as our childhood stomping grounds.

During our childhood, we only knew a handful of kids our age who would have been deemed "mixed" but now, almost every family we saw had a black relative with them or there were much tanner children following them closely. As these families have gotten darker, the jobs have not returned and the way people get treated has not improved. In fact, there are more empty lots, and it constantly reminds us that the places where people have access have consistently been predominantly white spaces. My brothers and I don't necessarily use words like "predominantly," but we knew that people perceived us differently if they thought we were white, or based on the company that we kept. Most of our company was black. Usually, if you saw us with our mother, people barely looked in our direction. My youngest brother was often spoken to in Spanish when Mexican people encountered us, but every time we were in a group with other black people, we clearly weren't treated any differently than other black people. I did meet white people who saw me with the same color and hair texture as my mother, and they enjoyed talking to me about books, movies, school, and other subjects, until they saw where I lived. Except for when I briefly married, I've always lived in places where black people live, so inevitably when a white person came to pick me up or dropped me off at my house, I would often hear "You live here?" or "Do you feel safe?" The coded language of race would rear up its head, and because I know I might be less threatening, I have often said, "Why? Are you afraid? I'm fine." I adopted this stance after a girl in a community college course that I took in high school drove me home. When she stopped in front of my mother's house, and she saw my black boyfriend, she stuttered through an excuse of why we couldn't go to the movies together next week. I had almost wished it wasn't so predictable, but at least I knew what type of person she was. Instances like this still remind me of how my mother was told by several people how she made her children's lives more difficult by having children with a black man. She was told this by white and black people.

However, as I have matured, and eventually taught at and visited schools, I saw more and more people who looked like me. Some of those students were just like me, but they encountered people who still saw them as problematic, confused, and misfits. Then there were others who were grouped into this ideal composite of what the future will look like, and many of us are aware of how faulty that way of thinking is when the traditional old school race problems have not abated. In Lauren Michele Jackson's 2017 *Buzzfeed* article "Why a New Mixed Race Generation Will Not Solve Racism," Jackson confronts what has been billed as a balm for race relations as a paper tiger:

> In advertising, on film, and on TV, there is a common prefer-
> ence for multiracial-looking people, along with the belief that
> they represent a utopian political future. Why do multiracial

children so often function as the antonym for racism? What is the political value of an interracial relationship? The notion that cream-colored babies will save the world is a popular one. Unfortunately, it's a myth.

When Jackson plainly stated that people – defining themselves as multiracial, interracial, mixed, biracial, multicultural, or other – would not solve racism by somehow diluting or eliminating race as it currently exists, she magnifies an important point. Race (and racism) does not disappear when people mix with other races. In fact, mixed identity complicates the discussion. Mixed race identity has the potential to enter family decision-making on a daily basis, as is evident in many of the essays here, which cover a broad span of African American, Asian, Caribbean, European, Latinx, and Native cultures. Although these essays show us how mixed race identity entails similar encounters within families with colorism and discrimination, there are moments of pride. These writers do not seem at all like Junot Diaz' short story "How to Date a Brown Girl (Black Girl, White Girl, or Halfie)" where girls can be grouped by stereotypes, even as the Dominican speaker tries to deny the Africa running through his hair. There are moments that defy the "tragic mulattoes" refusal on two different fronts by either culture or race. Many of the contributors find stable footing, and know exactly where they stand.

Those were the stories that I was waiting for and longed to hear. I started to see it in the novels of Mat Johnson and Danzy Senna, in the poems of Natasha Trethewey, and in songs from Cree Summer's *Street Faerie.* I started to see more of myself on the page when I met other writers like the ones on these pages – Janet Stickmon, Ross Gay, Adrian Matejka, John Murillo, Lisa Marie Rollins, Chelsea Lemon Fetzer, Rosebud Ben-Oni, and too many others to name here. It was as if all the people who were coming of age post-civil rights movement were passing each other in the constantly commingling circles of writers and creators. Hopefully, as readers explore this book they will see a range of themselves too – personal essays from people who occupy almost every major region of the United States, men and women, queer and straight, darker and lighter, bone straight and kinky, all approaching this behemoth of identity and claiming their firm positions in the world without sounding like "Kumbaya" or a vintage Coca-Cola commercial aimed at teaching people how to find harmony. Consider these pages a glimpse into the future with a resolute handle on the present, as each essay walks you through the circuitous misconceptions, and takes you to the clearing where the landscape is not nearly beige, or monotone.

—Tara Betts
Brooklyn, NY
March 3, 2017

Writing and Living as Racially Ambiguous

FROM AS EARLY AS I CAN REMEMBER, I experienced different periods in which I strategically claimed, like a bower bird, my many racial and ethnic heritages. My full name – "Sean Frederick Forbes" – is confounding precisely because it fails to accommodate my mixed identity. It bears no resemblance to my mother's Spanish name – Teresa Mercedes – nor does it cohere with my father's name (Hermes Delano). However, my name does connect to my parents' respective surnames: Robinson (for my mother) and Newball (for my father). When I asked my parents why they named me Sean Frederick, my mother stated it was because she liked the Scottish actor Sean Connery; *Never Say Never Again* was a popular film while she was pregnant with me. My father recently told me that my name reflected his own desire that I more easily "blend-in" with white American society.

Despite my father's initial desire that I "blend-in," my mixed race experiences make visible the degree to which I am read by others as problematically *blended*. Racially ambiguous, I am more than accustomed to the "What are you?" question; I am likewise used to being the object of ethnic casting, embedded in declarations that "I *must* be Dominican, or Egyptian, or Israeli, or Palestinian, or Puerto Rican, or Turkish." This latter point was evident in the following memory. Once, while visiting family in Stuttgart, Germany, three Egyptian men began speaking to me in Arabic. When I explained that I wasn't Egyptian, they switched linguistic registers and argued with me in English, insisting I was denying my Middle Eastern roots. I can recount many other explicit scenarios, but what remains implicit is that the confusion concerning my identity is inextricably linked to a complex, layered, and vast family history; such intimate narratives, as I subsequently maintain, intersect with a larger American history of racial mixing.

I first embraced the fact I was "mixed" in elementary school. As a young child, I initially sought to evade the complicated question of identity. In my first two years of high school, I claimed to be "Latino" (Colombian to be exact); in my final two years, I shifted to identifying as black (specifically Afro-Caribbean). I now identify as Afro-Latino, though such a claim necessarily omits my Anglo-Scottish ancestry. A more accurate characterization would therefore involve a declaration of being an "Afro-Latinx-Anglo-Scot" subject, which lays bare the truth of my being vis-à-vis many diasporas.

To clarify, my maternal and paternal grandparents, as well as my mother, were born in Isla de Providencia or Old Providence, a mountainous Caribbean island that is part of the Colombian department of the Archipelago of San Andrés, Providencia, and Santa Catalina. Providencia is east of Nicaragua and south of Jamaica; its total landmass is roughly five miles with a current population of 5,000. Many inhabitants claim West African, European, and mainland Colombian ancestry. It was the site of an English Puritan colony in 1629 established by the Providence Island Company; the territory was briefly taken by Spain in 1641. Since the end of Spanish rule, Providencia has been embroiled in a series of political battles involving Nicaragua and Colombia, which continue to fight over which nation has rightful ownership of the three islands. Such contestations over ownership, indicative of a multinational history of conquest, migration, and movement, uncannily intersect with the uncertainties embedded in my own mixed race identity. At the same time, while this history is seemingly unique to Providencia, it is one that coheres with the history of mixed race people in the United States, which—as this collection makes clear—involves multiple accounts of immigration, migration, and encounter.

My grandmothers frequently reminded their children and grandchildren that there was more European blood in our veins than African. I used to suck my teeth with incredulity whenever they made these claims: it seemed they both wanted to perpetuate the myth of our ancestry as largely white and European. Nevertheless, when I began to trace the Robinson-Forbes-Newball family lineage, there was considerable truth to my grandmothers' claims; more often than not, our family tree was marked by Anglican and Eastern European surnames like Venner and Birelski. Perhaps a DNA test from 23andme could help solve this puzzle that I have been trying to assemble for years, but then again, it might not. One of my colleagues grew up believing that his maternal and paternal families were mostly German based on family lore. His DNA test proved he was largely Irish and Scottish with less than 10 percent German ancestry, yet his surname and his family traditions and experiences prompted him to feel as if he belonged to a largely German culture and ancestry.

In the face of ongoing uncertainty, I sometimes wonder whether there are advantages or disadvantages to being mixed race; the fact that I have tactically chosen various identities over the course of my mixed race lifetime intersects with a human instinct to belong. Indeed, while I assert my mixed race heritage, I often find myself racialized as black or Latinx; such binaries are predicated on the ways in which others "read me" and refract a situatedness that is very much a reality for those of us who inhabit in-between ethno-racial spaces. I have noticed moments in which if I am with a group of African American or Afro-Caribbean people I will either affect black vernacular speech or an English-based patois to demonstrate that I, too, belong. If I am amongst Latinx people, I will speak more Spanish and sometimes Spanglish. I have caught myself in situations wherein I glorify my European ancestry to white friends. It hadn't occurred to me until I began to edit this anthology the many ways in which I had actively sought to be included as a way to challenge derogatory terms such as "half-breed," "mongrel," "tragic mulatto," and "mutt."

According to sociologist Chandra D. L. Waring, such terms associate "people with animals, questioning the very *humanity* of biracial persons, which is a common theme in racist ideologies" (303).[7] It rarely occurred to me that, in the aforementioned instances, I was actively attempting to prove my "humanity" to others who weren't bi/multiracial. An older white man once told me that he never agreed with "miscegenation" because it caused problems for the child, and asked how their parents could be so selfish as to not think about the child's well-being in society. This was also the same person who vehemently and hypocritically denied the existence of racism in American society. This problematic compartmentalization and ongoing classification of mixed race people is provocatively explored in Natasha Trethewey's 2012 collection of poetry *Thrall,* which concentrates its artistic attention on the personal, historical, social, and political tensions inherent in being mixed race. These tensions are most keenly examined in a four-sequenced poem titled "Taxonomy," which is inspired by a series of four *casta* paintings by Juan Rodríguez Juárez that depict the hierarchical system of race classification created by Spanish elites during the post-Conquest period in the eighteenth century. In the second section of "Taxonomy," Trethewey presents a family portrait: a Spanish man and a black woman who have produced a mulatto son. The final lines of the poem state:

"... The boy is a palimpsest of paint –
layers of color, history rendering him

that precise shade of in-between.
Before this he was nothing: blank

canvas – before image or word, before
a last brush stroke fixed him in his place."(21)[8]

Trethewey captures the reader's attention by directing the gaze of the entire painting to the innocent child born of this union, who is unaware that he is already categorized and involuntarily fixed to a specific racial space and place.

While I have spent a lifetime being "mixed race," I am also a (homo)sexed body; such intersections complicate an already convoluted subjectivity. "The body is, after all, how we determine what race, gender, and sexual orientation we *think* someone is and therefore, it has strong implications for how they will be treated" (Waring 305). I have been told by gay men, both white and of color, that my features are "exotic." With its sexual connotations, the hint of fantastic abjection, its feminized focus on the gazed-upon flesh, "exotic" trips wires of language, body, color, and gender, wires strung in childhood. I grew up in Southside Jamaica, Queens in a predominantly African American neighborhood in New York City. I was teased by my black peers because of my "good hair" and "light skin," features that are often associated with white standards of beauty. I was often asked – in an overtly sexual way by older teenage boys and men in the community – if I had a sister because they were positive that she was a "dime-piece," and that she would give them some "fine trim." I was often called "pretty boy," a term that was both complimentary and critical, facilitated certain sexual and sometimes reproductive expectations such as "with those high cheekbones and those almond-shaped eyes, you need to have some babies."

Such personal experiences with (non)belonging, coupled with the social and political dimensions of being "mixed race," function as an additional through-line for the varied pieces which comprise this anthology. It is a collection that provides an imagined community space for mixed race people to share their experiences. It is a space that does not revel in exclusivity or in the notion that mixed race people are somehow special or superior or detached from larger social and political issues. While there can be a strong sense of commonality and solidarity with other mixed race individuals, not all of the narratives are entirely the same since each presents varied and complex representations on being mixed race in the twenty-first century. ∎

— Sean Frederick Forbes
Thompson, CT
April 9, 2017

WORKS CITED

[1] See *Loving v. Virginia.* < https://www.law.cornell.edu/supremecourt/text/388/1> accessed February 13, 2017.

[2] See Hawkes, Rebecca. "Loving couple: the mixed race marriage trailblazers who inspired an Oscars favourite." May 15, 2016. *The Telegraph.* <http://www.telegraph.co.uk/films/2016/05/16/how-mildred-and-richard-loving-changed-america-the-true-story-be/> accessed January 31, 2017.

[3] See *Loving v. Virginia.* < https://www.law.cornell.edu/supremecourt/text/388/1> accessed February 13, 2017.

[4] *Ibid.*

[5] See *Obergefell v. Hodges.* < https://www.law.cornell.edu/supremecourt/text/14-556> accessed January 15, 2017.

[6] See Coleman, Arica. "What You Didn't Know about Loving v. Virginia." 10 June 2016. *Time Magazine.* <http://time.com/4362508/loving-v-virginia-personas/> accessed January 1, 2017.

[7] Waring, Chandra D. L. "'They See Me As Exotic ... That Intrigues Them:' Gender, Sexuality and the Racially Ambiguous Body." *Race, Gender & Class.* 20(3-4):299-317.

[8] Trethewey, Natasha. *Thrall.* (Boston: Houghton Mifflin Harcourt, 2012).

"By dismantling the narrow politics of racial identity and selective self-interest, by going beyond 'black' and 'white,' we may construct new values, new institutions and new visions of an America beyond traditional racial categories and racial oppression."

— Manning Marable

Carlos Adams

I Was Mixed Race
Before It Was Cool

WAS MIXED RACE BEFORE IT BECAME COOL, exotic, or desired and long before a person could take pride in their multiple-ethnicities; before *Loving v. Virginia* created a space for the offspring of interracial couples; before *National Geographic* announced the future of race in the late 1990s; before Gloria Anzaldúa's depiction of the borderlands; and before websites and Facebook pages were devoted to people like me. I was the unfortunate child parents spoke about when interracial marriages were discussed. I lived with racial intersectionality before it became an academic theory. I struggled to learn how to accept my multiple-ethnicities before anyone described the process of achieving acceptance.

I felt the sting of rejection when my siblings, who passed as white, would call me nigger. I felt the confusion, the alienation, the remorse caused by a sense of lacking some essential quality enjoyed by monoracial individuals, and those who could pass as monoracial like my siblings. I battled the self-hate, the self-doubt, and the self-pity until it consumed me, and often lashed out with unexpected rage stemming from the rejection of myself and my family. I clung to the denial of difference as I attempted to fit into either the structures of whiteness or non-whiteness. I withered from the fires of racial nonacceptance through individual and systemic racism. I felt then, and will always feel outside the structures of race in America.

I grew up thinking the issues surrounding my racial identity seemed normal. I thought it was just one of life's unsolvable mysteries. I rarely saw anyone like me on television or in the movies. I was taught to ignore the differences, hoping they would fade away. I never heard anyone who spoke truth to my existence. I rarely felt the touch of understanding by anyone who saw me as special. I lacked a site to speak from and a language to communicate what I was going through.

I was raised to not only deny the Mexican in me but to denounce it. My grandmother reinforced my shame in being brown. To her I was "Chucky" until I misbehaved; then I became "Carlos Antonio." I witnessed family members being punished for speaking Spanish, and men's names Americanized: Juan became "Johnny," and Romolo became "Rocky." We lived in white working class neighborhoods where white children hurled racial insults at me that they learned from their parents and relatives. My identity, founded on exclusion, always seemed to suggest I would never find a truce nor a peace settlement – wholeness.

One night, while talking with my grandmother, she spoke of attending segregated schools. She talked about her experiences with some *gringas* who bullied her daily after the schools desegregated. She described the shame of being brown in her homeland. So she stopped being Mexican and became pure Spanish in the hopes of receiving acceptance for her and her family. She passed on these feelings of inferiority to her children and grandchildren. Is it any wonder my mother, aunts, uncles, brothers and sister all married white?

It was much later that I understood her motives. She internalized the self-loathing that resulted from the daily negation. She understood how speaking English was only the first part of assimilation, speaking English without her Mexican accent was needed to ensure total assimilation; to remove any sense of otherness from her offspring so it would ensure her entrance into the American dream. What she never realized was that in America, being brown or black meant you could never fully assimilate into American whiteness.

I married a Mexican woman with three children. I thought my love, if you could call it love, stemmed from who she was and not who she represented. I was mistaken. I became the colonial Spanish father inflicting my will upon the colonized Mexican mother. I tried to turn her away from her culture, and her identity. I distanced the children from their culture, allowing for those brief moments of brownness to exist when surrounded by her family, when we worked and partied outside of the constraints of whiteness, or when she cooked tacos and tamales. I allowed for the air of my perceived racial superiority to soak into the spirits of my wife and children. I used her and the children to remind me of who I wasn't, to make me feel powerful, to allow me to embrace my Spanish "purity."

Eventually, I followed a different road. I enrolled in college and instead of rejecting my brownness, I embraced it and as important, its history. I realized in order to embrace my brownness, I had to know its history. Since there were few courses on Chicano/a history and culture, I realized it was up to me, has always been up to me, will continue to be up to me to understand the ways in which racial ambiguity has been written upon my body, infiltrated my mind, and eased its way into my soul.

I entered graduate school with a reputation for being a critical race theorist due to my critical exploration of race in America. My reputation evolved into a cultural nationalist as I immersed myself to understand Chicanismo. I developed a reputation as a cultural elitist as I took pride in being Chicano. Eventually, I became known as a race traitor when I moved in with a white woman. The pride some Chicanos and Chicanas on campus expressed about me for embracing my Chicano history and culture turned into scorn as I sold out to whiteness by loving its physical representation. Identity politics became a no-win situation. An environment that was once empowering became toxic. Friends who were once supportive became combative as love turned into dismay. No matter what I did, when I spoke, or how I felt, the judgment from my peers forced me into seclusion. I no longer wanted to deal with identity politics, nor did I want to compete for acceptance. My relationship with the white woman fell apart, and I ran away as soon as I could.

One summer I had an opportunity to study Spanish in my grandparent's homeland. It was six weeks of baggage filled with equal amounts of anticipation and anxiety. I felt something awaited me, some sense of who I was and where I belonged. It wasn't long before I realized I was an outcast in Mexico, what they called a *pocho*: someone who has become too American to be Mexican. My Spanish was never good enough, my accent too white, my clothing too American: shorts, sandals and tank tops instead of leather shoes, long pants and buttoned up shirts. I came to understand the limitations of the ancestral ties to my family's homeland. I realized I experienced brownness differently. Even though I had little contact with the culture or the people from Mexico outside of my mother's family, I experienced the racism they experienced. Yet, I had no historical or cultural foundation to support me.

I came back from my trip to Mexico more empowered and more accepting of my *pocho* identity. I found power in that marginalized space between two cultures, which came from the knowledge that I wasn't lacking some essential quality, rather, I was a part of that space where being brown and being white come together. I am a site of over-determination. I am not a soul deserving of scorn and ridicule but a spirit worthy of praise and celebration. I found the power to reposition myself within the structures of race, to embrace my ambiguity, and to end my alienation from myself.

Today, as a mixed race instructor who teaches about race and ethnicity, I come across mixed race students who feel like I did: confused and irrelevant in monoracial or monoethnic societies, they struggle to understand their dilemma and their right for acceptance. Like me, they had no one to speak to, no one who understood their confusion, and no one who appreciated their reality until those moments in class when a teacher described it. They became excited as they realized they were no longer forced by others or society to choose a monoracial or monoethnic identity. This excitement propelled them into an acceptance of their pluralistic identity, and the determination needed to change the existing framework of race and ethnicity from one of exclusion into one of inclusion.

Today, I have now reached a point where the inner turmoil is a ripple that only now reminds me of my unacceptability. I am not biracial because I'm trying to balance two competing selves. Nor am I mixed race because I'm trying to heal the split between two opposing selves. I am interracial, attempting to understand the fluidity of my identities. My identity, flows like shifting wind currents, taking me on journeys towards new and exciting discoveries. I am fluid – nothing is static – a constantly shifting sense of self – nothing is permanent – tolerant of my ambiguity – where nothing is unappreciated. ∎

Dedria Humphries Barker

The Girl with
the Good Hair

KNEW I HAD A WHITE GRANDMOTHER. I met her. Indeed, she looked white: pale, ghostly even; thin lips, straight hair delicately curled.

She was a relic with tissue paper skin, and a reed body. Her bones bent into a hunch-back. By the time I was born she was vintage, seventy-two years old. When she died in 1963, she was antique. I was nine. She might have had the life of a redwood tree if some black guy trying to snatch her purse had not knocked her to the pavement, breaking her hip. She was walking home from St. Cecilia's Catholic Church in Detroit.

Her name was Alice Donlan Johnson and she was from Ohio. She was my great-grandmother, the mother of my mother's mother. She visited and then came to live with us, her black family in Detroit. I can't say I ever had a conversation with her beyond saying, "Hi Grandma." There was no volley of words, that I remember. My uncle, who was twenty-five years older than me, said that when he was a kid she visited Detroit once a year and he never heard her say a word. His friends would ask about her, why she was so silent, and he would say she was deaf and dumb. To me she was a ghost.

I imagine my grandma and her mother talked to each other about people, friends and family from an earlier life in Ohio. They probably talked about what it took to make a family, what bound us together. But as a notch on that belt, I did not understand my white grandmother's role as the buckle.

■ ■ ■

ONE SUMMER AFTERNOON when I was eleven years old, I bounded out of the house, hair freshly washed and plaited. I was eager to find my friends.

My father's mother was visiting to take care of us. Maybe my mother was in the hospital having a baby—I am the third of what ultimately became thirteen children.

My father's mother decided washing and combing our hair was the most important task of her weekend with us, and so she did this on Saturday morning. She was a South Carolina Sea Island native, descended from the Geechees. These are people who retained much of their African heritage because they were isolated on the islands. They retained their own language, and a look that filmmaker Julie Dash misrepresented in her film, *Daughters of the Dust*. Geechees are not fair skinned with ringlet hair. Every Geechee I ever met looked like Lula Mae Orr Humphries Bryant. Her skin was pecan colored. She was my brown grandma.

Nimble as spider legs and shiny with Posner's, a heavy blue hair grease, Grandma Bryant's fingers crawled through my hair, gathering strands together. She worked a fine-tooth comb through and smoothed it with a stiff brush. Hair coated my skull in a thin layer.

The hair in Grandma's hand, she split into three-parts and, with the motion of a turning barbershop pole, turned that into a braid. Grandma pulled my scalp so tight my eyes felt slanted. I felt like I was viewing the world through slits, snake eyes, the lucky kind. My brown grandma believed in the paper bag test; that is, the acceptable color of skin was no darker than a grocery paper bag, and she was so proud of me, her first bright-skinned granddaughter.

Released from this torture I ran out of the house, and wonder of wonders, I, the clumsy scarred-leg one, stayed upright until I reached my friends across the street. They sat on the McClure's porch. I tried to join the group quietly, coming to a stop next to Joann, the daughter of that house who was tall and skinny, like me, but where I was yellow in the skin, she was bark brown. Everyone looked at me like I was a new coin.

"Ohh," JoAnn said, "Did you get your hair straightened?"

I shook my head, no, feeling the air cool on my scalp, wet from my braids.

Jo laughed, but then she touched the pale underside of her fingers to the fringe of baby hair above my ear. "You have good hair."

She could have said, your hair is pretty, or shiny or squeaky-clean. She could have made a joke, said my hair was spick and span like a pot, but what she said was "good."

Now everyone in the circle watched me in a way that made me watch myself. Too shy to turn fully to the car in the driveway, I cut my eyes into its window hoping to catch a glimpse of my reflection. I had viewed myself as a giraffe girl with my hair the largest spot. The wonderful way my friend said "good" filled me with the same feeling that stirred inside me when my father called me "princess." My hair transformed into a tiara, the afternoon sun igniting diamonds and dark sapphires.

It wasn't like my friend had never seen my hair, but maybe this was the first time she had seen my freshly washed hair. My mother's routine was to wash our hair on Saturday evenings, bringing my two younger sisters and me to the bathtub in turn. By the time the CBS network played the opening strains of the theme song of *Gunsmoke*, Mama was sitting in a chair in front of the television set with me sitting on the floor, the back of my head between her knees. While actor James Arness played Marshall Dillon, she greased and brushed my hair into plaits—one top-knot braid and two other braids on the back—perfect for church and visiting relatives.

By the time I reached school on Monday my hair was stone dry, the gleam gone dull. Mine was the type of hair that loved water. With water, it relaxed and got all wavy and glistening like a seal rippling through smooth water. When my hair was wet, it excelled, definitely in a class with Esther Williams, whose arching front dives into an Olympic-sized swimming pool gained her fame in front of Hollywood's bright lights and rolling cameras.

As a light-skinned black girl standing on the dry earth of Detroit's west side, I just wanted my friends to like me.

At home, my hair was the worst of the lot. My mother's hair was black like charcoal poured from the bag, and soft and full down to her shoulders. One sister's hair was white-girl thin; the other was blonde. My lush-haired sister never failed to remind me that I had been a bald-headed baby.

Yet, on the street, I was the girl with the good hair. I felt pride at being singled-out in this way. My friend liked my hair because it was good. Yet, our hair was nothing alike. Hers was short, coarse and stick straight, exhausted from the strokes of a hot comb. A rainbow of bright rubber bands caught her hair into tiny pigtails that frizzed on the ends. If my hair was good, then was her hair bad?

Good was a moral pronouncement, like behavior in prison, like a stairway to heaven, like saving it for marriage. Good hair was more than hair. It was life.

I ducked my head and mumbled that my grandmother washed my hair.

A woman's crowning glory sparks no end to compliments. That childhood incident was the first of many I enjoyed for no effort of my own. My hair was handed down to me from the DNA of a silent ghostly grandmother who floated through the side-yard of my life. Good hair was what my white grandma gave me. She helped make me what my brown grandma wanted, what my black friends admired. I was the girl with the good hair. ■

Carly Bates

French Vanilla

L IKE A LOT OF THINGS, I've had to learn to love coffee. My earliest
memories of coffee are the sound of the coffee grinder early in the
morning as my father prepared a pot and I was still in bed. The smell
of beans as I stepped groggily into the kitchen, my father standing in his
pajamas. Endless iterations of beverages as I stepped into a Starbucks, my
palm placed in my father's.

I worked at a café for a summer; coffee was the job. When the time
had come to have my first latte one Sunday morning, I stepped up to the
espresso machine, pulled a shot, steamed some milk, and added a little flavor
of... vanilla. The bitterness of the beans saturated my tongue. But as the
creamy blend slid down my throat, and warmth spread through my insides,
I was left with the sweet, smiling aftertaste of syrup.

I found myself frequenting coffee shops more often throughout the following months, comforted by the warmth of that first sip, as I ventured to
try other espresso drinks, always with a hint of vanilla.

French vanilla.

Like a crayon boxed away in a set of "24," I stood among a number of
individuals on a tram in the Seattle-Tacoma Airport.

"'Scuse me." I looked over at an airport employee who had been tasked
with the responsibility of getting the woman in the wheelchair, whose handles
he gripped to where she needed to be. He continued, "Are you mixed?" I felt
familiar anxiety and apprehension, knowing that I was going to have this
conversation again, here and now, yet curious about how I might be made
uncomfortable this time.

"Yes," I said, glancing at him, desperate to know what our witnesses, who said nothing, were thinking.

"With what?" I gave my well-rehearsed and truthful answer: "I'm half black and half white."

"Which parent is which?" he asked. Like it matters. I could feel this complete stranger trying to figure me out, as if with each question he was fortifying a box around me, perfecting corners, adjusting dimensions. Again, the truth, "My mom is white..." "And your dad's black." He finished my truth for me.

He had all the facts he needed to know exactly who I was. I could see the mental notes he took with each riveting question, his brain calculating algorithms of genetics and pigmentations.

"Girl, you're too light. You're like French Vanilla! Ha! You need more sun." There it was. I had waited my whole life to hear those words out loud, words that I had only thought. Even better, those words were coming from a perfectly credible source: a black man in Seattle who didn't even know my name.

Not knowing how to respond, I slid my eyes to the ground in front of me. "Thank you."

The tram stopped, the doors opened, and I followed our audience out. Like a crayon boxed away in a set of "24," he gave me a label: *French Vanilla*. The next tram arrived, and as people spilled out of the cars in front of me, I found myself baffled: this man just told someone from Phoenix, Arizona that she needed more sun! Reeling, playing this 30-second exchange over and over in my head, cataloging his words and my reactions, clenching my brow tightly, feeling tension in my gut, I, like in every other moment like this one, thought that maybe, instead of a "Thank you," I could have used that moment to tell him that:

> there isn't a day that goes by when those words don't cross my mind;

> I've had white friends tell me that they're darker than me;

> if he didn't know, "too white" translates to "not black enough";

> if he didn't know, not being black enough is an upsetting

reality when you are the byproduct of interracial love, and everyday you are a witness to interracial hate in your country;

like a lot of things, I've had to learn to love every inch of my skin;

my blackness has nothing to do with him;

my whiteness has nothing to do with him;

the beautiful blend of color and characteristics that were gifted to me by my white mother and my black father have nothing to do with him; and that

these thoughts and questions that will continue to shift and maleate as I grow older has absolutely nothing to do with coffee. ■

Jackson Bliss

When Words Make You Real

1.

When i was a boy, I felt disconnected from the kids in Northern Michigan. I played with *Star Wars* action figures and Japanese robots, creating intricate storylines inside my head about galactic invasion. Sometimes, I flipped through manga my parents brought back from Japan, even though I couldn't read *kanji*. I showed up to school dressed in a *Miami Vice* outfit (my classmates taunted me, a few threatened to beat me up for "being a pussy"). I also played soccer and pretended I was a spy. On Saturdays, I went to my Obāsan's trailer and played Mozart and Sakura on her piano. Sometimes, she sang along. One year, I dressed up as a samurai for Halloween. Another year, I was a ninja. In junior high, I crushed on girls quickly when they smiled at me in the hallway, and I always had a girlfriend (partially because they were open-minded and understanding, and partially because they accepted me as someone who believed he was part Japanese but not Asian).

2.

All throughout junior high, I regularly daydreamed about living in Tokyo and having robot guardian angels. I spent hours by myself at home after school and on weekends, playing Atari games and old school RPG's on the family PC. I wrote pop songs on my synthesizer and biked through the neighborhood by myself, pretending I was in the Tour de France. I learned to chant *itadakimasu* before meals like my mom showed me to, which often raised eyebrows when the words slipped out of my mouth away from home.

Once, I brought a Japanese medallion to class for show and tell after my parents returned from a trip from Nippon. When I started to explain that my family was *nikkeijin* and that I had Japanese cousins, the teacher told me to sit down. More than anything, I wish someone had told me back then that there was a word to describe people like me, people of mixed Asian ancestry who would often—almost religiously—violate the rules of cultural identification. I wish I'd known other hapas in my childhood who could have encouraged me to celebrate and not sublimate my own racial hyphenation.

3.

BECAUSE I LOVED LONG BATHS as a kid, I didn't take my first shower until I was in sixth grade (which I found mildly traumatic). One of my favorite meals growing up was Sapporo Ichiban ramen. My mom would add raw eggs, *kamaboko* (fish cake), *nori*, shaved bonito, and scallions to the broth, transforming the meal of poor college students into a perfect Japanese dinner for four. The language we used to talk about family was as different as the food we ate, which was normal to us. On my mom's side, my family had Japanese names that rolled off my tongue: Yukiyo, Eikichi, Chie, Shizuko, and Hideo. My Obāsan had a thick accent when she spoke. Sometimes, I had to translate her English to waiters who looked confused, sometimes even hostile, when she spoke. My hapa mom occasionally wore a Tina Turner wig to work, just for kicks. My dad made Jackson Pollock T-shirts in the backyard with a toothbrush and acrylic paint, which he later sold at our store on Front Street, which became an endless source of gossip in the town. In so many ways, my family was straight up different (both racially and culturally), and although it took me twenty years to grasp, I was more than just another Nisei after school special. For most of my life, I wanted to understand how much of me was based on how I looked to the rest of the world and how much was based on who I was inside, including the Asian part no one could see (which, by the way, is the entire premise of my second novel, *The Ninjas of My Greater Self*). As it turned out, confusion was the easy part of being a nerd, an emotional artist, and a secret Asian.

4.

I DIDN'T UNDERSTAND until much later that like my hapa mom and my Japanese *Obāsan,* I'd always been different than the community I lived in, and that my difference was one of the most painful but also one of the coolest and one of the most crucial aspects of my metamorphic identity, slowly emancipating me from the fairytale of cultural normalcy. As an adult, I slowly realized that being both hapa and a (secret) nerd gave me the space to negotiate my own cultural, racial, professional, and gender identity: I was equal parts Asian, American, and European, committed writer and accidental heartbreaker, rebel and romantic, klutz and athlete, sensualist and intellectual, pretty boy, composer, inconsistent vegan, gamer, permanent student, and travel junkie. I was the very face of cultural hybridity, even though it would take me years to see the importance and the beauty of identifying myself as a mixed race American in a country that has traditionally used race as a way of classifying and dividing communities into castes and gradations of colorism against their will.

5.

ONE OF THE FIRST THINGS I've learned as a nerd and a hapa (who once pretended he was neither) is that violence is not intrinsically masculine or American even though we still construct masculinity in precisely that way. In America, "being a man" is still synonymous with enduring hardship, locking down emotions, accumulating wealth, and using violence to resolve conflict. But this (culturally relative) definition is destructive because it simplifies – and in fact, rejects – the inherent complexity of my hapa masculinity, ignoring my male interiority and also my Asianness. Our default definition of masculinity in America is almost entirely physical, external, and Anglo-normative, which is deeply problematic (not to mention insulting). During the 1980s, the nerd was the anti-male archetype, the skinny, zit-faced white dweeb in thick glasses wearing ugly cardigans and pocket protectors. The nerd was always that Asian dude getting thrown into a locker and slapped around by Paleolithic white jocks in the hallway. But the 1980s nerd, the different standards of APIA masculinity, and the *otaku,* have collectively paved the way for the transgression of my default gender roles as a hapa fiction writer, helping me subvert cookie-cutter gender templates that also expand the repertoire of my own racial and cultural subjectivity.

6.

THE SECOND THING I'VE LEARNED is that while I may have suffered intense alienation, racial erasure and illegibility as a teenage boy (not to mention cultural isolation growing up hapa before that was even a word in the mainland), I was simply ahead of my time. As a hapa, I am the quintessential story of multicultural America in all of its permutations, narratives, and contradictions. I may not have been the face of this country's hegemonic past, but I am certainly the face, the story, and the phenotype of its demographic destiny. It took me my whole life to understand not only why I was so different from my classmates, but also why I'm so essential to America's cultural biography as a thriving multiracial democracy. As a hapa artist, I'm literally rewriting the plot structure of American life every single day with my own life, with the stories of my childhood and the reimagining of my identity, with the timbre of my own voice. Of course, I do so with intense love and devotion now, but also with yearning too for all the years I was completely and utterly lost, always fractional, always splintered, and always incomplete in a country that couldn't see my wholeness and couldn't honor my racial hyphenation. It wasn't until I discovered words like hapa, multiracial, and *nikkeijin* much later on in my life that I felt real in an existential sense. Until there's a word for you coined by people like you, it's like you don't exist in the world. In a very literal sense, you need language to sanctify your struggle. ∎

F. Douglas Brown

How to Father Mixed Children as a Mixed Parent: A Zuihitsu After Sei Shonagon

1. Start with the truth.

WHEN TRANSLATED, your mom's last name means "stranded," as in a ship on a sandbar. Tell your children this is not them. *Your Nonny married three black men to get off that island in her.* When they see her alone and wonder, rebuke this image of loneliness altogether with a meal. Fill their bellies to the brim with the comfort food of your upbringing: rice and fried chicken; eggs and day-old spaghetti doused in hot sauce.

2. Use the math in their favor.

SHARE WITH YOUR KIDS the stories of people trying to put you together: Black and Tan; Black and Samoan or Tongan; Creole (as in, "mixed"); Black and... The stares are figuring out an equation that is upright and off paper. Tell your children it is funny *but it really isn't,* especially when in Phoenix or in Santa Clara or in Madrid, places you have lived. Have them prepped for the confident ones in all places who will stop them, and boldly ask. If these people are mixed themselves, they will breech all social space. Tell them these folks know the stares too, and should know better not to invade so swiftly. Caution your kids on the risks of solidarity, but at the same time teach them empathy: *When this particular set of gawker steps to you, it is not because their curiosity got the best of them. What is really happening is a path toward not being alone or different. It is some lonely soul who has found another mixed blood – skin and hair, and a wonderful multitude gathered in one body. Don't flinch at,* "Goddamn it! I've been looking for you." Tell them, *"It's all good."*

Ex Wife = Black + German + Irish + Mexican

You = Black + Filipino

Kids = 2 Black + Filipino + German + Irish + Mexican

3. Make a Re-Mixed Mix tape.

GIVE THEM THE MIXED MIX, consisting of songs by Prince, Bob Marley, Switch/DeBarge (let them know the difference), Vanity 6, Sheila E. (include the story of how your mom, their Nonny, had a fling with Sheila E's dad before she was born. Tell them how every time you listen to her, you think, "could've been my sister"), Al B. Sure, Lenny Kravitz, Rage Against the Machine, Sade, TLC, Alicia Keys, Ne-Yo, Kelis, Faith Evans, J. Cole, Drake, Bruno Mars, Toro y Moi, Karen O, Norah Jones, and Ben Harper. So many more to add but this is the first Eclectic on Eclectic jams you create for them. Take your son's suggestion and add The Blue Scholars, a black and Filipino hip-hop group. Let it warm your heart because not only does your son listen to conscious hip-hop, but to music that reflects him in ways beyond beats and lyrics.

4. Take all parts of them deeper than their skin.

Hair and eyes : mother :: skin and hands : father

THE BEGINNING OF WHAT YOU KNOW of Mississippi is skin-related. Your dad's friends tell you how lucky you are to be mixed. "Man, when I was your age this light skinned girl had a crush on me. But her mama ran me off and out of her life real fast. I can still hear that woman shouting between her shotgun's double barrel crack, 'don't ever bring yo black ass round here! She gon stay pure. She gon stay away from niggas like you.' What can I say, I'm that *old* black."

Included in what you know about Mississippi are the two small facts regarding your grandfather who was half black and half Natchez or Choctaw:

1. His vigorous fear of ghosts ("haints" in Mississippi); and

2. His hair reached down passed his belt ("You have hair like my daddy," your dad would say. "If I had hair like that, I'd let it grow to the floor.")

Could your grandfather have talked to an onion-skin colored girl? What were the risks for a mixed man in Mississippi when "pure" means washing your life out? Would he have shrugged off the insults your cousins hurled with a shotgun force? "Burnt toast," they would say, "you look like burnt toast." The hurt and anger burned, even though you were in love with your skin, then and now. You have always been in love with the coolness of chocolate that matched the cool of your daddy, or the beautiful temperament of Mamaw. Privilege has everything and nothing to do with skin. Prep them for being the darkest amongst whites, and the lightest amongst blacks. Remind them that their skin is always in jeopardy, and that taking precaution doesn't have to lead or even light the way. It means not to be surprised if some make it an issue, or if they are afforded opportunities you never had because of their lightness. When your son tells you, "If you have another baby, I'll be jealous if they are as dark as you," know he feels there have been opportunities he has never had because of his lightness. *You'll always be "Number 1" son. That's deeper than anything.*

Don't avoid the topic of hair. Even though there is nothing to hide in your daughter's hair (declare to her if perfect hair exists, it is hers: summer streaks of gold, mixed with brown, mixed with strawberry blonde, mixed with wave or curl... *sweet girl, you can take your pick*), reveal to your kids that you should have cut your dad's cotton white hair when he died. Everyone who knew his Isaac Hayes baldness of later years would have recognized him faster during his open casket, and kept that lasting memory of him. Only you know he decided to grow it out, and at the very least, you should have been the one to pick his afro to a clean boof and round sheen. You should have made it spring forth, ready for a Saturday night. You should have cared for his thick rows of white that gently swayed to a comb and spray, the way you cared for your son's hair when he was four. You were so tender with your boy's curry colored curls. The fine wisp of his hair made C's as you cut it away. Your hair, somewhere between the two: Black oiled blood, and ube root soaking each strand, will one day need a sheering without you offering direction. To prepare them for that day, start sending pictures of your haircuts to your daughter with the perfect hair, and your son with majestically auburn coils. Ask them their thoughts. Better yet, ask them what they would have done differently. Ask for future suggestions. How often has a mixed child been fated with a parent who didn't know what to do with their child's coif? Save your kids' kids the embarrassment, and let them practice on you.

5. Learn to love all opposites.

WHEN YOU TALK POLITICS, tell them about your Uncle Normy, Filipino Republican for life. Replay for them the names of the black Republicans he would throw at you: Booker T. Washington, Shelby Steele, Armstrong Williams, just to name a few. "You can be like them, Dougi," he would tell you, glee in his teeth and a vodka soda in his hand. Tell them that anyone promoting confusion is not to be trusted and they should politely back away (uncle or not). Tell them being mixed is confusing enough, so why would anyone black want to be a Republican? *I guess even Conservatives have a purpose, kids.*

6. You are what you eat.

Pork, rice, soy sauce : your mom :: Beef, rice, gravy : your dad

OPTIONS INCREASE WHEN MIXED—times two for you when they both lead to rice. The rice your mom makes is sticky with a crispy bottom layer. That layer, a silver mine or the first rain during a drought, is coveted and sought after by you and your siblings. The rice your mom makes requires a process of rinse and repeat. Rinse the white grains until the water is clean, until the dead rice or bugs are gone. Drain the old water without spilling any of the rice; rinse, then drain again. Repeat. Repeat. Repeat until the water is no longer cloudy. "You should be able to see the top of the rice." Rest your finger on the top of the rice and fill the pot with enough water to reach the first line on your index finger. Emphasize with your mother's importance of water-to-rice ratio. Explain how this is as true a cultural measurement as the cubit. Teach them how to cook the tradition of dishes this way—hearsay and codes, secrets and historical trial and error turned to truth.

This is the same way your father has taught you how to barbecue. "Make the whole neighborhood want some," he has told you time and time again. But when he is the one making rice, you reconsider his advice. The rice he uses is out of a box, and only takes a minute to cook. It is wet and each grain stands alone and separate. When you explain this to your kids, remind them that this is not a metaphor. Offer less about his style of rice making, and emphasize his gravy. There is always a skillet on his stove as black and heavy as night. He will melt butter or heat oil. He will add flour and mix in water, season to taste, and stir until it is thick and bubbling. "Make sure it be the color of your kids—light and creamy." Don't be afraid to laugh or use his joke when explaining this to your children. It will help them remember when the gravy is done. Spoon the gravy and its directions over the rice.

Strangely enough, your kids will want neither. They love your fried rice. They love the way leftovers are repurposed and transformed. They love how the nothings in the fridge have turned into a something so gratifying and tasty. Like the fried rice, their Asian selves blend with everything else inside them, and their many parts meld into one, flavor layered upon flavor.

7. End with the more truth.

WHEN TRANSLATED, your mom's last name means "stranded," as in, a ship on a sandbar. So far, this applies more to your dad, because he has died before he could pass on his family history to your children. The number of times he invited you to Mississippi haunts you because every time you hear that an aunt, uncle or cousin has passed, a piece of you dies with them—"stranded."

Before it's too late, replay your dad's basketball days following a Chitlin' Circuit. Let them understand that, "Freddie B. could shoot the rock!" Bring his quest from the South alongside your great-grandparent's odyssey from the Philippines to Hawai'i just to give birth to your grandma. Let your children see your grandma's courage that started in a boat, and kung-fu kicked an off duty sheriff. Your grandma's boldness transferred to your mother, and to her brother, Normie, the one who introduced your mom and dad. Your kids need to understand that the blood that courses through them is more mixed then they know.■

Alison Carr

Brown Like Ali

MY MOTHER LIKES TO TELL a story from my childhood. The star of the tale is my sister, who is six years my junior and technically a half-sibling, due to the fact that we have different fathers. But growing up together as one nuclear family in rural Maine, we rarely made such distinctions, with the exception of my stepdad's occasionally puzzled friend, for whom he would explain away the extra melanin in my skin and the frizz in my hair. "This is my stepdaughter, Alison." The curious strangers would nod their heads and smile, seemingly comforted by the confirmation that their eyes had not deceived them. I was the little girl with the olive skin. The one with the dark eyes and those beautiful curls that they admired. The one who gave them pause. In these moments, the instantaneous reality check was inescapable: I am different. Unique, exotic, interesting, mysterious, no matter the descriptor, being "othered" was a concept that I understood even before I had time to form or claim my own racial identity. Outside of these occasions, race was almost never discussed within my white American, Euro-descended family. Though it was always present, it became invisible, until the hidden elephant was thrust into view and we were all reminded that someone must be held accountable for this brown child.

With such picturesque surroundings, as kids, it was easy to take the landscape for granted. From the colorful leaves of fall, to the haunting, snowy winters, the outdoor lifestyle is one of adventure and discovery for a child. I was no exception. A city dweller these days, I cannot help but crave the easy lakeside summers and impromptu September hikes that were a childhood standard. The slow pace. A perfectly starry sky. Peaceful country silence. These are experiences that I cherish. Being a Mainer is a large part of my identity, but often when I return home to visit, those who don't know me assume I am an outsider. It is an assumption that I have come to expect, and I often try to find entertaining ways to burst the proverbial bubbles about who I am and where I come from. Being an anomaly has become something of a forté. As a self-identified woman of color, I have grown to embrace the qualities of myself that were once embedded deep inside the psychological walls of my white experience.

My hardworking, blue-collar parents raised us arguably well amidst ongoing family stressors and humble financial means. I can only imagine what an experience it must have been for them to witness as both of their daughters learned to move through the world. I wonder what they thought with regard to how their children would grow and change as individuals. The obvious physical differences between my blue-eyed, freckle-faced sister and I have always come second to our starkly contrasting personalities. I am not sure that my parents were prepared to consider race as a factor in raising children, but there they were with the two of us, different as could be, in so many ways. As my mother tells and retells of a memory that must be one of her favorites, I cannot help but think that she is continually processing the unique lived racial experiences of each of her daughters. And so the story goes . . .

> One brisk Maine day in the late 1980s, my family makes the hour-long drive to my Aunt Faye's place, which is an enviable ranch-style home on a dead end street with a nice yard and an above ground pool. During such visits, my mother and aunt commonly talk for hours in the kitchen while my sister, cousins and I play and watch TV in the living room. My sister, who is about three and a half at the time, is painfully shy and a notoriously picky eater. Feeling hungry, she goes into the kitchen to request an afternoon snack. While Aunt Faye is preparing something for her to eat (most likely chicken nuggets or strawberry Yoplait,) a conversation begins about grownups and jobs and my sister's impending future. Although I was not present for this conversation, I have heard the story so many times that I will never forget my sister's answer to the age-old question: What are you going to be when you

grow up? In her quiet, but utterly assured toddler voice, she proclaims, "I'm going to be brown like Ali when I grow up."

This is the place in the story where my mother typically pauses for a hearty laugh, while her audience giggles and is genuinely tickled by the sweet and profound innocence of the child's reply. My sister, in her developmentally-appropriate consideration of our aesthetic differences, wholeheartedly believed that because her big sister has brown skin, she too would grow to be bigger and taller and browner. It must be inevitable.

I still laugh at this story. It is not a surprise anymore; I know the punch line, but it warms my heart to think that out of all the responses she could have given, my sister spoke her truth. I am fairly certain that at the time, the adults in my family did not recognize this as an effort on my sister's part to make sense of her own racial identity juxtaposed with the image of a mixed race sibling. And yet again, the topic of race was front and center in our lives, not by choice, but by necessity.

Looking back, I recall the efforts the adults in my life made to try to shade me from the potentially difficult realities of being a racial minority in our family and community. My mother did not want me to feel different from anyone else, and yet, she had a constant undeniable awareness that I was her brown child. My mere existence in our small town challenged people. It challenged my family. My presence forced everyone to expand their world view enough to fit me into it. ■

Mona Lisa Chavez-Esqueda

Race for Dinner

EVERY SUNDAY WE WOULD ARRIVE at my maternal grandmother's house for spaghetti dinner and the same announcement would be humorously shouted upon the arrival of my family: "The Mexicans are here."

Usually one of my uncles or an older cousin would fulfill this tradition; a town crier of sorts warning the villagers of intruders. The outcry would be followed by another not so funny joke of "what took you so long, did you swim here?" It was odd. It was off-putting. It was racist. The Sunday greeting was the norm growing up as a mixed person with a family that held a monoracial ideology of race. Some families greet each other's arrival with hugs and kisses. My familial experience came with a racial slur as a greeting; slander overtly packaged as witty banter served up for the comedic entertainment of others.

My mother's family ancestry is one of Italian immigrants. My grandfather left Italy due to the political unrest during Mussolini's rise. My Italian relatives were proud of their heritage, even after being marginalized and racialized in the United States. Being 100 percent Italian was a badge of honor for them. Additionally, their need to assimilate and be accepted was important to becoming full-fledged Americans. My grandfather did not want my mother to marry someone who was *not* Italian. Instead she married my father. My father is not Italian.

Quite un-Italian, my father's family hails from Southern Colorado and Northern New Mexico. Comparatively, when visiting my paternal relatives, there would be a discussion of the historio-political origination of how our family became who we were. My paternal family also shared stories of the marginalization and prejudice experienced in the San Luis Valley. My father took pride in his roots; much like my mother's father did, except my father's ancestry was 100 percent Spanish. I grew up understanding that blood quantum purity had something to do with pride. When my father would introduce me to his side of the family he would refer to me as a "coyote." An old term with roots from the early Spaniard caste system, "coyote" refers to a person who is mixed Indian and European. The first time my father introduced me this way I did not understand. My thought was "why are you introducing me as an animal?" I felt angry, offended and confused, it felt rude. I remember looking over at my father bewildered.

I grew up. I married. I had children. Like me, my partner identifies as mixed. When my children would get the "What are you?" question, we would discuss what that question meant. Usually at home or in the car the discussions would occur, after they had been at school or at an activity with their playmates. The first time my daughter got this question she was in second grade.

She got in the car and said, "A boy at school asked me what I was today." I asked her, "What did you say?"

I told him, "I am a girl. But then he said, "No where do you come from?"

She didn't understand. This would be one of many, in-depth discussions we would have about race and what they were. I told my children they are mixed. My children began referring to themselves as "Mixicans." For Mother's Day this year my daughter, who is now twenty-seven years old, gave me the gift of a DNA test available through popular genealogy websites. It was a thoughtful gift; she is aware of my interest in my family roots. I was excited to find family members and connect with them. The DNA test indicated a contrary fact; I am not Mexican; the test indicated I am Native American, Asian, and have roots in the Iberian Peninsula. The largest part of my DNA indicated Caucasian with Italian/Greek origins.

In the 1600s, Spain forced Indians in North and Central America, including my ancestors, to become Christianized in order to survive. Technically my father's family is Mestizo. The unspoken, but well-known facts in my paternal family history acknowledged that the Spanish did not bring women with them to the New America. As a result, they married Indian women. Theirs is a story common within colonialism. My father's family spoke Spanish, the language of their colonizers. The Treaty of Hidalgo was a real document to them, part of history and their physical existence. One document shifted my father's family origins from being part of Mexican territory to becoming part of the United States of America. The land that changed hands through Hidalgo was purchased and the residents came along with it.

I grew up comparing my different experiences with my maternal family versus my paternal family I found a glaring reality: I could see how race was structured. My mother's family, although they had suffered many injustices, saw their "other" status begin to change.

Their category of race, as Italians, shifted to an ethnicity. They became recognized as "ethnic Caucasians." They transcended race into whiteness.

Like converts to a new religion, my mother's family became zealots in their efforts to adopt and enforce white perspectives. Now, re-examining those Sunday greetings, I would interpret the "Mexican" comments as part of the maternal family embracing their white privilege. They weren't the "other" anymore; we were. I was.

My father's family has not transcended race. The categorization label for my paternal family is Hispanic non-white. They are not regarded as white; they are the perpetual "other."

Having my racial status "called out" upon my arrival created a self-awareness and social awareness at a tender age, even among my own family. I didn't know, but somehow understood, that monoraciality would be an unachievable status for me. I felt "not enough" simply because I was mixed. In certain contexts, I felt a tremendous amount of pride about being uniquely mixed, while in others I felt shame, confusion, and a certain level of rejection. After all, my maternal family had our blood only through marriage; my paternal family, on the other hand, came from what was Mexican territory.

My history and my identity have been sculpted by policy and legal precedent when my parents married and anti-miscegenation laws were technically still on the books. Not only did my grandfather not approve of my parents union, but society didn't either. *Loving v. Virginia* passed two years after I was born. It has been a surreal experience to live an identity that had been decided upon by society, and to be aware of the laws and sentiments reflecting society's disapproval of my identity.

I identify as a woman of color. Because I am ethnoracially ambiguous in my appearance, I could "pass," except at certain times of the year when I "brown up." At such times, there is no denying that I am something "other" than white. People are confused by my appearance. Are you a light skinned black woman? Are you Japanese? Are you Indian (dot not feather)? Are you Persian? These are just a few of the questions I have been asked. Am I offended?

According to the DNA test these observers weren't totally incorrect about my origins. Other observers, those who related to me as an object of race (including my maternal family), were compelling constructors of race. Which approach of interacting with me is more forgivable or more palatable? At the end of each type of encounter, my identity is defined.

I am a woman of color.

These family memories have left me with a lot of questions about the concept of race. I continue to wonder "What is the problem with being "Mexican"?

And I ask, "Why is being "Mexican" used as a rationale by privileged whites' cruel greetings under the guise of comedy? Why is it appropriate for family (or anyone) to use the identity of a person of color in a pejorative way? Is it a form of microaggression?

It felt like something more than a micro-experience to me. And why is being monoracial so important anyway?

I won't pretend to have the answers. Instead, I turn on the news and hear the echoes of my childhood from our leaders, from our presidential candidates, and from white nationalist groups.

The media espouses the idea that we are a post-racial nation. It doesn't feel that way. Not to me.

A final, haunting question ambles through my mind: Can we, as humans, get to the other side of "race"? ∎

Fredrick D. Kakinami Cloyd

A Black Japanese Amerasian Being

A WARM SUMMER DAY in Albuquerque, 1966: I was ten years old. I and an African American friend who lived across the street weren't on speaking terms. My Dad and I had been working outside on the lawn when my friend came out of his house and yelled at me, "you Jap!" So, immediately I yelled back: "you nigger!"

Dad grabbed my arm firmly with a steely look: "Don't you EVER use that word ever again." My heart sank. I felt betrayed by my own father. *How come he can call me a Jap but nigger isn't okay?* I thought. Although I was on American soil, I was not only "American." Transnational mixed race, mixed nation military kids like myself, cannot be easily labeled, tamed or forced into dominant American norms. The "melting pot" is a lie. Americans like me are both desired and a threat.

1950s Japan, my birth town, Ōme: A small mountain forest town west of Tokyo. Temple bells echo through the green and the brown wooden houses with paper lattice walls woven by dirt roads. *Tatami* mat floors, the fragrance of *miso shiru, oden,* or *takuan* and *oshitashi* breakfasts enveloped in red and gold misty autumn mornings. Steam trains chugged by our house and deer played in the hills.

Most of the neighborhood women wouldn't talk to Mama or I, because we were pariahs—women who married American servicemen and their children. Yelling *ainoko* (love child), *kurombo* (nigger/black-sambo), *konketsuji* (mixed blood), or *saru-no-ko* (monkey kid), the neighborhood kids would run after me, throwing stones. I was beaten unconscious by baseball-bat-wielding boys by the creek near our house. A few times, women would yell, *"yoru no onna"* (woman of the night) at my mother and she would sometimes scream at them and hit them. Many Japanese considered any "self-respecting" Japanese woman sleeping with the former enemy to be a whore.

Dad, 1950s Occupation: A Black-American soldier in the Jim Crow system of the U.S. Air Force, stationed in Japan and Jeju-Do Korea during the Korean War and Occupied Japan; meets a woman, who is a Japanese national of upper class, mixed heritage. I am born to them. I had never heard of A-me-ri-ka and spoke only Japanese. But because of those times and my racial/national mixture, I've been made acutely aware of being haunted by war, devastation, and occupation. This makes it particular, not just "Black-Japanese" American.

Movement, 1960s–1970s: Albuquerque in the 1960s, I was treated much better than many folks in Japan up until then. However, to some American kids – and even some teachers – I was nigger, mutt, Jap, chink or half-breed. I was bullied via three "identities" not of my making. During this time, I began to question "why me?"

After living in Albuquerque and Hawai'i, and now in Japan again in the late 1960s, the types of violence against my mother and me had become more subtle. By the 1970s, racism in the U.S. was largely subtle, indirect and institutionally enacted. Hawai'i in the 1960s remained the single place my mother and I remembered as being a happy place, until her passing away in 2011.

Now: Although decades have passed, racism in both the United States and Japan still remains. Also, I have never been confused about who I was, as others like me sometimes do. If someone asks, "what are you?" I answer that my father is Black-American and my mother is Japanese. At other times, I respond with, "why do you ask?" And at other times, I would say: Black-Japanese Amerasian military brat, or Blasian Amerasian. I never say Black-Japanese – a race-only response devoid of history and context.

In combating intergenerational conflict and the forgetting and refusing of histories, I think that it's important to acknowledge we are more than racial identities. As I acknowledged my sexuality, it was also interesting that some guys would retort: "you're a faggot, everybody knows that Asians are faggots." Identity carries the ghosts that create and hold the violence of colonial-constructed hierarchies (from human to sub-human to non-human). The hierarchies are always, in some way, shape, or form: genocidal.

As I grew into adulthood in the United States, the primary mode of difference through which racism was used on me, was and is, African American hetero-blackness. The police and their entitlements to violence through racial and sexual profiling, was a norm for me. Driving a car was a nightmare, so eventually I stopped desiring a car. My Japaneseness continued to be disallowed by many Japanese nationals as well. In one instance, when I was a Japanese language instructor at Berlitz in Upstate New York, I befriended another Japanese instructor. She and I would hang out together, share meals, joke around and we would exchange small gifts, as do most Japanese in the forming of ties. Since language centers call teachers in for work by availability, I was puzzled when I began getting less and less work. One day, the administrative assistant at Berlitz called me aside and proceeded to tell me that this Japanese instructor I befriended had been calling meetings with the bosses there to plead to get rid of me because I was not really Japanese, and that I created a bad image for Japanese culture at Berlitz.

These and other incidents continue for me today, as they do with many mixed race people I know. From "you're not one of us" to "how dare you talk about yourself as if you were ..." to "you're confused" and other such monoracially-induced nationalisms and essentialisms. On the other end is the "I don't see you as a person of color" and "I don't see you as different, I see you as human," or "why do you keep bringing up race?" color blindness. By excluding you, a person uses difference to exclude from the "pure" race, culture or nation. In color blindness, difference is trivialized in order for them to then condemn you for not thinking or acting like the "normal" people. These forms of racism shifted from the direct name-calling type of racism of the past. Being "the United Nations" or "a smorgasbord" or "everything" is meant to be both amusing and condescending, or at the very least, exoticizing.

Through different periods in my life, I would also attempt to reach out to find community. When I reached out to Japanese American communities, I found that often, I was excluded. In one university club I attended, the leader told me I "wasn't Japanese enough." It was hilarious yet painful, because no one in that club spoke Japanese or had been to Japan. They were thoroughly "American." Where's the Japanese part of Japanese American?, I thought. Some Japanese Americans told me to my face that my mother betrayed both Japan and the United States and so she shouldn't be allowed to live. Unbelievable.

And African Americans would sometimes call me "black" and question why I would even mention being Asian. "Black is black, quit mixin' stuff up" I was told on numerous occasions. At other times, African Americans would say: "You can't speak for us about black issues. You're part Asian."

Wanting to explore a mixed race social movement, I reached out to mixed Japanese groups forming in the 1970s and 1980s. I found out quickly that the White-Japanese would take over all duties, and decide all matters. Whenever we spoke to matters differently from their way of thinking, I and other Black-Japanese would be shut down via the unspoken white privilege and built-in Japanese yellow supremacy. In their unwillingness to look at certain assimilations into mainstream Americanism, they created spaces that wouldn't tolerate Black-Japanese. However, the present situation seems to be a little better than those days when I first tried to join those groups.

Living in the U.S. affords me a freedom of identity that I wouldn't have in Japan. I know from reading the words of Ariana Miyamoto – a Black-Japanese woman who was voted Miss Universe Japan in March 2015, recounting the racism she endures in Japan even now. In understanding the knowledge of ongoing issues of mixed race babies in the Asia-Pacific, abandoned by American soldiers today, I feel my identity connected to these larger issues. Studying society through post-colonial and post-structural ways of thinking, has given me more hope in ways to work as a social change agent for better worlds. I entered a Zen monastery in upstate New York to save my own life from disappearing completely, which nourished me to finish writing a decades-long project that is now a book to be published in fall 2017. In the current climate of social change movements in the U.S., I hope we make our concerns connected to non-U.S. movements and globalized issues, to shift the global color lines as we work to decrease racism within and without, through inter-generational communication. Without making our differences the culprit, to interrupt our forgetting and our disconnection from each other through homogenizing nations, we need to confront the repetitions of narcissism, injustice and cruelty in our world. ∎

Santana Dempsey

An Impossible Feat

EVER SINCE I WAS A LITTLE GIRL, being loved by someone seemed an impossible feat.

When I was three years old, my younger sister and I were taken away from our home. One morning, these two big white ladies came into our apartment and snatched us away. I screamed at them to leave us alone. I knew strangers were bad. My mom would have strange men come over sometimes and every time she'd get hurt. I didn't want my mom to get hurt again. These ladies said they were social workers and were there to help us. I cried hysterically, yelling for my mom to come save us from these evil women, but she wasn't home. Sometimes she'd forget us and stay out for a few days. Whenever this happened, I took care of my younger sister.

My dad wasn't around either. I don't really remember him. I wish I did. Juan Manuel Santana. That was his name. My grandma used to say he was a bad man for getting my mom into trouble all the time. She'd say, "Juan is a low life wetback that is no better than a nigger." I used to giggle when she'd say "wetback" having no clue what it meant but knew the word sounded funny.

Once, I asked my grandma if I could see a picture of Juan so I wouldn't forget him. Secretly, I wanted to see if I looked like him. I look like my mom but not all the way. She has strawberry colored hair and freckles. Her skin is also a lot lighter than mine.

My skin is a light caramel color. My hair is brown, thick and curly. Probably one of the thickest types of hair in the world. This is not a joke. My sister looks the same as me. I must have upset my grandma because she looked me dead in the eye and said, "All you need to know about your daddy is he gave you your color and left you with his burden." Then she took all the photos we had of him (which was only two), and burned them. I was so mad at her I couldn't stop crying. That was all I had left of my dad.

How was I suppose to remember where I got my burden?

When my dad used to speak, he sounded a little different from my mom. I found out later Spanish was his first language and he was not born in the U.S., which explained why my grandma would always tell me to never learn "that language" because I was American, not some border nigger. That was probably the first time I heard the word "nigger." It would not be the last.

After my sister and I were carried away and put into a van, we were placed in the custody of the state. Days later, we were living in a foster home with seven other children in Southern, Missouri. Everyone who lived there was white like my mom. Even our house was white. I may not have really felt like I was different if it weren't for my stupid hair. My foster mom, Tammy, despised doing our hair mainly because she didn't know how to do it. She would always say we had "nigger hair."

Since I had heard that word before, I knew that meant my hair was bad. I wanted to change my hair so she wouldn't think I was bad, but I didn't know how.

During my nightly prayers, I prayed that God would send me easy hair. I'd pray to him that I'd be a good girl forever if he could just please change my hair. Then, I'd envision opening my eyes, going to the bathroom, looking into the mirror and seeing myself with long, silky, beautiful blonde flowing hair. Hair like my mom. Not hair that would break every single Walmart wide tooth comb Tammy would buy.

One morning, my foster mom was trying to comb through my hair. She became so annoyed with the struggle that she stormed out of the room. Minutes later, Tammy called us into the bathroom. She was sitting on the toilet seat and told me to sit between her legs on the cold tile floor. My foster dad, Ron appeared in the doorway with a pair of big, red, shiny scissors. He handed them to Tammy and she began cutting my hair. Not a trim. Not even a cut. No. No. No. It was a big chop kind of cut. A cut that only left inches of hair from my scalp. A cut that made me look like a boy. After she was finished, Tammy looked so relieved and satisfied with herself, whereas I sat on the floor wailing for my hair to jump back onto my scalp. When Tammy left, I peered hesitantly into the mirror looking at myself. I finally saw what they saw. A nigger.

For me, deep down, this was when my hatred towards my mixed race hair began. No one seemed to understand it. It made me feel ugly because I felt ashamed that my foster mom didn't like my hair. More than anything, I wanted her to like my hair. I'd convinced myself, if she liked my hair, she'd love me.

My sister and I stayed in the foster home in Carthage, Missouri for three years. Not once did I encounter a person of color. I may have even stayed in foster care longer, but on October 15, 1986, my mother Sandy Saunders Santana was pronounced dead. My foster parents yelled at everyone to go outside except for my sister and me to stay. I thought I was in trouble because I had stolen extra Pringles in the middle of the night. I was always hungry in the foster home. I would sneak into the kitchen after everyone went to sleep to get my sister and I more food. I was never caught!

It was an unusually warm autumn day. Ron told me to come sit on his lap and asked my sister to sit on Tammy's. We just sat. I sat all tense, waiting for the belt. Sometimes, if we did something really bad, Ron made us pull down our pants and bend us over his knee. He took off his long, brown, leather belt and would smack it across our bare asses until we cried. This time, he didn't take off his belt. Instead, Tammy started talking. She said our social workers called. Her voice started to sound all scratchy. She abruptly stopped talking and looked away from us. Ron quickly picked up the conversation talking very sternly. He said there was an accident and our mom got hurt. She had to go live in heaven to be with God, but she loved us very, very much. He started saying the same thing over and over, "You did nothing wrong. She loved you girls. You did nothing wrong. She loved you girls." No matter how many times he repeated those words, I didn't believe him.

Years later, I discovered the truth about my mother in a newspaper article. She was found dead in a strange man's house with a single bullet to her chest. Her death was ruled a suicide. I don't remember the last time I saw her. She was suppose to see us once a week to prove to the state that she was a fit mother to get us back. She barely showed up, and often left my sister and me waiting.

I only knew one thing: I was not wanted by my parents. I was not wanted by anyone. The only rational explanation was that I had bad hair and brown skin, which meant I was unlovable.

What else was I suppose to think? This is what made me different. My foster parents wouldn't even adopt us. We weren't white enough. They wanted kids that could "pass" as their own children. With our hair, Tammy said, we would never be able to pass. So they would pass on us. My grandma wouldn't take us either. We reminded her too much of Sandy's mistakes, although she told social services it was for financial reasons.

From the moment I was brought into this world, I experienced love differently than most children. I learned that if I loved someone they would leave me. In turn, I couldn't comprehend how someone would be able to love someone like me. It seemed an impossible feat.

Then one evening, the phone rang. To my surprise, Tammy handed me the phone. On the other end of the line my social worker excitedly told me that she had shown a couple looking to adopt my photo and they wanted to meet me and my sister. I remember wondering if she got the photos mixed up with different sisters. Before I could entertain another thought she said: "They love your curly hair"! ■

Timeka Drew

Nigger Lover

"WHY IS YOUR MOTHER a nigger lover?" I was five years old when I was first asked this question. I was in the first grade, and all of the fire and agitation and rage behind the eyes of the young child asking me this question perplexed me perhaps as much as it hurt me. This was not the first time I had heard the word "nigger," but it was the first time it was so intimately directed at me. The demand for an answer about my nigger-loving mother was made at the fence on the playground – I learned that hanging near the outside boundaries wouldn't keep me safe from social interaction and I assumed nigger would be a word I might encounter any day and every day from that moment on.

Nigger is a word I heard out of the mouth of young girls and immature boys, adults I respected and adults I feared. Nigger would become a word spit out of the mouth of past lovers when they wanted to hurt me by trying to make me think they made an exception to their racist rule in coupling with me – a word I have never felt comfortable uttering or hearing no matter if it ended in "er" or with an "a." I learned what the word "nigger" meant in context – the context was that I was black, and the people around me were not. To them, I was black for one reason – because my white mother loved a nigger.

I realized quite quickly that this one question was actually a series of questions – questions that didn't have real answers, like, "Why? Why would my beautiful white mother from a respected, well-known Catholic family love a nigger? Were there not white men willing to love her? Did she hate herself so much that she felt the need to love someone beneath her? What was she lacking that led her down the path of nigger-loving? Did she think it was rebellious to love a nigger? Did she think she was starting some kind of nigger-loving trend? What about the kids? Did she ever stop to think about the kids while she was nigger-loving?!"

Some of these questions about my white mother and her choices were uttered out loud to me, others silently sizzled between the snarky lines generally spoken by elementary school kids but clearly stolen and regurgitated from the mouths of their confused parents.

Questions lead to conversations.

I was not a very talkative little girl, but I wasn't fearful of interacting with my peers either. I had plenty of white family members; it was obvious white members of my family (and the people they married) found my existence difficult to deal with, so I had become intimately accustomed to the way they felt. I was used to changing the air by entering a room. I had grown familiar with people modifying what they were talking about or editing their tone when I was around.

I acquired glasses when I was five; after I had my tonsils and adenoids removed the same year, my hearing was far better than my sight, so I could hear the things people said about me, and what they said about people of color in general more than I could see their expressions from across a room. I went from blurry vision and muted hearing to having four eyes and hearing more than anyone assumed I could. At the time, it felt like the sharpening of my senses was a subtle form of torture.

"Why is your mother a nigger lover?"

blank stare

"My mom said that your mom is a nigger lover, and that I can't go to your house to play…"

"I never invited you to my house."

"Is your mom white?"

"Yes."

"Is your dad black?"

"Yes."

"So what does that make you?"

"I am mixed. I am both."

"But…you are black."

"Yes, I am black. But, my mom is white…just like your mom."

But, my white mom wasn't just like their white mom. My mom was a nigger lover. Not only did my mother have the audacity to love a nigger, she married and had children with one.

My mom was the mother of black children. No matter what we called ourselves, we would never look like our mother in the way these other kids would look like their mothers. I could be modeling a carbon copy of my mother's face and most people would only see a black girl being taken care of by a white woman – not a mother with her daughter.

■ ■ ■

I SPENT THIS TIME in my early childhood with eyes, ears and spirit wide open. I was soaking in not just words, but the unspoken feelings inside rooms containing the turbulation and agitation of intolerance. I never needed to be taught about people hating us, and the danger it brought, because I could see and hear people taunting us and threatening us earlier than I can remember. This survival instinct taught me to take racists seriously. When this happened, I began planning an escape early on because I knew it was imperative to make the people around me feel I was one of them in order to survive this part of my life without drowning in treachery. I first implemented this tactic at school, and quickly learned that I could easily manipulate them effectively.

"Why is your mom a nigger lover?"

"Why are your parents racist?"

"My parents aren't racist!"

"Your parents are obviously racist if..."

"It is wrong to mix the races and my parents said it is a sin! I..."

"I have two uncles that are priests and I can assure you marrying someone that is a different color is not considered a sin."

"You have two uncles who are priests!?!"

"Yes. They are old, and they are white, and they know a lot more about what a sin is and what a sin isn't than you or your parents do. So you should speak about what you know."

This conversation about my nigger-loving mother did not happen once. It didn't happen twice. The discussion about my mother loving a nigger was a theme throughout my childhood from kids who were jealous or bored or mad or evil or obsessed or whatever to revisit at their leisure.

When I was in the first grade, I ran to a teacher and cried once. Someone had asked why my mom was a nigger lover and several older kids laughed. I felt the tears rushing to my eyes, and I ran on the hot pavement to someone I thought was a safe authority figure.

She happened to be the mother of one of the kids in my class—a particularly pale skinned, somewhat sickly looking boy. That teacher comforted me by hugging me, but she did not alert a higher school authority like the child's teacher or the principal. She didn't confront the child and tell her it was unacceptable to say such a terrible word, and that it was certainly not acceptable at school. I thought, in my knee-jerk reaction as a five-year-old, that this was just kids being mean and it didn't extend to nice, Catholic teachers at my school. In that moment, while she was hugging me and drying my eyes and telling me not to cry and to run along and play with someone else, I realized she was not going to do anything, and right then and there, I knew I was not safe. I knew I would never be safe in a space run by white people, and those were the only spaces I knew existed in our town.

As I continued to contemplate the situation, I realized that even if that teacher had alerted the principal, or the child had to face repercussions that would not have made me safe. I figured that she was in a position to call attention to the taunting. Instead, she weaved a rug with her silence—a place others could sweep things under every time this black girl ran into the many forms of racism that were inevitable by people perpetuating and enabling them to fester and flourish in this community. This teacher might even think of my mother as a nigger lover herself, which made it ridiculous that I would run to her with my tears in the first place. She might have been thinking to herself while cradling my lanky body, chest heaving from awkward sobs, "It might not sound nice, but the truth about your mom being a nigger lover is something you have to come to terms with…" Did I just embarrass myself by running into the arms of an ideological enemy?

Tears dried. Eyes opened. I went home and hugged my mom. ∎

Naomi Raquel Enright

From One Exile to Another

FROM ONE EXILE TO ANOTHER." This is what my mother once asked Chinua Achebe to write in her copy of *Things Fall Apart.* I stood right next to her and in that moment I realized the impact of my mother's experience coming to study at Tulane University from Guayaquil, Ecuador at the age of nineteen in 1965. She subsequently married my Jewish American father, had two bilingual children with multiple citizenships, and was an impassioned, influential educator for many years. Her entire adult life has been spent in a foreign land, and when she returns to Ecuador, she has become the foreigner.

Growing up, discussions of race, culture, and identity were commonplace. In fact, they were encouraged as a way for me and my brother to feel confident in a world where we could and often would be questioned or challenged. My parents ensured that my brother and I knew who we were. I am the daughter of an Ecuadorian mother, a Jewish American father, born in Bolivia, and a citizen of three countries. I have two native languages, and I do not fit any box.

Nevertheless, it is not at all easy to exist on the fringe of this color-conscious, deeply racist and divided society. My parents never emphasized the difference in our skin tones, which to some might seem naïve, but on the contrary, it was revolutionary. By not buying into this country's obsession with skin color and by talking about our cultural identity and mixed origins instead, my parents in fact imparted to us a strong sense of self. My parents always let me know that the issues people had with our family were a reflection of them, not of us. It was a crucial lesson, one all children need to learn, but one mixed children in this society particularly need to learn.

I am now an adult and a parent myself to a bilingual six-year-old boy this society deems as "white." My husband is of Irish and German ancestry, and with my genetic mixture, it really is unsurprising that our son was born blond, fair-skinned and green-eyed. And yet our relationship as mother and son is questioned or challenged everyday. I do not exaggerate. And now I am left to ponder how to raise my bilingual, multiethnic son in a society that due to his physical appearance, dilutes him as "white." How is it that I, the woman who carried him forth, am to consider myself a person of color but he is to consider himself white? It is cognitive dissonance and as far as I'm concerned, reflective of this country's unresolved racist legacy.

Not only would this society dilute my son's truth, but it would afford him privileges he has never earned solely based on his physical appearance. This is the bedrock of our racist society and one I cannot allow my family to be complicit in. I have been told by many how "lucky" I am that my son is so light, and every time I hear it, I cringe. I am lucky that he is physically healthy; I am lucky that he is intellectually able; I am lucky that he is loving, energetic and entertaining. To feel lucky because of his physical appearance is to (a) think there is something wrong with my own physical appearance, and (b) to allow systemic racism to thrive. I have no illusions about dismantling systemic racism, but I do think I can make a difference in my own life, and certainly in how I raise my son. Yes, my son will reap the benefits of being read as "white," but if my husband and I have any influence, he will learn *why* he is reaping benefits, and he will know it is inherently wrong. And hopefully, he will join the fight against the very system that puts him on a pedestal, but would demonize his own mother.

"From one exile to another," my mother said. It is clear how my mother could feel that she is in exile, but strangely enough, I feel similarly. Albeit for very different reasons but being of mixed heritage, I am never quite at home anywhere. In this country, I am consistently reminded of my "otherness," particularly now that my son and I elicit questions both implied and voiced simply by our existence. When visiting family in Ecuador, I am constantly reminded how American I really am. And to add further complication, I was born in Bolivia. I am a conundrum, which certainly creates my own sense of exile, but I truly couldn't imagine another story for myself. I am very thankful that I was taught to embrace the totality of my ethnicity.

I am now teaching my son to also embrace the totality of his ethnicity. I could easily have him be read and defined as "white," but to do so would be a disservice to him, as well as hurtful to me. To do so would be a form of erasure. To do so would be allowing this society to have more power. To do so would be giving in. My son may be blond, fair-skinned and green-eyed, but he is not white. He is an American of Ecuadorian (West African, Incan, and Spanish), Jewish (Eastern European), Irish and German descent. He is a native English and Spanish speaker. He has a name spelled and pronounced in Spanish. He is multiethnic. His story is not written on his face. And neither is mine.

I hope my son will continue to feel pride in his truth, and will never allow a divisive, destructive system to define him. It is no doubt challenging for us in this society, and growing up, I often felt very alienated, angry and hurt, but I was lucky that my parents raised me to know that those feelings were the result of how I was being treated or viewed, not the result of who I am. Who I am is who I am supposed to be. I am a revolutionary. I am an agent of change. And I am proud. ■

Anika Fajardo

None Taken

1.

NO OFFENSE, but you don't look Latina. These are the Mexicans, the Colombians, the Minnesota-born, second-generation Latinos who grew up visiting their grandmothers in Texas. They speak English with chopped off syllables and drop in words like *mi'jo* and *tortas* but still say "ruff" instead of "roof."

No offense, the white people say, but you don't look Hispanic. They look at my Banana Republic cowl neck, my Gap jeans, my fair trade necklace. I don't fit into their box. Do you speak Spanish? Do you eat *tamales?* Do you watch *telenovelas?* Nope, not Hispanic. Not Latina. You must be white.

2.

THINGS I GOT because I'm Hispanic: a college scholarship; a seat on a non-profit board; my job; followed around the mall.

Things I got because I'm white: a college education; a recipe for potato salad; my husband; a fitting room at Nordstrom.

3.

"VAMOS A BRONCEARNOS," my father's wife said. We had towels, swim suits, and midday tropical Colombian sun.

"Don't let her burn," my father said. He was thinking of the pale skin of my mother, her straw-colored hair, and the red starbursts on her shoulders after a day at the lake.

"But she's a *Colombiana!*" my father's wife protested. His second wife is brown like a cup of chocolate.

"You don't know what the sun is like," he said, "for white skin."

He doesn't know either. His hands, face, back are the color of saddle leather.

4.

THE IMMIGRATION OFFICER at the Bogotá airport wore a little hat and spoke in Spanish to me through the glass.

"Where is your Colombian passport?"

"I don't have one."

"But you were born in Colombia."

"Yes."

"Where is your Colombian passport?"

"I grew up in the U.S."

"Where are your naturalization papers?"

"I'm not naturalized."

"Then where is your Colombian passport?"

5.

MY FATHER IS A PAINTER.

His brushes are fanatically cleaned and organized, bristles up, in glass jars. Only the smooth wooden handles bear clues of their uses. I am a brush handle splattered in paint. Look at me from one angle and you see white. Look from another and you see scarlet and orange and tourmaline. Spin it between your fingers and watch the colors blend and soften.

6.

I DIDN'T KNOW THERE WAS A NAME for what I was until I was in high school. Given the choices, I checked the box that said: Hispanic: A person of Cuban, Mexican, Puerto Rican, South or Central American heritage. Before the 2000 Census, you couldn't be both white and Hispanic. You had to choose.

Actually, it wasn't a box. It was a round bubble that I filled in with a number two pencil. Race: *Hispanic*.

Even though Hispanic is not a race.

7.

THE ONLY RACE I EVER WON was the 55-meter hurdles in a sixth grade track meet.

I was twelve years old, the tallest girl in the class (the only time I was ever the tallest). I was a horse clearing the steeplechase fences, I was Tipperary Tim, Red Rum, National Velvet.

I leaped over hurdles.

8.

IT TAKES A YEAR to get a *cédula*, a state-issued ID card. And then it takes another year after that to get a passport, my father explained. The flimsy little card would have my picture and name on it, with two surnames. In Colombia I have two last names to prove that I have both a mother and a father. But you can see that I had a father who was small and dark, whose eyes were black pools and whose nose was flat as a river rock. You can see my mother's smile, her pale skin, her choices.

9.

"SPAIN IS A SECOND-WORLD COUNTRY," my American classmate insisted while we exchange students shifted in our hard plastic chairs.

"No es," the history professor argued. This classroom was on the second floor of a university building in an industrial city in Spain in a time before the European Union. One floor below, a little café sold *cervezas* and *café con leche* in between classes.

"The U.S. is a first-world country. So Spain is a second-world country," the student said. She was white, came from blue collar folks in the Midwest.

"No," the professor told her. He was a Spaniard which meant he had a Roman nose, Arabic coloring, and a lisp.

"Spain's not third-world, though, is it?" she asked.

"But it's not called second-world." He pulls at the cuffs of his corduroy jacket and sat on the edge of the desk. "It's called developing," he told her.

"It's a second-world country," she repeated. He sighed.

10.

MY SKIN IS PALE, my accent is solidly Minnesotan, and my mother cooked casseroles. Maybe the white people are right; maybe I am white.

My hair is the color of a coffee bean, I was born in Colombia, and I have my grandmother Doña Rosa's nose. Maybe the white people are wrong; maybe I'm Latina.

11.

"I DON'T HAVE BROWN SKIN," I used to tell my playmates when I was a child. "But when I get tan in the summer, it just lasts longer."

I believed I was sun-kissed, blessed with a tan that lasted all winter.

But in Minnesota, the winters are cold and white. For weeks at a time the sun disappears behind clouds as dull as bath water and nights as long as God, and then when it reappears, its reflection on the snow blinds you until you see spots.

Now I have age spots that are as dark as my father's skin.

I look in the mirror. Along my forehead strands of grayish-white hairs are threaded into the dark brown. When my hair turns silver, and all the color has gone from my lips and cheeks, and my skin has turned the same sallow gray of elderly people of all races, will I be as white as the white people think I am? Or will I dance a *cumbia* in front of the bathroom mirror?

12.

THROUGH THE GLASS, I watched the immigration officer's mouth move—open and closed—like a goldfish in a bowl.

Behind me, the lines were long, filled with black-haired mothers and toddlers and bent-over grandparents. Brown-skinned women in precise red lipstick and narrow blue skirts smiled and directed the queues. Only the walls were white.

The officer held up a finger (*just a minute*) and left his post.

And when he returned, he handed me back my passport and let me pass. ∎

Liberty Ferda

The Other Side
of the Street

ON A WARM EVENING a few months ago, I stood holding my fifteenth-month-old daughter outside a house with a For Sale sign in the yard. A police car pulled up as I scrutinized the brick exterior. "I'd buy on the other side of Stanton Avenue if I were you," said the officer.

"Why, is there a lot of crime here?" I asked. Calls were rare, he said, and mostly for minor problems – petty theft and the like. So what was the problem? Then I remembered earlier seeing an African American boy riding his bicycle two doors down, how I'd felt heartened that this was, within a fairly segregated city, a racially mixed neighborhood – the kind my husband and I wanted to raise our daughter in. But my kinky-curly hair was pulled back. My daughter's skin is on the fair end of olive-toned, like mine. The officer had assumed I was a fellow white person he could speak between the lines to.

But I am an undercover other.

Much of my life I have passed as white. For a while, this was unknowing and my movements were unguarded against racism's realities – which is to say, white. I was adopted into a white family in rural Illinois under the auspices of being born to a white woman and a white man, which is what the adopters requested. Before you gasp at the couple who became my parents, their request was based with the acknowledgment that this homogeneous region would prove difficult for a child of color. And yet, children of color – even mixed ones with fair skin, light eyes, and barely a wisp of hair at birth – were harder to place in families (for years their files were labeled "special needs"), so the social workers fudged my birth father's race to secure me a home swiftly.

In elementary school, kids would taunt me by whispering the word afro like a bad word. This may have been when my double-consciousness emerged, tangled with the adolescent desire to be like everybody else. It was true that my hair grew "up" instead of "down," puffing out into a veritable Angela Davis crown, which confused me, my parents, and any beautician that ventured near my head. What was a white girl doing with hair like that?

Not everyone was confused. Once when I was ten and walking on Main Street of our dusty town, a man pulled his car alongside me and said, "you got nigger blood in you, don't you?" It was not a question but a threat. I said no, the only possible answer for survival. At that moment a deep sense of shame and fear burrowed into my bones. I searched fervently for ways to straighten my hair to acceptability, finding chemical relaxers and flat irons and "anti-frizz" products galore. Once my hair was straight, there were fewer questions about my identity. I became privy to the way some people talk about race when they think only white people are near. By high school, I could share lunch with a friend who said one day, casually, that he wasn't racist but he could never date a black girl.

In college, I encountered Henry Louis Gates Jr.'s memoir, *Colored People,* and felt a flush of familiarity and relief when I read the chapter on hair – the cultural obsession with hair and different black styles, the way his mother would apply chemical relaxers to hair in her kitchen. I gathered in and held close black literature as though it were long lost family. I made contact with my birth mother, who confirmed that my birth father was black. Eventually I found my way to black salons, the first place where someone knew exactly what to do with my hair. Soon I quit relaxing it, and began to come to terms with my identity.

So when a white college boyfriend said, "My mother loves your hair and says you look exotic," I felt a thread of uneasiness. I wanted to take it as a compliment, as he clearly meant it to be. His mother, whom I'd never met, had posted a photo of me – my skin summer bronzed, hair unbound – on her refrigerator. It may have been the first time I knew I was being seen as different but not too different, a touch of "not white" but not enough to be threatening or perceived as "other." Something new and interesting to sample for a moment, then toss aside when it gets boring or too complicated.

Later I found my birth father's side. The feeling of being accepted by that black family, of being seen, was indescribable. No matter how many friends of color I had made as an adult, I was often conscious of my white upbringing, and wondered if they thought my thoughts and feelings about race were legitimate. I couldn't claim an experience of struggle against racism that many in my bloodline could, and it's not fair that I *can* be undercover, even if I don't *want* to. For example, I've never, to my knowledge, been discriminated against for jobs because of my ethnicity. (Though in my first interviews, I wore my hair slicked back into an innocuous bun just in case.)

Around the time I met my black family, I was dating a black man and found an email he'd sent to a friend with my photo attached to it: "She's black but look how white she looks." He actually wrote that.

It's in these brief moments—hearing a misguided hair compliment, a covert comment about a neighborhood, an offhand remark about dating—when my fault lines have opened widest. I never told my high school friend that dismissing an entire race from your dating pool was racist—I needed him, and the town at large, to believe I was white. I could not explain to that mother how her comments made me feel small—I needed her to like me. I never confessed to reading that email—I didn't want to discuss my whiteness or lose affection even though that affection was tied to a warped fascination with my appearance.

I didn't call out the police officer in front of the house up for sale for his racism—I was afraid of him.

But I did buy the house. ■

Chelsea Lemon Fetzer

Speck

WHAT DO I LOOK LIKE?" I asked Mom before she pulled the keys from the ignition. The sun-bleached house she rented for the two of us waited beyond the driver's side window. Fistfuls of sand spotted our sidewalk between snowbanks. I was fourteen.

Mom turned to check me for a surprise tattoo or something. One eyebrow rose above her prescription sunglasses. "What am I missing?" She liked to keep it moving. She liked to hurry up and get the groceries in. But she was stuck humoring me in the Corolla. We still had our seat belts on.

"Just . . . what do I look like? All the time."

"You look like Chelsea."

"Do I look exotic?"

It's embarrassing telling you this. Here's what I looked like when I was fourteen: Metallica shirt, tangle of hippie necklaces, crystals and beads. My hair was wide enough to hide both hands. A few curls even reached past the middle of my back, when stretched. High bangs in front was nonnegotiable in Carver County, 1991. Every morning I straightened mine with a flat iron, teased them up, then sprayed with Aqua Net Professional until the sculpture was hard as plastic. I wanted to be like the girls I hung with. Still, my friends' parents looked at me like I was going to steal their purses or what remained of their kids' tolerable behavior. Though it was the Minnesota way to never directly comment on my evident non-whiteness when I was in the room, now that I'd entered puberty some lady at the grocery store just said I was "so exotic-looking" like it was a compliment, like I was so lucky. The word stuck like a burr in my mind. *Exotic.*

Mom took enough breath for a lengthy answer. She exhaled. Silence. Her eyes searched my shoulders. The windows steamed up. "I can understand how people might see you that way," she said.

"Do *you* see me that way?" *Is there a name for beauty that includes me? Could I be lucky for this strange body?* I wanted her to just say yes.

"No. You're my kid, that's how I see you."

Mom's eyes were grey-blue. Winter blue. She wore her hair short and out of the way. Though she was barely thirty-eight that day, the dark curls I'd seen in her high school picture on my grandparents' kitchen wall were already outnumbered by greys because being a single mom will do that.

Like plenty of Minnesotans, her great-grandparents settled in the Midwest from Scandinavia and Germany. My father's family, regular American black folks, cannot trace the origin of our ancestors farther back than two men freed from slavery, plus a Cherokee great-great grandmother, an Irish orphan left on a black family's doorstep, and French brothers who grandma says "had an affection" for slave women. Before my father was born, his parents fled the South during Jim Crow. He was eighteen when they returned to Georgia and he decided to stay in Minneapolis. A few years later, he and Mom met working at a health food co-op. They were in their early twenties when I was born, never married. Whether my parents loved each other or not is a detail they keep to themselves.

When I was two, my father moved to New York City to pursue a career in dance. Mom became a plant pathologist. She raised me alone in blizzards and slush, in vegetable gardens and lakes that could hold you in green. I loved her deeply. And I loved Minnesota. I was usually happy as a kid.

I was also the only black person in my town, in most of my classes at school, and in my home. I was The Black Girl. Chelsea with the Afro. I was Nigger. Medusa! Medusa! on the school bus.

Weekday mornings, I screamed while Mom tore through my hair with the big brush and the squirt bottle. I screamed when she got fed up with the work of it, then cut it as short as hers. When she had some extra money, I screamed in the Cost Cutters waiting area after the indignity of paging through catalogs on the table, the ones they put out to help white people with style ideas. Neat bob, the pixie. Layered, feathered, fountained…

"I am not represented here!" I stormed.

Mom tightened her lips and ushered me toward the stylist who could professionally smile you to death at her sink.

I'd seen some parts of *Clash of the Titans,* how the serpents on Medusa's head had their own tongues. Their own instinct and choreography. She was magic, even if it was her doom. My hair had its own choreography too. Some days it looked struck by lightning, others it coiled like a pile of phone cords. It defied gravity. It reached for the wind. It obstructed views.

Though it wasn't exactly like my father's (his hair rippled so tightly all over), I came to think of my hair as *my blackness.* Rooted. All my own. If I was the doomed witch for it, then maybe I was magic too.

"Nothing wrong with being different. Better than normal boring."

"White people only everywhere! That's a disempowering environment for a person of color! My race was pointed out to me e-v-e-r-y single day."

"You never told me that. I didn't know."

"Couldn't you have just looked around sometimes? Why would you choose to raise me here?"

"Because ... it's home."

I was nineteen this time, on winter break from Sarah Lawrence College in New York. I had a nose ring and a botched super-short haircut courtesy of my dorm roommate. Mom and I sat in the car again, seat belts on. Our Corolla – littered with Minnesota roadmaps, was a cherry red speck on the face of the earth, on the scroll of human history, where now I wanted to blame her. Accuse her. Explode! How could she presume we were simply mother and daughter when our country demanded us in opposite corners? Then again, all my life my throat gripped "black" like it did curse words in her presence. I sensed, even as a young child, that conversations about race were conversations about separation. I didn't dare bring it up in our house. Not in public. Only in the hush grey interior where Mom and I sat shoulder to shoulder. Where we had to keep close. Like these times I'm telling you about in our car.

At Sarah Lawrence College there were enough black students on campus to form a group called Harambee which demanded there weren't enough black students on campus. Somebody counted close to twenty; I didn't say that was a whole lot by my standards. I sat every meeting before the chalk-board that read "ACTIONS," all geared up just to be in the room. Our skins were a gorgeous spiral of browns. Our hair, every texture a curl could dream. Though they were strangers, this reflection must have mattered more than how I looked like my mother. They were not ashamed, slumped, or silent. Call them exotic and watch what happens. They knew what blackness was.

First semester, I handed my roommate the pair of scissors. She recommended I go to the mall instead. "I don't do mall haircuts," I informed her. "Bad experiences." And so she cut it all off while I sat on the lid of our hall toilet. It looked like I'd been in some kind of lawnmower accident. I was satisfied.

In my mid-twenties I moved to Brooklyn, New York. My neighborhood looked like Trinidad. Calypso and roti. My landlord was black, my neighbors, my subway stop, my laundromat was black. A few train stops away, I worked as a bartender at a soul food restaurant that featured live jazz. My boss was black, my co-workers, my customers. My soundtrack was black. Occasionally, I enjoyed (*really* enjoyed) saying, "The White Lady wants her collards to go." or "Don't give the White Guy anymore Hennessy. He's cut off." Sure, my feet ached in rum soaked, orthopedic galoshes. Sure, I'd have to force most smiles after 1:00 a.m. I hadn't planned to take orders for a living, I wanted to be a writer. But one night the band played "Chelsea Bridge" and a regular said, "Hey, they're playing your song." And maybe my first try at a novel was far from perfect, but I could make one hell of a martini. I knew I stood where I was supposed to be. And life was funny, playing me in extremes while the saxophone slipped from discord to harmony. Music belonged to both ears.

■ ■ ■

"REMEMBER Cost Cutters, Mom?"

"You screaming, I remember. Plenty of you screaming."

"Those magazines in the waiting area. Heads up their ass! Nobody in Carver County knew what to do with black hair."

"Black hair? But I always thought ..." Mom paused, careful. "You got *my* hair."

She kisses my oldest daughter's honey curls. She kisses my second baby's sleepy brown eyes. She waits outside the driver's side window while I buckle them in and start the car. Since becoming Grandma, Mom has grown her hair out long enough to twist into hair combs or braid.

Sometimes it looks struck by lightning, sometimes despite the straighter greys, it still coils. Perfect white phone chords reaching for the wind. My mother is beautiful.

Maybe one day my children will hold me captive by my own seat belt and accuse me of failing to see the ways their bodies depart from mine. I know our country will want to simplify them in a way I cannot. I have faced plenty of mirrors by now, realizing again Mom is right about my hair. Though my father's ripples gather at the edge of my forehead too like a council of waters. At forty, I am glad my reflections refuse to settle it. My hair. It's all up in the air. It always wanted to be. ■

Wayne Freeman

The Question

*My mom took my brother and me to visit my Jewish paternal
grandmother when I was a child. As we walked out to leave the
house, she said to my Mexican American mother, "You know.
There are Mexican families moving in here. And its fine with
me! They are good! They are not the kind with dirty faces and
snot coming out of their noses." My mom bit her tongue, but
when we got in the car, she vented to us kids. "Gimme a break.
I mean, what about you guys?!?! Do you have half a dirty face
and one nostril with mocos (Spanish for snot)?!?!?" Her joke
diffused the tension, and we laughed at the ridiculousness of it.*

*"Are you Mexican or white?" A Chicana girl in high school
asked me point blank. "Uhhh, both" I replied. My mom's
Mexican and my dad's white. "Your last name is Freeman?"
"Yea." "Do you speak good Spanish?" "Nah." "Oh then you're
white," she said. I chuckled awkwardly.*

*I got a job working at a local park shortly after high school. One
day, I got in a conversation with an older Mexican man. He
switched from English to Spanish, "Wait, you are Mexican right?"
he asked. I recalled the conversation with the girl in high school
recently, so I hesitated to say yes. "My mom is, but my dad's white."
"So the answer is yes," he said. "How can your mom be Mexican
but you are not? You don't have a problem with being Mexican
right?"*

Recently, my daughter began playing with a neighborhood boy who had a Latino father and a white mother. His father and I would sit outside and watch our kids, and we eventually developed a friendship. Months went by and he never asked me about my racial identification. Then, one day, he said, "You know what man, how does a Hispanic guy get a name like Wayne?" I laughed. "My father is white. And actually my last name is Freeman." "Wait, what???? You are half white?!?!?" "Yup," I said. "No way!!!" He exclaimed. "I never would have guessed it! I don't see it man." He stared at me hard. "Nope, I just can't see it!"

Ronnie is the older brother of an old friend. I have known Ronnie, who is half African American and half Chicano, for many years. Recently, Ronnie and I both attended a wedding, where Ronnie saw my parents for the first time. The next time I went to visit my friend, Ronnie said, "Hey man, I had never seen your mom before, I had no idea that you were half Mexican!" "Yeah," I laughed. "You didn't know that?!?!" "No!" He stared at my face very intently. "Holy shit! I can totally see it. I can't believe I never saw it before. Now that explains a lot!" We shared a good laugh, though I never figured out exactly what it explained.

I recently attended my cousin Rudy's wedding. Rudy is on my mother's Mexican American side of the family. My wife and I sat across from a Latin@ couple, a man and a woman who were friends of my cousin. We had never met before. As we began to talk, the woman looked at me puzzled. "Wait, you are related to Rudy?" she said. "Yeah," I said, "he's my cousin." "Whoa," she said, "I didn't think you were Mexican." She pointed at my wife, who is Latina, and said, "I thought you were the one that was related!" We all laughed, but it did feel weird that someone thought that I didn't look like I belonged among my own family.

CONFUSE PEOPLE. Race, much like gender, is one of the main classifications that people make when they meet somebody. Even mixed race people
like Ronnie do it. Some question me because they see me as racially ambiguous. Some, like the woman at the wedding, are sure I'm white. Others, like
the neighbor in the apartment complex, are sure I'm Mexican. Some rely on
things other than appearance to make up their mind. Language, name, clothing, etc. I laugh a lot in these interactions. Sometimes I find it genuinely funny,
and it's a good laugh. Sometimes its awkward laughter. Sometimes a mixture
of both. Being mixed race is a blessing and a curse for me. It has spurred me
to curiosity, made me more observant of arbitrary social classifications, and
more committed to racial justice and equality. But it has also been a source of
confusion and frustration. It has been an advantage, allowing me to sometimes
"pass" in the white world, and a disadvantage, rendering me unintelligible, a
social anomaly. I believe that mixed race people have important insights to
share, but many don't listen to social anomalies. They should, though.

I am frequently asked "What are you?" I understand that many mixed
race people dislike "the question," and I agree that it can be frustrating.
However, I generally welcome it. I look at it sort of like asking somebody
their preferred gender pronoun. I do not expect people to be color blind in
a society that is not. And though the question can be awkward, it can also
feel like a relief to get it over with, avoiding a future situation like the one
I had with my neighbor or Ronnie, when I can feel someone that I have
known for some time get new, shocking information and recategorize me.
Now that's uncomfortable. Sometimes I will find a reason to just casually
say it, and help people out if I sense it is on their minds.

I understand, however, that there may be certain factors that make me
not completely opposed to the "what are you" question. As a heterosexual
male, I am not asked this question in sexualized or exoticizing ways like many
women describe ("Ooooh you look exotic, what are you?"). Furthermore,
those who have grown up in mostly white spaces, unlike myself, may feel
a sting when asked this question by whites, a reminder that racial mixture
drops one down a peg in the racial hierarchy, and makes one feel inferior.
Of this I can only speculate, but I can say that "the question" from people
of color can feel like an authenticity test, or a sign that one is suspicious
of me. But I do not blame this on people that ask questions. [I blame this

on a racial hierarchy that places whites above non-whites, leading whites to feel superior to all others, leading all others to be suspicious of whites, and leading mixed white/non-white people like myself to have feelings of inferiority when questioned by whites, and feel distrusted when questioned by non-whites.]

What I do expect is that my answer to "the question" is accepted and respected. For mixed race people, any racial identification may be contested (well, you're not really . . .). In addition, many challenge mixed race as a legitimate category. They may, in their desire to maintain order in their world, attempt to tell you how you should identify yourself. Like the girl in high school and the man at the park, this often leads to contradictory messages. We need, then, collective social change, not individual strategies. We must create space for legitimate hybrid identities in our society, but instead we continue to see racial categories as discreet and mutually exclusive.

I believe, however, that we must go beyond just opening up space for hybrid identities, because it is not only the discreetness of racial categories that troubles me, but also the hierarchical nature of those categories. Again, the "what are you" question is uncomfortable not only because it is probing and makes one vulnerable in a racially polarized society, but also because it brings with it feelings of either inferiority or suspicion, feelings that are rooted in the history of colonization and its accompanying racial hierarchies. As long as racial categories continue to be hierarchical, they will remain crucial distinctions and sites of struggle. The push for mixed race legitimacy, then, must also involve a struggle against white supremacy and racial hierarchy, as racial polarization and racial hierarchization are intricately intertwined. How can we even conceive of hybrid identities when different parts of our identities have unequal power relationships with each other in the world around us? How can that ever be psychologically healthy?

A struggle for hybrid identities that does not seek to dismantle racial hierarchy is also socially irresponsible because it only serves to move white/non-white mixed race people up the hierarchy at the expense of monoracial non-white people. The reality of colorism among colonized and racialized people, or the vertical spectrum of hierarchical *mestizaje* throughout Latin America, shows what results when more nuanced racial categories exist without challenging white supremacy. White supremacy does not end because of racial mixture, it only becomes more complex. And besides, why push for hybridized identities that really only solidify a position for us below whites and above non-whites, or as my mother put it, half a dirty face and one nostril with *mocos*? That's the question. ■

Frances Frost

There Are Levels to This

DON'T GO TO THE PLAYGROUND 'til I get back from school. And do not eat that outside." These were my older cousin's instructions to my brother and me when we first arrived in Baltimore. Why did we have to be stuck in the house or confined to the front stoop until the 3:00 p.m. school bell when our summer had already started? And why couldn't we eat our favorite *kimbap*, rice rolled in seaweed, while sitting outside? The snowball truck didn't even come until after all the neighborhood kids got home from school and there was not much else to do until then.

We had moved from San Antonio to Baltimore and were staying with my father's brother and sister-in-law while waiting to find our own house. Our dad, uncle and aunt went off to work each day. My mother, brother and I stayed home. I thought my parents would veto my cousin's "rule," but not only did my parents think waiting for him was a good idea, my mother was a bit nervous about heading out in this new city by herself, too. So the three of us waited each day until the kids came home from school, and the adults came home from work.

It was in those couple of months of living in Baltimore that I realized how uncommon being biracial was. Or at least, in Baltimore City. We had moved from an Army base where my friends were various percentages of Thai, black, Korean, Puerto Rican, Mexican and white. My classmates were as likely born in a foreign country as they were born in the United States, with two parents of the same or different race. My black and Korean brother and I, our Korean mother, and black father fit in fine. But that changed when we moved out of the Army base gates.

Baltimore, or at least the part we lived in, was a predominant race city: black. And it was here where I stumbled upon the telltale signs that we were something other than that. The long straight ponytails and almost almond shaped eyes gave me away. My brother with the same eyes, the curly hair. People thought we were Hawai'ian. Our mother of course was the dead giveaway. When people saw her, they thought we were Chinese. Those were pretty much the options. But whatever we were, they were sure we weren't black like them, and we weren't from Baltimore.

My cousin's warning made sense once we realized how much of a curiosity we were. And how everyone wasn't too crazy about us not-from-around-here kids. There were always questions. What are you? Where are you from? Do you eat rice everyday? Do you speak English? You think you're cute with that long hair? There were the pulled-back eyes, the miming of hair flips that I've never done in my life, and the mimicking "ching-chong" sounds that were supposed to approximate a foreign language that wasn't even ours. My cousin was there to deflect the many questions and stares so we could swing and go down the slide in moderate peace.

Moving to the county was only the B-side of the same record. Our new neighbors were black and white, but we still remained the only biracial kids in our neighborhood and school for a long time.

We realized that there are levels to this status of being biracial. The next level is being bicultural. What's the difference? A big difference.

A child with a black parent and a white parent, both American, is biracial. There is a debate about sweet potato or pumpkin pie, The Beatles or the Jackson Five, the Bunkers or the Jeffersons, afro or blond French braids. Being biracial is getting someone to cornrow your hair, but they don't really stay unfrizzed like everyone else's. It's having some family from the north and others from the south. Listening to gospel and country. You have a mix of features from all the grandparents, but clearly, you are seen as some kind of American mulatto.

Bicultural is having an American parent and a not-American parent. The conversation is in a mixed-language, there is macaroni and cheese and seaweed on the table. You are the only black kid listening to Donnie and Marie because your mom thought they looked like nice people. You celebrate Christmas, New Years, the Lunar New Year, and commemorate your ancestors (the not-American ones.) You wear your native dress to your piano recital because it is, after all, a very important event. Your mother doesn't really understand what the teacher is saying and you don't have enough native language skills to translate. It's being asked all the time "What are you?" "That's a country?"

It's a little bit different, as it turned out, than having a different religion. Many of our classmates practiced this new religion I had only read about: Judaism. I'd never had real live Jewish friends before. And I soon came to discover, they ate some odd foods, too. Come spring time, they ate these flat crackers and a bready-ball soup. They were allowed to bring their foods to school, but my rice and kimchi stayed home. They went to school and learned another language, but their parents spoke English, and only spoke Hebrew for religious reasons. No one ever asked them what they were or where they were from. They were all white and there were a lot of them. Everyone knew their food and why the boys wore those little hats. Their differences were part of the fabric; ours totally clashed. There were levels to this bicultural thing, too.

As we settled into our new home, we came to understand that being bicultural meant being good in math (as people expected) but not at basketball (what a shock to many.) It meant playing the piano, but having no dance rhythm. It meant eating all the food you loved at home and taking peanut butter and jelly to school. It was living up to—or not—all the stereotypes of a culture everyone was familiar with and one that people really weren't. Being bicultural is having a guilty acknowledgment that you harbor some of those same negative stereotypes against your own race. Both of them.

As a biracial and bicultural child, you one day realize that you possess this duality of race and culture and heritage. You realize that there is the race of your parents—and that there is a third one. There is the amalgamation between the two races of your family which is uniquely yours and your siblings. Adults understand that biracial is a different thing, with its own beauty and stories, as well as challenges and peculiarities. And its own history, because in all blendings of races, there is some history. But monoracial people really don't understand all the complexities of this third race that is separate from their own.

But when you are a little kid, who has moved into a new city where it seems that no one else looks like you, you are just making this discovery. You are coming to realize that you need some protection around you. You learn to guard your feelings against those who don't fully embrace all that you are. Who don't accept the other half of you. You get tired of answering the same questions over and over and standing up against the same teasing over and over. You begin to welcome someone to stand guard around you.

You leave the *kimbap* inside until dinner. Instead, you sit on the stoop and come to love salted sunflower seeds you bought from the snowball truck yesterday while everyone was home. You learn how to suck the salt off of them, crack and spit out the shells and enjoy the seeds. And you wait for your cousin to come home from school because all you want to do is not think about race. You only want to go play on the swings. ■

Wendy A. Gaudin

Raceless

I AM A CHILD OF MIXTURE. I have no black parent. I have no white parent. I have no Asian parent, I have no Middle Eastern parent, nor Pacific Islander, nor Micronesian, nor Indian Oceanic. I am not the product of American troops in Vietnam or Cambodia, Korea or the Philippines. I am not the child of a Cuban mother and a Russian father, an Israeli father and a Palestinian mother. I am not Sudanese and South Sudanese. I am not half one thing and half another.

I am the product of the bayous and the deltas, the tenant farms and the sugar fields. I spring from the curving levees that are the burial grounds of convict laborers and the disappearing islands of the Gulf, I am the child of the oyster shell streets and dirty brick roads of Louisiana: the neglected backwoods of France's western empire, the unwrapped gift to Imperial Spain, the cheap procurement by the expansive kingdom of the U.S. The state itself has existed in a kind of territorial binary: the north Anglo, English-speaking and Protestant; and the south Latinate, French-speaking and Catholic. The north, hilly with piney woods, and the south, below sea level and sinking. Louisiana, the colony stolen from the Houma, the Chitimacha, the Tensas, the Opelousa, the Pascagoula, the Tunica. Stolen from the Natchez. Louisiana, the colony: settled violently, painstakingly, lustily, involuntarily, and incrementally by Europeans, Africans, Caribbean islanders, and Asians of various extractions, class positionings, various ethnicities and upward mobilities.

My upwardly-mobile people planted this place, its roots mossy, its branches languid. They were French, Fon, Yoruba and Fula; Haitian, Choctaw, Natchitoches and Cherokee; Spanish, Scots-Irish, German, and Chinese.

They were laundresses and seamstresses, they were printers and carpenters, they were farmers and oystermen, day laborers and pharmacists, root workers and healers. Shredding every line that time and space and sovereignty drew around their bodies, my ancestors – the named and the unnamed, the dominant and the raped, the settlers and the settled upon – turned completely upside down what was familiar in the world. They made something brand new: the first intercontinental tribe. They made the people who made me.

My mother and my father are both mixed, both children of Louisiana people who left the Jim Crow South behind and settled in Los Angeles. All four of my grandparents were mixed. They held on to their fancy Louisiana accents and Southern grammar for decades out on the West Coast, my grandmothers with skin the color of coconut rice, my grandfathers brown like *injera*. Of my eight great-grandparents, six were mixed. Of my sixteen great-great grandparents, ten were mixed. Grandfatherlessness defined both of my parents' childhoods: two grandfathers having been white men, visiting their hegemonic sex upon two young, mixed girls and then vanishing. The other two died in the old country, taking their final rest in the concrete tombs of Orleans and Ascension Parishes: one of them being half mulâtre and half Choctaw, standing tall and thin, and the other looking like P. B. S. Pinchback.

I was reared in the white flight suburbs at the base of the Santa Susana Mountains. My childhood friends were Kleins, Steins, Buchwalds, Malamuds, Baxters, Schneiders, Horlicks, and Haases. While many of our neighbors were ethnic Jews, celebrating Seder and Shabbat, Bar Mitzvahs and Bat Mitzvahs (some of my friends' fathers wearing Yarmulkes, Mezuzahs nailed at an angle next to their front doors), we were the racially ambiguous family with the French surname. We weren't clearly anything except Catholic and middle class. Like our neighbors, our father went to work every day (him being a biology professor), and our mother stayed at home, packing our lunches, washing our clothes, shopping for groceries, driving us to CCD, brushing our long, curly hair. Our cousins came to visit us on the weekends, and we spent our afternoons sitting on the covered back patio, swimming in the pool that was often littered with pine needles, dancing to black music in the living room, our cousins, sporting their dark brown, light brown, pale and alabaster skin, their blue eyes, their freckles and red hair, arriving in someone's red Opel GT, with Eric Clapton blaring from the speakers.

I was the darkest of my mother's three daughters, my oldest sister look-ing Polynesian with long, straight, black hair, and my middle sister looking somewhat Caucasian until the 1980s, when people decided that she looked like Jennifer Beals and told her so. As a young girl, I was almond brown with two long braids hanging down my back. Now, as a middle aged woman, my face is the pink of the rosacea that I've inherited from my mother, and the almond-brown of my youth has faded to cashew.

Once, when I was a student at Alfred Nobel Junior High School, a black classmate asked me a silly, adolescent question, "If there was a race war, which side would you be on? Would you go with the blacks or the whites?" I remember thinking, I have no idea why you're giving me those two options. He must have assumed that I was biracial. I do, indeed, have a brown-skinned father and a white-skinned mother, a father with a long pointed nose and a mother with wavy jet-black hair, a father who is mistaken for Eritrean and a mother to whom people speak Armenian, and display their disappointment when she tells them, "Really! I am not Armenian!" I recall people telling me, "Wow! You look just like your dad!" Aside from my skin color and my curly hair, I don't resemble my father, but I do look a lot like my mother, whom service workers always assume is the woman in front of me in line. "We're together," my mother or I say, with a clear intonation of correction.

When people learn that I am mixed, or when they ask me, "What are you?" and I reply, "I'm mixed," they conflate mixedness with biraciality. I must have a mother who is one thing and a father who is something else. Often, I have encountered an understandable hostility from my black comrades, an assumption that blackness is something I cower away from, or something that I don't have to claim because of my presentation or my upbringing. But my explanation, either aloud or to myself, is one that reaches back to my history, my family prior to their migration to California, my family all the way back to the American Revolution. I am a child of mixture, I enunciate just like that, with my Southern California, mall-loitered, beach-dusted, Valley-decorated accent not nearly as strong as my grandparents, I am the result of generations upon generations of mixed people seeking each other out, mixed people arranging their children's marriages, mixed people finding refuge in the middle ground that they shared, mixed people meeting each other at dances and at novenas, choosing mates who looked like themselves or who shared their local culture, choosing mates whose skin color matched their own, who ate gumbo on Sundays and red beans and rice on Mondays.

So when that classmate of mine asked me, "Which side would you be on?," I struggled to answer because I knew that my answer was not what he was looking for. If I'd said, "the white side," I would be immediately rejected, called out as a traitor, a brown-skinned girl who thinks she's white; if I'd said, "the black side," I would be claiming a loyalty and belonging that I'd never felt. It was an impossible question.

The question, too, took a war-like stance: its weapons were the context of race in America, its harm was the impossibility of an answer. The question was a weapon aimed at my body, which represented in its very physicality the violence of history, the transgressions of sexuality, the byproduct of power, the illicitness of desire. My body: a question seeking to be answered, a problem that needed to be solved.

After the classmate at Alfred Nobel Junior High School walked away from me, the question he asked hovered in the air like an unexploded bomb as I walked through the gates, climbed into my mother's red Oldsmobile, and quietly knew that I would be asked this question, one way or another, for the rest of my life. ■

Herbert Harris

Multigenerational Identities

MY FIRST CONSCIOUS AWARENESS of racial identity occurred at the age of four. I was attending a black preschool where I was one of the lightest children in the class. It was only a matter of time before the difference between me and most of the other children would be noticed. One day, another child placed his hand next to mine and said, "I'm black and you're white." I was terrified at the thought of being different from the other children. The fear and isolation I experienced in that moment remains one of my most vivid childhood memories. It was a scene that would be repeated many times. I was often the lightest child among various groupings of playmates and schoolmates. A consciousness of color had been awakened in me and in my peers, that would remain with me throughout my life.

I have very light skin and physical features that are mostly suggestive of Caucasian ancestry. However, the overall impression that I convey is sufficiently ambiguous to be interpreted as either black or white. As an adult, I have found that the way others recognize me depends largely on context and expectations. Racial perceptions are never projected onto a blank slate. They are filtered and distorted by many lenses. My skin color and features usually serve to corroborate people's assumptions or confirm their suspicions. The person we think we see is rarely the person who is actually before us. Throughout most of my adult life, I have lived and worked in predominantly white environments. An assumption of whiteness usually biases how others see me. Without additional cues, most people tend to identify me as white. This is very far from who I am.

My racially mixed heritage came to me through many generations. My ancestors were slaves and slave owners. Researching their history has given me many insights into my own identity. Mixed since before the Civil War, my ancestors migrated to Washington, D.C. after Reconstruction. Here they formed a very diverse society that was part of a larger black community. Looking back as far as the photographic record permits; my ancestors had visibly mixed features. Many could have passed as white and escaped the segregation that surrounded them. They chose instead to remain part of a community with which they had very strong ties. Within this community, my family's identity has always been a complex and evolving question. Each generation struggled with its issues, and each found its own solutions. My parents, grandparents, and great-grandparents all had very different perspectives of who they were, and how they fit into the interstices between black and white. Some lived in times when being of mixed race conferred significant privileges. Others lived in times when mixed race was a major disadvantage. Their struggles, attitudes, outlooks, and conflicts about race were passed down from generation to generation to become a vital part of my heritage.

As a result of multigenerational mixing, I grew up in a family where race was not a dichotomous matter of black and white. If it was anything at all, race was a continuum of tones, colors, and textures. There were no natural divisions between people. I had aunts, uncles, and cousins who represented a spectrum, each gradation blending imperceptibly into the next. Some of us were darker and others lighter. I was aware of being a part of this continuum, but I had no conception of black or white. It was not until my preschool experience, when I began to move away from my circle of family and neighbors, that I became conscious of the racially polarized society that surrounded us.

I was born in the midst of the civil rights era, nine years before the *Loving v. Virginia* decision struck down the last of the anti-miscegenation laws that prohibited interracial marriage. The idea of a distinct mixed race identity was almost inconceivable at that time. People of mixed heritage existed everywhere around me, but the outside world recognized us only as black. We lived in a society governed by the one-drop rule that defined as black anyone having any African ancestry. A sharp color line divided Washington into black and white. My family had been members of the city's black middle class. To outsiders, we were essentially invisible, living within the margins of a marginalized community. That invisibility increased as a more Afrocentric spirit animated black consciousness throughout the 1960s. As black became beautiful, beige receded further into the background.

The year after my preschool experience, my parents made great financial sacrifices to send me to a predominantly white private school in Washington. The civil rights movement had opened unprecedented opportunities for us to go to schools that our parents could never have dreamed of attending. Because of my ambiguous appearance, race did not seem, at first, to be a salient issue. I was happy just to blend in with the other children and forget about the color consciousness that I had experienced the year before. Yet, I was increasingly aware that something separated me from these white children. I could not fail to notice that each day I crossed the color line that divided Washington on my journey to school. I went from the decaying black neighborhood of my family and friends to the amazingly affluent white neighborhoods of my school and school friends. The material contrast between the homes and cars was stunning, but so was the racial divide that separated these worlds. For a time, I was accepted into this privileged and sheltered place, but some part of me knew that I was only a guest. Where did I really belong?

The question of belonging would not go away. A nagging awareness of difference festered and grew. I could not name it, but it was always there. I wanted very much to belong. In the fourth grade, an event occurred that placed race at the center of my awareness. I had a falling out with a friend. I can't recall what we argued over, but tempers got out of control. "Nigger," he called me. I felt a blinding rage. What happened next was a blur. We fought; parents were called, conferences held, apologies exacted. The school worked very hard to smooth things over, but nothing would ever be the same for me. The secret that I didn't even know I was keeping had gotten out.

How did I know this word? Where could I have heard it before? How could I have grasped its significance? Somehow, I did. Somehow, I knew all of its terrible meanings. This single word opened a fracture line that split the two worlds I inhabited apart. All of the feelings of anger and shame and fear now had a name.

These experiences framed my early racial identity development with book-end-like symmetry. Among black children, I had been identified as other; among white children, I had been identified as other. Each experience was associated with significant emotional trauma, and each had lasting effects on my relations with others. Race seemed to be a game that I could not win. I was constantly on guard, constantly wondering how others saw me. Did I blend in among my peers, or was I recognized as other? Who was I beneath the camouflage I presented to others? Where did I belong?

These questions followed me through college, medical school, and well into my work life as a mental health professional. At every stage of my life, new variations on my childhood experiences have arisen and constantly challenged me to rethink and reframe the fundamental issues of identity. At the same time, I have witnessed profound societal changes that remapped the terrain between black and white. No longer a disturbing paradox to be passed over in silence, mixed race is becoming an increasingly acknowledged entity within our society. Yet that society still offers us only limited modes of recognition, and we continue to be seen primarily through filters of black or white.

Identity is a dialogue between self and others. How is authentic self-expression possible when others see us in such divergent and contradictory ways? For me the answer continues to unfold against the background of my experiences. A major source of strength has come from knowing that others have traveled this path before. As I have learned more about my family history, I have come to appreciate that it has always been possible to create authentic identities within this liminal space between black and white. My mixed race ancestors lived through times of slavery and emancipation, Reconstruction and Jim Crow. They lived through race riots. They built a community and participated in the transformation of our society. What enabled them to succeed was the capacity to live with the paradoxes of identity, and to turn paradox into a creative force. The identity that I have today is a product not only of my own personal experiences, but also of the experiences of all the generations that came before. ■

Rena M. Heinrich

The White Wilderness

EVEN I THOUGHT IT WAS WEIRD that there were Filipinos in Alaska.
How they ended up there is still a mystery to me. Sure, I knew the
history of the Alaskeros who worked in the canneries in the 1930s.
I knew that Alaska was one of the easiest entrance points into the United
States, following the 1965 Immigration Act. Yes, it was paradise for a culture
in love with fish. But when these islanders from the Tropic of Cancer landed
and stepped onto the ice fields in perpetual darkness, I would have thought
that they'd have headed south. They didn't. They stayed. Hundreds of Filipinos migrated to Alaska and made the Last Frontier their home, my family
among them. As a child, I grew up carrying bamboo poles through two feet
of snow for the annual Filipino community banquets. I took off my Moon
Boots and danced the Tinikling barefoot, although it was twenty below zero
outside. I was carted around to every Filipino Mass, spoken in a tongue
familiar, though at times indecipherable. My blood knew I was in the right
place, knew that I belonged there, but I was still on the outside somehow.

There was a reason for this.

Try as I might, I failed at being accepted by the other Filipino children.
This was to be the running theme of my youth in Alaska. It was not because
I didn't really speak Tagalog or Ilocano. It was because of one simple fact,
something about myself I loved, but something the others could not recon-
cile – my father was white.

It was my light complexion, my German surname, my European jaw
that betrayed the Ilocano features and made me look more Japanese than
anything else. Forget the fact that I couldn't speak the language. Take one look
at me and right away I looked like the nisei neighbor from down the street.

The adults loved it. They petted me, smiled at me, and told me I was beautiful—a *mestiza*. I was something novel to them. My tito lovingly called me "Snow White." But to the kids my age, I was an outsider, trying to lay claim to an inheritance that wasn't mine. The irony was that I was culturally more Filipino than the other pinoy children I knew. My mother, who had a Masters in bilingual education, made educating others about the Filipino culture her life's work. She pulled me out of my Catholic school to don butterfly sleeves and to dance the *Paru-parong Bukid* at multicultural fairs. I grew up receiving "blessings" from my grandparents, aunts, and uncles. I listened to the lore of the acacia trees and the *nipa* huts, proud that these stories made me who I was. I had aunties, not aunts, and they didn't have to be related to me. I had actually been to the Philippines and played with my cousins in the province. I was constantly reminded that my mother was the oldest of seven—the brilliant one—and that being her eldest daughter gave me certain leverage, a leverage that came with dire responsibility. For me, the word "family" meant every single member of the extended tree as well as some neighbors you annexed in. Rice went with everything from tacos to spaghetti. Christmas was not only about turkey and mashed potatoes. It was also about *lumpia* and *pancit*. I looked forward to the *polvoron* in my Christmas stocking.

Somehow, this wasn't enough.

The Filipino Community of Anchorage, Alaska sponsored banquets, picnics, potlucks, and Masses, and one year they hosted a teen dance. It was held in the dead of winter, but I wanted to go. I begged my mom to take me—my protective Filipino mother who normally wouldn't let me out of the house. "What curfew?" she always quipped. I had no curfew because parents in their right minds didn't let their children out of the house past nine o'clock. But a dance, sponsored by the Filipino Community? She would let me go to that. She braved ten degrees below zero, the snow crunching under her tires as she backed out of the garage, and drove on black ice to get me there.

I was thrilled. Finally. Finally, there would be a place where I would fit in. Of course! I could dance! Everyone can fit in, can blend in, at a dance. I really wanted this. They would see that I was one of them. I tried to slip into conversations. I tried to be as friendly as I could, surreptitiously hoping my black hair and brown eyes could carry me all on their own. In the outside world, these traits were dead ringers for my ethnic background, giving me an easy pass into Asian circles. But here, they were of no use to me. I couldn't understand why their racial alchemy didn't work. Mostly, I couldn't avoid the fact that none of the other kids would dance with me.

These were the children of my mother's friends. I knew them all by name. I smiled. I tried to call them to me, and all that happened was a large group of the "full" kids, the full Filipinos, on one side of the room and me, the *tisay*, dancing alone on the other. I knew for sure then that my "whiteness" was unforgivable. It was my "not being Filipino enough" that held me at bay. This solidified my understanding of my "otherness" forever. I was not like them. No matter how much I tried. My DNA would not allow it. They would not allow it. I tried to pretend this didn't bother me. The Cure and Depeche Mode were all that I needed. I was fine. I danced solo for awhile. Then finally, I convinced myself I had to go. I had things to do. I just stopped in because my mom had made me. I called her to come get me. "Why so early?" she said.

I left the dance with the snow swirling around me, the spirit of *mabuhay* abandoning me in the darkness of the frozen north. I was the Snow White in slippery shoes, turned out to brave a white wilderness alone. ■

Velina Hasu Houston

Cinnamon and Pearl

TAKING A TRIP TO A STORE with my mother was always a big event when I was a child in Kansas. Probably such a trip produced excitement in many children, but the trip for me was a Big Adventure outside of the Japanese culture that reigned inside of our home and into the American world outside. Let me note that by "American" I am referring to the United States-centric usage of the word to mean citizens of the U.S.

I am five years old. I am in the midst of the first year of an American school, Westwood Elementary in Junction City, Kansas. I am wearing a yellow and white gingham dress with black rickrack that my mother has made for me. Watching her sew on the rickrack, the meticulousness of her fingers holding the trim and hand-sewing it into the bottom of the skirt of the dress before she hemmed it had been a meditation, a meditation on how different my life was from those of most of the other children at Westwood Elementary: me with my cinnamon-hued skin and wavy hair, my mother with her pearl-colored skin and straight, fine hair; me with my Japanese, African, Native American Indian, and Cuban heritage; my mother with her Japanese heritage. Having been reared in Japan, she had learned to sew, embroider, knit, crochet, and tat, arts fairly lost in the U.S. I felt privileged to have a dress made by her expert and caring hands versus something that was bought off the rack at a local store.

My mother takes me to a department store on the main street of the town. As we disembark from the maroon Pontiac sedan that my father deemed safe and big enough for her to drive, my pearl-skinned Japanese mother takes me by the hand as though I am made of gold. When we enter the store, the white ladies that work there look us over as if we have wandered into the wrong place. One nods to another, and that one proceeds to follow us around the store as we strive to shop. Their presence concerns my mother. Finally, she decides that it is safe to let go of my hand. I watch the white ladies watching me and have a sudden, quick urge to do something to upset them since they are looking at me as if I am going to do just that. However, I quell the urge and try to ignore their eyes tracking my every movement.

While my mother looks at ladies' gloves, I look at handkerchiefs in the next aisle. My mother often wears gloves, something that I find so elegant and feminine.

Because she is the only woman that I have seen wearing gloves, I have come to believe that glove-wearing is Japanese and not American. I like gloves, but there are not many choices for little girls, just plain black or white, and my world is oh-so-much-more colorful than that. Handkerchiefs held a different kind of fascination because I could use the ones designed for adults. I stood in front of the handkerchiefs gazing at the different styles. There was not much color differentiation, but there were different kinds of lace on the white ones, and there were beige, lilac, and baby pink ones. My mother had brought such beautiful handkerchiefs from Japan. None of these truly compared, but I scrutinized them trying to decide which one I preferred. Even as I admired them and imagined myself using one at school, I could hear the American children laughing at me for using something that they felt was so ridiculous, unnecessary, and old-fashioned. Were handkerchiefs Japanese, too?

Then I saw him.

He was a tall white man wearing a black suit, white shirt, and matching tie. His blond hair was slicked back with some sort of pomade. Except for a slight forward bend in his right shoulder, he stood straight, but on his tiptoes. The reason for this is that he had come to a sudden stop, his breath caught by the sight of something that had completely arrested his attention. I followed his gaze. He was staring at my mother; in fact, he was gawking. The intensity of his gaze caused my mother to look up from the gloves in his direction. I watched through the displays from the next aisle.

Stammering a hello, the man approached my mother and stood too close to her. "Where are you from?" he asked.

"Japan."

"So you're Japanese?" My mother nodded.

"If you don't mind me saying, you're the most beautiful thing I ever saw."

My mother bowed and stepped back. Looking toward the aisle in which I stood, her brow furrowed with concern. I walked slowly into her aisle and bowed.

Smiling at me, she took my hand. The man's gaze turned from lovelorn admiration into suspicion.

"Who's that?" he asked.

"My daughter," my mother said.

The man's expression turned into horror. "This is your daughter?" Clearly, he did not believe that cinnamon and pearl skin belonged together, and definitely not in the same family. "You adopted her?" Now his tone sounded impertinent, as though he could process the notion of adoption, but not the adoption of a dark-skinned child and certainly not a child that had any shred of African descent.

"This is my mother," I said.

"My daughter," my mother affirmed.

"You mean, you're married to a…a…" The man could not look more disgusted, a state of being that only further repulsed my mother and me. He was not our kind of people. "But you didn't have to do that," he lamented. "You're so beautiful. You didn't have to do that." Turning so quickly that I thought he would fall down, he spun around and dashed out of the store.

One of the ladies in the store apparently had witnessed or eavesdropped on the entire episode. She looked at my mother and me as if we had done something to offend this offensive man.

I realized that my being and looking different was always going to be a point of consternation for many people that thought of themselves as having only one race, people I call monoracial. The idea that diverse cultures could blend into a new kind of being that did not fit into any known racial category and that, in fact, defied categorization was above and beyond what Americans could absorb.

When it comes to mixed race individuals that also have African heritage, I think this problem grows exponentially.

I have always thought of being and looking different as assets. My differences enrich my outlook, humanity, worldview, and writing. In my grade school, there were many other mixed race persons that had Japanese, African American, Native American Indian, European American, and Latin roots.

Because of that, I did not feel alone in my mixed race identity and interracial, international family, but, in the outer society, I did feel that race was reduced to an overly simplistic duality of white and black. That reduction meant that mixed race people were erroneously lumped into one category or another, never mind the fact that they did not belong in those categories, nor did they fit and they definitely did not fit. Both white and black people are guilty of trying to reduce mixed race into one or the other, and therefore, I guess, understand it and are able to rest easy in that understanding, despite the inaccuracy. I was blessed with the fact that in my inner society, the society of my family if you will, I did not face difficulties with regard to being mixed race. My father and mother both supported the fact that I was a product of both of them and, on that basis, multiracial and multicultural. Whenever the "what are you" question was asked of me – and it was asked often – my parents encouraged me to claim my blendedness and explain the wealth of my ethnicities.

My mixed race and multicultural identity and my mediation of them emanate from living the truth of my identity. I have never been interested in passing for black, Asian, or Latina; if asked, I like to address everything that I am without apology or fanfare. I support a "no passing" zone. Humankind constructed the idea of "race" to be able to categorize human beings and understand/limit them better. Those kinds of boundaries do not hold salt with me. Over the years, my explorations as a writer – fed by explorations of ethnicity, gender, sexuality, and intellectualism – have guided me into a deeper understanding of who I am ethnically and why it is critical that I honor that in the name of my ancestors, for my children, and for future descendants.■

Mark S. James

Living Color in a Color Blind World

WHEN I FELT DISCOURAGED AS A CHILD, my white maternal grandmother would sometimes tell me that I could become the first black President of the United States. I don't know if she actually believed that, but I do know she intended to make sure that I would never feel inferior because I am black. Obviously, I did not become the first black President, but the professor who welcomed me and my cohort to graduate school did. Fortunately, I have never had any interest in being a politician, let alone President, but I did go on to get the education my grandmother implied I would need to protect and defend myself against a culture still dominated by white supremacy.

I think Grandma drew on her own experience with oppression in order to relate to me. Because my grandmother's mother had gone to college and became a teacher, Grandma expected to go to college and dreamed of becoming a poet. But the Great Depression dashed her hopes and she was compelled to skip college and support her younger brother as he went to college and then law school. Afterward, she married my grandfather and became a stay-at-home mom. But she was not happy. As my mother described her own childhood, it sounds like Grandma became one of those upwardly-mobile but deeply discontented and self-medicating housewives that Betty Friedan describes in *The Feminine Mystique*.

Then along came me. I was Grandma's first grandchild and because my skin color could no longer be used to deny me access to any college or university, she wanted me to pursue the finest education available. When she would look into my eyes and say, "Mark, they can take everything from you – your money, your house, your job, *everything* – but the one thing no one can take from you is your education and the person you become because of it," I intuitively understood her to be warning me not to place too much value in money and things, and not to assume that the opportunities available to me at that time would always be available to me. As she surely knew, the end of state-sanctioned racial discrimination did not mean the end of white supremacy, just as women winning the right to vote hadn't meant the end of patriarchy. After all, Grandma's mother had gone to college and yet Grandma couldn't. She had spent her childhood in the Roaring Twenties and witnessed how quickly everything was lost in the Crash of 1929 and the Great Depression, and she had seen young women like herself contribute enormously to the war effort only to be pulled back into the domestic sphere and marginalized once the war concluded. Now she lived in a nice, beach-front home and always had two new cars in the driveway, but she knew that it all could be snatched away in an instant and she would have nothing to call her own. So she pushed education as my path to freedom.

I was only sixteen when Grandma died and, to put it mildly, I did not take it well. Growing up, I saw my grandparents a great deal in the summers and I drew on their unconditional love and support year-round to combat the indifference or outright hostility I often felt in my daily life. To be sure, there were white cousins, friends, and teachers who were also supportive, but I felt that my grandparents understood what I was up against and were firmly on my side. I would even call on them to intervene on my behalf when I felt that my own mother was being unreasonable.

Nothing in my mother's background prepared her to be a single mother of two black children, so it was hard for her. She and her sister grew up in an upwardly-mobile middle-class family in a conservative, predominantly white city in central Illinois. My grandparents wanted to make sure that their two daughters had a more secure and privileged upbringing than they had, so they pushed their children to go to college and get a degree. My aunt became a veterinarian, but my mother, rebelliously impatient with formal education, dropped out of college after accumulating just enough credits for an Associate's degree. She became a social worker, and that is where she met my father. He was from a black community in Detroit, and so my parents became fascinated with each other in the heady context of the Civil Rights movement. Nevertheless, they retreated back to their respectively segregated worlds soon after I was born, so I only had contact with my black family members a few weeks each summer. So my mother struggled with single parenthood as well as a loss of class and racial status. As far as she was concerned, the demands of the Civil Rights movement had been accomplished with the legal dissolution of Jim Crow segregation, and as black women were promoted over her at work she began to complain that maybe racism was going the other way. Additionally, because of the failed relationships with my father and my sister's father, my mother swore off black men. And since she believed that no white man would want a white woman with black children, she waited until my sister and I graduated and left home to begin dating again.

I felt responsible for my mother's hardship and unhappiness, as any child would. I also felt responsible for the general unease I sometimes sensed among her family and friends. I am certain that my mother's friends and family felt they were doing a kind thing by ignoring race, but as I grew into a young man this "colorblindness" increasingly made me feel that there was something wrong with me. Even though I had never developed what might be called a black identity, nor had I been aware of experiencing much in the way of explicit racism, I still felt a certain tension, as if my skin was some intrusive reminder to politely change the subject. These microaggressions went unremarked, like summer lightning with no thunder, no rain, and no relief. While I know that no one intended to insult me or make me uncomfortable, I sensed that their concern was less about me and more about reassuring and supporting my mother as she continued to suffer for her youthful indiscretions.

Like most children, I felt that the relationships with my mother and everyone else were "normal." For the most part, my mother was charming, smart, and fun, and, like I said, her friends and family were kind and tolerant. Yet, because these relationships still made me feel invisible much of the time, I chose to pursue my college education as far away from home as I could get, and to the surprise of exactly no one, I flunked out my first year. But I pulled myself together and, with the help of part-time work and a condominium's worth of student loans, I managed not only to earn a Bachelor's degree from the University of Southern California, but a Master's degree from the University of Hawaii and a PhD from the University of Chicago.

Yet, whenever I went back home things only seemed to get worse. As long as I was genial and accommodating all was well, but the moment I said anything that made anyone uncomfortable my family would circle the wagons as if against some ill-mannered intruder. The last straw came after a cousin declared on Facebook that race played no part in Michael Brown's murder or in the prosecutor's refusal to indict Darren Wilson for it. I challenged that and after an increasingly bitter exchange I soon found myself trying to explain to my family how white privilege and white fragility were making it impossible for them to hear me. When they cast themselves as victims because I called the racist things they said "racist," I finally accepted that in their view silently tolerating my blackness in their family meant I had no right to demand anything more from them.

Fortunately for me, early in my life my grandmother bestowed me with a counter-narrative about who I was and what I could become that contradicted the seductive but degrading narratives of black masculinity that percolated through my environment as I was growing up. Who knows what I could have done had she lived longer, but I think she would be pleased to know that I still heard her through all of the noise and confusion. I think she'd be proud that the education she wanted for me helped me understand my personal struggle as part of the struggle that is America. As the election of Donald Trump proves, that struggle is still very far from over. ∎

Allyson Jeffredo

A Half Tale

There's no imagination, actually. Many of the anecdotes in the book were gathered by asking friends of mine to tell me moments when racism surprisingly entered in when you were among friends or colleagues, or just doing some ordinary thing in your day.

—Claudia Rankine, on where she acquired some of the stories in *Citizen*

ARRIVE AT MY FRIEND'S HOUSE late one Saturday evening. It's March. The evening chill still lurks in the trees at night. Everyone's hiding from the crisp air in the living room, casually drinking beers. We spent many weekends together like this, but since school started—we're all instructors of miscellaneous grades—we didn't have as much free time to gather.

As I settle in, our conversations inevitably turn to our students—what we're doing in class, which lessons have been successful, which lessons we're struggling with, and cool articles we've read. It's no different when my (white) friend, Stephanie, starts talking about her class.

She's in the midst of her first year teaching high school freshmen at a charter school in a predominantly white area in a Southern California desert. Loose and tipsy already from the beers I missed out on, she says, "Yeah! I've been talking to my students about racism lately and I told them it's okay to be racist because we're all a little racist! I mean, I'm racist. We're all racist!"

Stephanie's confident this is the best way to make her students feel comfortable, she doesn't realize (or doesn't care) three-fifths of the room are Latin@s, us being fairly light skinned or acceptably tanned, without accents and educated. Stephanie continues, "Like, sometimes when I'm talking to a black guy or Mexican guy, I immediately think they're criminals. For some reason, it just pops into my head." My eyes are probably as wide as serving platters.

I'm uncomfortable when no one speaks up, so I say, "I don't think everyone's a 'little racist,' but that's racist." She turns on me accusingly, "I'm racist? Oh, so you don't think you're racist?" I hesitate under this blazing inquiry, "No, I don't." To which everyone in the room, my Latin@ friends included, begin, "No, yeah, everyone's a little racist." "I'm racist too." "What about when Mexicans are racist towards other Mexicans?"

"I think you guys mean prejudiced."

Being half-white and half-Latina, in a room full of white people, I wouldn't stand out. In this regard, I'm hyper-aware of my privilege: I fit in, I easily blend into the idealized white sphere with my toasted marshmallow skin, my chestnut hair and gold-brown eyes.

I was fourteen when I realized how white I was. I had painful cystic acne, which kept me away from most mirrors. So, when my friend, Phylicia, who was half-black and half-Mexican, made us try on clothes in front of her full length mirror, I was captivated by our differences. Her beautiful, smooth, mahogany skin made my skin look translucent, sickly and enflamed. Afterwards, I would slap any exposed skin to get some color in the morning; I would lay out in the sun collecting only burns; I would dye my hair black (oblivious this contrast made me look whiter), all in the hopes I would gain some semblance of the sweet, rich coffee-colored skin and hair like Phylicia's. Then, no one would call me *"pinche gringa"* and my grandma would never have to explain my whiteness as *"solamente es gringita"* again.

When Stephanie was incredulous I didn't feel racist, she didn't care I grew up in an area 98 percent Chican@/Latin@, where many people found jobs in the agricultural fields, like my dad and mom, uncles and aunts, and grandparents, permanently or at some point in their lives. My parents worked for decades in agriculture. During season, they worked long hours, 12-14 hour days, six or seven days a week. Because of this, my brother and I were raised by our Spanish-speaking grandparents in a place where Spanish was the primary language on the street and in businesses. Stephanie didn't care about any of this.

In fact, a year before, when Stephanie taught at the middle school I went to at the east end of the Coachella Valley, she referred to the school and the students as "ghetto." The drive paralleled with citrus groves, a place where most families the middle school served worked in the ranches picking rows of grapes and other fruits and vegetables in triple-digit days when they were ripe and heavy on the stem.

I tried to explain all of this again, but none of it sunk in. I couldn't be there any longer, so I set my half-finished beer on the porch and left. The next day, and for weeks after, I was enraged about Stephanie's unapologetic racism. The way whiteness permits a confession that indicts black and Mexican men whose only crime is the color of their skin; the way whiteness remains unchecked and, in fact, accepted and defended even by people who could be those men to someone wearing similar lenses.

I was reminded of the desert and the Coachella Valley, where I grew up. A place with such disparaging gaps in wealth spread across 45 miles. The range of impoverished to working-class people of the East Valley ("ghetto"): Mecca, Thermal, Coachella, and Indio, versus the West Valley: La Quinta, Palm Desert, Rancho Mirage, and Palm Springs, where the impoverished and working-class are obtrusively barricaded by tourists and unimaginable sums of wealth, but this is where jobs are found.

This is a place where a white person can find comradery in my appearance. Once, when I worked in a hair salon in La Quinta, all the hair stylists were Latinas speaking Spanish in the backroom or to one another in passing. A white client asked, "That doesn't make you uncomfortable?" as she jerked her head in the mirror towards my coworkers talking in the back. The sharpness in her whisper assumed she knew how I felt. Another time, while in line at Starbucks as some young kids came in loud with jubilance, the guy behind me moved in close and said, "Fucking, wetbacks." Or the times when I would take my grandma to the doctor's office and the nurse would ask what company I was with, my grandma more likely to be my duty, my charge, than my relative with her brown skin.

In these instances, and many others, I have to defend those around me and myself against this invasive realm of hate, just as I had to do with Stephanie. Therapist Brené Brown, in her TED Talk, "Listening to Shame," says, "We heard the most compelling call ever to have a conversation in this country, and I think globally, around race, right? We cannot have that conversation without shame. Because you cannot talk about race without talking about privilege. And when people start talking about privilege, they get paralyzed by shame." Sometimes the privilege of being light-skinned manifests in heart splintering ways. Instead of being the subject of these ignorant, thoughtless remarks, I become a shameful spectator. I become an unsuspecting white form colonized and integrated into the framework of devaluing my friends, my loved ones, and strangers. My body is somehow not mine and belongs to the agenda of others.

To write this, I feel shame. The shame taking hold like a dandelion with its roots anchored deep beneath the surface. Even when it's plucked, the broken roots continuously regenerate. I'm ashamed to admit I have become an accomplice to the debasement of human lives. Blackmailed by the color of my skin, I don't have the choice to be excluded. ∎

Nadine M. Knight

The Luxury of Ambiguity

TO BE BIRACIAL IN THE UNITED STATES is to be exhaustively familiar with the identity quiz: the faux-polite, "Where are you from? No, really?" line of questioning about your background, along with its ruder cousin, the dehumanizing "What are you?" My mother is white, a German immigrant. Her accent prompts many to ask or guess where she's from, but she's never asked what she is; likewise, my black Jamaican immigrant father is sometimes subjected to exoticizing or patronizing comments about his "cool" accent but is also never a "what." They are immediately humanized and understood in a way that biracial people frequently are not.

However, to be biracial (and especially in the United States, to be black-white) is to be the subject of an entire nation's racial anxieties, a blank canvas upon which strangers, schoolmates, teachers, coworkers, friends, and neighbors project their racial assumptions, confessions, and preoccupations. This line of questioning, this manifestation of double-consciousness, reaches as far back in my memories as I can delve; I cannot remember a time when where I came from (and no, "Baltimore" was never the satisfactory answer) was not a curiosity.

On the one hand, it has been refreshing that the twenty-first century is catching up to people like me with the "beiging of America." On the other hand, in the wake of the ongoing horrors of police and political violence against communities of color in this country, I think that it is more important than ever for biracial people of all backgrounds to increase our visibility and our activism. I learned to derive pleasure from playing with the identity quiz; but it is increasingly important to use the quiz to correct the persistent assumption that to be biracial is to not be truly accepted as part of American society.

When I was a child, the limited American imagination fixed my identity to one half of a binary. I can no longer recall how or why the topic came up, but once when I was very young my mother attempted to explain this to me. It's now a bit hazy, honestly—there was a clunky metaphor about black and white bunnies—but here is what I do remember clearly: "You will have to choose," my mother said firmly. "You will have to pick one or the other." She explained that things like the census, and school applications, and my driver's license would only let me tick one box. (Eventually, there was the option of an "other" box, but I felt like it made me sound non-human). Even at such a young age I resented the paucity of choices, this demand that I willfully sever one part of my identity. So that day in the car I decided that I would not, in fact, choose; I'd just let other people see in me what they wanted. I would regret this very quickly.

Biracial people are never actually granted the luxury of ambiguity. I was not even in high school before I realized that my passivity gave strangers far too much narrative power: to speculate, to marginalize, to undermine my family's ties. On countless occasions in my youth, strangers doubted that my parents were my parents; not "seeing" me in just one parent, they would ask where my parents were. I learned that my identity was often situational, and absent any other evidence I would be categorized through contrast with my companions. I can't recall a conversation about race with my father like I had with my mother, but I have watched carefully over the years as he navigated American society with a wife and children much lighter than he is, and saw how people assumed that we do not fit together despite this country's long history of interracial relationships.

There was a time, perhaps in fifth grade, when one friend told me, confidently and bluntly, that another friend's parents didn't like me because "they don't approve of mixed marriages." This was during the 1980s; not the 1950s or 1880s. It felt as if a veil was lifted, and I began to see exactly how unlike most of my friends I was at my predominantly white private school. I tried to keep my head down and blend in. But of course I never actually blended in, and a final lesson stunned me the most: eighth grade biology class, when I was forced to stand up before the entire class so that they could observe my "negroid nose," apparently the best example to be found. I was beyond mortified (what eighth grader wants to be put on display?). I'm not even sure any of us really understood the term "negroid," or how breathtakingly racist this moment was. But it sounded ugly in his mouth, and he had made it very clear that I didn't belong.

After that, I worked on my icy stare. I started to deliberately obfuscate when people asked me where I'm from. I began to enjoy the fact that my racial ambiguity makes people uncomfortable. Of course it is often annoying—if I had a dollar for every white person who touched my hair without permission...well, I might not be a millionaire, but I could certainly foot the bill for a nice vacation. (And as a college professor, if I had a dollar for every time a well-meaning colleague of a certain age told me that they "marched with Dr. King" before then saying something offensive, well...).

I now like that I intimidate people who fear that they can't "read" me. And I like collecting the identities that are offered, the vision of alternative selves I could be in another universe. I've learned that white people pretty much never think that I'm white. Their favorite guess is Mexican, and I wonder if it's the default "nonwhite" category when they've ruled out black or Asian but still need to put a name to threatening foreignness (see Donald Trump's dream of a wall).

Black and brown people claim me as their own: I'm most frequently deemed Dominican, Boricua, Cape Verdean, Cuban, Mexican. It can be fun, except for all of the times when I am met with looks of disappointment or distrust when I explain that I'm not Latina and don't actually speak Spanish. The Jamaicans get it (half) right. My racial ambiguity is even global: I have been taken for Moroccan in Germany, Maori in New Zealand, Brazilian everywhere when there's World Cup soccer on. The most exotic guesses include Fijian, Egyptian, and Israeli. This broad range gives me new perspectives on different cultural expectations and receptions around the world; I am certain that the novelty of my ambiguity has sometimes worked to my benefit.

But novelty wears off. These days I challenge the inevitable line of questioning, calling out people who demand an explanation of my race(s), making clear how marginalizing and demeaning something like "what are you?" can be. Curiosity is not inherently wrong. But context matters. Timing matters. Intent matters. This influences my belief in teaching my students to deconstruct a question before they can ever hope to arrive at a satisfactory answer. Most importantly—something that can seem quite odd from a literature professor who believes in generating numerous questions of texts – I tell them that not every question has to be answered in the first place. To some extent, I became a professor and my students are at a selective liberal arts college because we are good at answering questions. We like answering questions. But not answering can be powerful, too. Absolutely no one, except perhaps my physician, needs to know "what" I am. It has taken me decades, but now I own my appearance and I owe you nothing.

As I look in horror at the current political emboldening of xenophobia and white supremacy, I no longer believe in passivity or silence. For me, this includes setting aside "biracial" as my first descriptor in favor of the simpler, more confrontational black. While I'm glad that the binary has eroded and there are finally more boxes to check, "biracial" seems inadequate to me. It's too polite, too easy, too vague. To be solely defined as biracial, for me, is to often be dismissed as merely exotic, a curiosity. It frequently lumps me among other mixed people with whom I share few cultural ties. Biracial doesn't actually tell people anything about how I experience the world, complete with the "negroid nose" that once so caught a teacher's attention. Black, on the other hand, puts people on political notice about my place in American society as someone who is constantly forced to negotiate other peoples' racial (and often racist) assumptions. I want my fellow Americans to be confronted with the complicated and nuanced intricacies of who looks – and is – American today. I want the curious to ask not where I'm from, which can signal distrust or ignorance; I want the curious to ask instead where we are going together. ■

Jewel Love

A Beige Christmas

IT WAS CHRISTMAS AGAIN. Time to put on my nice sweater. My sister is putting on her nice dress. As my twin sister, she and I are getting ready to visit our white grandparents, Grandma and Grandpa Stewart. Scottish-Canadian lovely folks who were warm, emotionally distant, yet formally present.

Mom's ready so we loaded into the "boat," which was an old green Chevy that kept close ties with call boxes and local mechanics. We'd find our way up the Oakland hills where upper class members of the "Town" resided. Before the Oakland fire, we journeyed up there on special occasions for grandparent visits. These visits were always similar. Starting with a handshake or hug at the door. Chatting with grandpa while grandma finished dinner in the kitchen. Always warm, cozy, and clean in their home.

As it was Christmas, we'd expect presents to open and play with. They were always good for that, and we loved them for it. Not a lot of talk or affection between them and us until we grew older, but as six year olds, we took the back seat to my mother. Two black kids. Two mixed kids. The first generation of black infusion to the always white Stewart family. We found ourselves both a part of their lives, and separated from their social circles where race mixing was still novel.

A large chicken was cut into by Grandpa Stewart, the patriarch. And for the next hour we'd listen to stories about the railroads, World War II, and other interests of grandpa. He held court, while my sister and I snickered at Grandma's comments on the far side of the table. The food was always good, flavorful, well-proportioned. Obesity was never an option due to our portion sizes, and frowned upon as well. Yet, always dessert afterwards. Soon we'd leave, having put on our coats, given hugs or handshakes, heading back down the hill into the flatlands of Oakland. The ghetto where black lives mattered, and gunshots were a cacophony of street notes. The 'hood that welcomed a white mother with her mixed kids, and our unit greeted neighbors with cuteness and pamphlets on joining our Buddhist religion. Both of these were protective measures from the danger around us, and genuine connection points with the good hearts of those living on our street.

Getting home, sleep would take over after the solid meal and subtle family time, with our new toys being the highlight of the evening, as kids ought to believe. Tomorrow we'd visit Grandma Johnny, on our black side. We never called it our black side until we learned about black, and that people outside of our family cared about such things as race. When that point arrived, race became everything, and the distinctions became important to tell you who I am, by describing their colors.

Waking up, we'd prepare to see Grandma Johnny in whatever form we'd prefer. Jeans, T-shirt, and loose sweater were sufficient. The currency where we were headed was love and Southern good eats. Never to be disappointed we found love in abundance upon our arrival. Hugged to death and cheeks sucked by Grandma Johnny, we were initiated into the family. Uncles, aunts, new boyfriends, girlfriends, kids from around the way, friends of our cousin were present. "Kids outside, and keep your hands off the walls!" Away we went with our cousin for an hour long adventure of cartoon tag and run-over before we checked on the adults back inside. Here the informality of dinner, family members eating off of paper plates, sitting on the couch, on floors, or standing. All watching basketball or a recent flick, drinking Kool-Aid or Pepsi. Laughter rife, smiles plentiful, my father tall and dark, handsome with an off putting sense about him, wafted in and out of the party. Him and my sister with an odd relationship never to heal, and he and I pressured for connection. Yet love prevailed, playfulness commanded, and food piled up high in the eyes of children just taller than the table. Seconds and thirds of macaroni and cheese, greens, fried chicken, cornbread, biscuits, yams, stuffing, corn, was present, straight from the South. Grandma Johnny never disappointed. Heaven had a name and it was Grandma Johnny's house on Christmas. Jewel Junior was lauded for getting another plate, and their encouragement was part of the reason for my decision. These gatherings lasted for hours, and eventually with full plates wrapped in tinfoil, we'd journey back on the "boat" to our East Oakland home.

These were our two family experiences growing up, my sister and I, as mixed youngsters of African American and Scottish Canadian descent. Both valuable, both shaping our experiences as kids and as young adults. Today, I still struggle with an African American identity, and an emerging mixed one. My sister seems to be comfortable as brown and mixed. Forever, I will have a sense of the calmness presented at our white grandparents' house, and the fun in my African American grandma's home. Both pieces add to my personality. Boisterous and stoic, formal and loving, boundaried and eclectic. All in proper proportion, and unfortunately sometimes off, they all came together to honor my ancestors' voices. Through this, my ancestors speak through me. ■

devorah major

Educated to Shy

IF YOUR MAMA WAS WHITE and your daddy a Negro, you'd look like a zebra."

"If your daddy was colored and your mommy white you would have one half of your body white and the other half Negro." I stood in the school yard, in second or third grade, yelling denials and refusing to cry while I withered inside. The landlord's youngest daughter Lora was at my side fiercely defending me to the white children who circled us, taunting and teasing. Lora and her sister, the only other black girls I remember in the school, were "real" Negroes. I was the fraud. I did not feel like the special child my mother proclaimed I was, the incredible person my father insisted I was. I felt wrong.

My parents married in 1949. Their marriage made the Chicago newspaper. Her father was moved from supervising a milk delivery crew in an affluent white community to serving the coloreds, since his daughter was a "nigger lover." The father and daughter didn't speak for another seventeen years. Soon after my brother was born, my parents took the train to Berkeley, California where I was born in 1952. My parents discussed the realities of race in America and agreed that we were to be brought up as the colored children we were, as the Negroes the world would see us as, as members of a community that might tease us for our heritage but would ultimately accept and love us as my Caribbean grandparents did, and as her American-born parents and immigrant grandparents did not. She was not to teach us her faith and he would not advocate for his religious beliefs. Rather, we would be free to learn and choose what truth was for us. We were told to understand ourselves as biracial, as multicultural and as Negro. We were not white, as pink is not white, or strictly speaking red, but instead a particular blending of them both. We were Negro because that was the way the world saw us, but we were to always understand and acknowledge our heritage. When people asked what race we were, and they did with irritating regularity, we were to assert that we were "human."

From Berkeley to Marin City to North Beach, San Francisco, my father held at least a dozen jobs and my mother half as many. Finally they stabilized and moved from North Beach and their almost all adult artist community to a large flat in a "family" neighborhood. We had black landlords whose three children were neatly spaced around me and my brother. In my memory, the Simmons were wonderful people. Mrs. Simmons allowed me to go to evening church events with her daughters. There was singing and playing and running around the church, which I enjoyed. Before the evening ended, we children would stand on the stage and sing a song or two as we practiced. I usually had a bird's nest of wild hair while all of the other little girls were neatly oiled and braided. As I remember I was the only one with eczema rashes running down my legs and neck and covering my inner elbow joints. Still I felt accepted. I was different because I was an individual, because I was not a member of the church, because I was not with my parents or grandparents, but not because I was colored.

During this time my mother chose to put my brother and me in a summer day camp run by the Jewish Community Center. She had obtained two scholarships and was relieved to have a safe place for us that summer. We were divided into tribes and would spend the morning session in our little groups.

Every time there was a partner activity in the morning session I was never "picked." Instead, a child would be assigned to be my partner. I could never figure out what was wrong with me. I was, admittedly, incompetent with ball skills but I was good at almost everything else. I could run fast, loved to climb, could figure out the clues to a scavenger hunt, was never mean, and lived by my father's mantra, "It's nice to be nice." I could be the slave girl in a reenactment but never the queen. I was always uncomfortable but would not tell my mother because she was so proud of the center and the "wonderful opportunities" it offered.

The after lunch session included the entire camp where we sang songs and learned Bible stories. After that the early pick up children would go home and those of us who had to wait until our parents got off work, could play, swim, or sometimes work in the art room.

When the late session was offered I was alone. I could be alone in the pool while others splashed and swam around, ignoring me or alone in the halls. An art teacher saw me in the hallway one day and had me come to her room. She took out tiles and told me she would show me how to make a mosaic. This was a special activity just for me she smiled. And I would sit gluing on the tiles afternoon after afternoon. It was not unlike the Russian preschool where a teacher pulled lonely me aside and put me in front of an easel showing me an approach to painting flowers. My mother was a skilled painter and I loved learning how to work like that and didn't question why I was alone. But in day camp I knew it was because of who I was, how I was. I did not know it was because of my color. I was proud to be Negro. These were, after all, the family who loved me, the neighbors who accepted me, and the children who played with me.

Somewhere around eight or nine years old I took to being alone as a way of life. I felt the problem was me and I became shy and reclusive. I read voraciously and found worlds in which to disappear. I looked for the places where I could slip into the magical, and I believed the world of Oz was real. I knew that among the cast of odd characters I would fit in with my half-combed hair, rashy limbs, shy smiling, and quick-witted, tan self.

Besides Negro, the few friends I had were from many ethnicities, Korean Jackie who took care of her wheelchair bound mother after school, Filipino Margie, the eldest daughter who had all the chores, and white Melody, whose divorced mother worked like mine did. All of us were, in different ways, outcasts. It wasn't until high school, a college prep high school I hated, with a population of 1,800 with less than 1/2 percent of black youth, that I felt not black enough. I thought it strange as I was more politically aware than most of the blacks, and whites too for that matter. I had been on the front lines of demonstrations my father and his friends organized for (then) Negro rights since the age of eleven. But when Martin Luther King Jr. was assassinated and we walked out of our high school the next day in a planned protest, me in my black boots, black mini skirt and dark blue beret (I didn't have a black one) I was welcomed as a sister. A small group of us ended up at my house, which was replete with jazz records. Suddenly I had substance, "You listen to this?" I pulled out the Dinah Washington and Billie Holiday albums I loved. The young piano player was talking about the Coltrane,

MJQ, and Miles. I like "My Favorite Things" and "Greensleeves" I opined, and found those albums. For a while I was black enough, but it didn't last. I was still a bit too different, pretty but quirky and I hung out with all the odd balls and misfits.

By then I knew that the role I didn't get in the school play was due to my blackness, the fact that I never saw a high school counselor despite excellent grades and high SAT scores was due to my blackness, the not being called on to have my questions answered in geometry class was because of my blackness. And my not being invited to all black parties, never being talked to by the black boys who I had crushes on was because of my brownness. The pattern was inescapable and the damage was done. I was painfully, almost pathologically, shy. I rarely reached out to others and rarely noticed when others reached out to me. I had found the place for me. I learned to love to walk alone, dance alone, write alone, be myself alone.

As the years passed I learned to love the self I formed, multiculturally true, but steeped in African-rich rhythms, which form the melody of my song. My world is filled with accepting friends of many ethnicities, although African diaspora remains the majority voice. I am still shy, not the worst thing for a writer, but have found myself adept at diving into our ocean of possibilities, retrieving pearls and buried treasures that know no boundaries of caste or class. ■

Jane Marchant

A Century of Progress

WINTER IS HERE and there are no leaves in sight. I am standing in front of what was once 684 East 39th Street, once part of Chicago's Ida B. Wells housing projects. Gray dust swirls to the sides of the roads; it also covers cars. Gray light shines through gray clouds and gray glass litters Bronzeville's streets in the South Side. The Chicago Housing Authority demolished my Grandma Barbara's first home. In place of the two-bedroom apartment that housed my Grandma Barbara, her two siblings, and their mother – and generations after them, as the city's public housing projects shifted from idyllic dream to dangerous nightmare – are three-story apartment buildings for rent or sale. Demolition of the Ida B. Wells Homes began in 2002 and construction for the Oakwood Shores replacement development is nearly complete. A manufactured park cuts the new housing development in two, Lake Michigan breaks against the shore barely a mile east, and skyscrapers rise in the distance. Barely five months ago, I did not know my Grandma Barbara grew up in Chicago's first housing projects segregated for black residents. She kept many things hidden from me, and the outside world. Among Grandma Barbara's secrets was the fact that her mother was black.

I love my Grandma Barbara. I loved her as I grew up in a predominant-ly-white neighborhood; I loved her when I wasn't allowed to play with her hair, when she ate peanuts and jelly beans at our dining-room table, and when I understood she and my mother were somehow different from the white mothers around us, but I did not understand why. I loved Grandma Barbara in her hospital bed, as she told the nurses she was from Spain, as she lay dying. I love her as she rests in a jar on my aunt's mantelpiece. But Grandma Barbara told her children and grandchildren lies about who we are.

I find myself, repeatedly, asking, "Why?" Slavery's dangers do not exist anymore. The segregation of Grandma Barbara's youth does not legally exist anymore. When she was on her deathbed in 2007, she was no longer called a mulatto, my mother no longer called a quadroon; I am not called an octoroon, my children will not be named mustifees and my grandchildren will not be mustifinos. We are not in the French Southern States of the 1800s and my great-grandchildren will never be called quarterons, and their children sang-meles. Our one drop will no longer enslave us all. So what was Grandma Barbara hiding from?

My grandmother's lies have spread across our family tree. Her lies cut my mother and her siblings off from their family. My mother said to me, "The lies have hurt us for too long." And so I have set out to find the truth.

I understand that I am only at the beginning of my journey, as I ask relatives about our family history and search through archives to confirm their tales. I am first led to the towns of Louisville, Kentucky, and Jeffersonville, Indiana, which face each other across the Ohio River. Kentucky was a slave state. Indiana was not. Swimming or boating across the river's murky water resulted in freedom only once touching Indiana's shore. The two communities segregated themselves into white and black. A myth says my ancestors moved their church board by board across the Ohio River and into Indiana, where my Grandma Barbara's mother, Jean Allen, was raised.

Government records list my great-grandmother, Jean, as "Negro." Sometimes she is recorded as Jane Allen; sometimes her birth date is 1906, sometimes 1903. She was beautiful, with a graceful neck and piercing eyes. One relative said that when Jean was sixteen years old, she got into trouble with her mother for riding a motorcycle. After finishing four years of high school, she spent a semester at mortuary school. A corpse sat up on the table, due to a buildup of gas, and Jean dropped out to move to Chicago.

Somewhere between 1925 and 1929, friends introduced Jean to John Maurice Galvin; he was born in 1902, went by "Maurice," and was one of thirteen Irish-Catholic siblings. In his early twenties, he lived in a small town in North Dakota, where he and a friend stole a steer and tried to sell it to a local butcher. The butcher knew immediately whom the steer belonged to, and a warrant was put out for Maurice's arrest. He skipped town, at some point joined a rodeo, and ended up in Chicago. Perhaps Jean was impressed by his story about the steer, or by his sense of adventure. Perhaps it was true love.

I have learned that since Jean Baptiste Point du Sable – a black man – was the first settler on the Chicago River in 1779; since the War of 1812's battle at Fort Dearborn between U.S. Troops and Potawatomi Native Americans; since Abraham Lincoln was a candidate during Chicago's Republican National Convention of 1860 and someone whispered to the chairman of the Ohio delegation, "Swing your votes to Lincoln, and your boy can have anything he wants;" since Reconstruction; since the largely-forgotten fire of 1874 that burned downtown, forcing displaced black residents to the less-populated South Side; since the Black Codes and the establishment of Jim Crow; and since the Great Migration began and ended, Chicago has been one of the most segregated cities in America. City officials drew lines through neighborhoods and placed people on either side. Jean Allen and Maurice Galvin were segregated into different streets of black and white. There was no gray.

And while anti-miscegenation laws in Illinois were overturned in 1874, it was illegal in Indiana for a black person to marry a white person at the time of Jean and Maurice's relationship. Until 1965, the Indiana Constitution provided that "when one of the parties is a white person and the other possessed of one-eighth or more of Negro blood," the marriage is "absolutely void without any legal proceedings." Indiana's Constitution went on to legislate that "every person who shall knowingly marry in violation of the provisions of this section shall, on conviction, be fined not less than one hundred dollars nor more than one thousand dollars, and imprisoned in a state prison not less than one year nor more than ten years." The same monetary fines were applicable to those counseling or assisting interracial marriage.

Yet somewhere between 1929 and 1930, Jean and Maurice went on a double-date to Crown Point, Indiana. The town's justices of the peace advertised in Chicago's newspapers that couples could marry twenty-four hours a day, seven days a week, at Crown Point's marriage mill. From 1915 to 1940, approximately 175,000 couples married at its Lake County Courthouse. And on Jean and Maurice's double-date in Crown Point, someone suggested they get married.

This can't be the full story: I wonder how, with anti-miscegenation laws in place, Jean and Maurice could have married. Some family members say that Maurice asked his friend to pretend to be a justice of the peace for the ceremony, or that the license was falsified, or Maurice and his friends thought it all a fun joke. My family is full of mysteries and I don't know how much Jean knew about the law or men, but I know that when she declared her marriage vows, she gained an ephemeral husband and lost her family—they disowned her because of her relationship to a white man.

Family lore says Maurice took a different wife, instead of Jean. This story has been told to make ourselves feel better about Maurice's actions, to make us feel like he loved Jean and met her after he had already had married another woman, the wrong woman. But I found records. The U.S. Census of 1930 lists John Maurice Galvin as a yard clerk for the railroad, while living with his parents at 6937 Calumet Avenue. He had married a woman recorded as white, named Charlotte Galvin, who lived with him and his family. And on October 16, 1930, Jean gave birth to her first daughter, Norma Galvin.

In the depths of the Great Depression's absent fathers and bread lines, on November 10, 1931, Jean again went into labor. My grandmother was born first. A doctor used forceps to pull her twin out of the womb and Jean named her babies Barbara and Robert Galvin. Jean had no family besides her children; they were effectively homeless, living off the kindnesses of friends.

While interviewing my grandmother's twin brother, Robert, in Chicago, he shared his first memory with me: He was in a hospital. It was all white. He was an infant and he was being dunked into a bathtub, scrubbed, and passed to another woman in white to dry him off. There was a long line of children being bathed and dried. Jean couldn't get out of bed to care for her babies, due to heartbreak or exhaustion or both. Her children had been sent to an orphanage. Robert was too young to have a clear memory of time, and does not know how long he and his sisters lived there.

Outside the orphanage, carpenters, bricklayers, and electricians set up Chicago's Century of Progress World's Fair, to take place from May 27 to November 1, 1933. Wooden boards were nailed to form the Dragon Ride. The Village of "Darkest Africa" brought Nigerian royalty and Belgian Congo pygmies from the African continent to show "Real African Life in a Real African Village." The Infant Incubator Company arranged premature babies in rows. The "Plantation Show" portrayed happy slaves dancing bare-breasted and a concession called "African Dips" involved throwing balls at live, black men.

Two miles directly south from the fairgrounds, from 22nd to 63rd Streets, in between Wentworth and Cottage Grove Avenues, Jean regained custody of her three children. They – along with two-thirds of all black Chicagoans – were segregated, the vast majority in poverty, in what had become known as the "Black Belt." Between 1920 and 1930, the U.S. Census reported an increase of 124,445 black residents in Chicago. Jean was not the only mother desperate to shelter her toddlers, as she moved from cheap, temporary apartments to friends' couches, taking in odd seamstress work.

The Depression had halted the housing industry and almost all construction: only 137 new units were built in Chicago in 1933. A special census in 1934 showed the average black household, such as the one that Jean and her three children had stayed in, contained 6.8 people, compared to 4.7 in the average white home. That year, the city demolished approximately seven-thousand black housing units they had deemed "sub-standard." Many still-standing black homes lacked plumbing or entire apartment floors shared one bathroom. Men and women and children squatted in the abandoned Pythian Temple at 37th Place and State Street. On New Year's Eve, 1935, *The Chicago Tribune* ran an advertisement for mascara that withstood cold-weather tears; the weather that day oscillated between eleven and twenty-five degrees Fahrenheit. There was no heating in squatted buildings such as the Pythian Temple. Unsanitary conditions led to rat attacks on sleeping children, frequently resulting in maiming or death. No one can tell me exactly where Jean's small family slept during these times.

When President Franklin Delano Roosevelt won a landslide reelection in 1936, his New Deal political reforms brought forth the Chicago Housing Authority. Chicago's first three housing projects opened in 1938, with space for 2,378 white families. In 1939, engineers, plumbers, steam fitters, and structural-steel workers broke ground on a forty-seven-acre property that would cost nearly nine million dollars and shelter 1,662 black families. The Homes were segregated in accordance to the federal "Neighborhood Composition Rule," which required housing developments to mirror the racial composition of the neighborhood they were being built in. Named after the renowned black journalist and social reformer, the Ida B. Wells Homes were composed of two-to-four-story buildings; the community even had space for vegetable gardens. Some 17,544 applications were received, including my great-grandmother's.

Jean miraculously received a housing assignment and she held her head high as she walked through Chicago's South Side, her three adolescents in tow. They were tired, they were poor, and it was 1941. They had essentially been homeless for a decade when they entered 684 East 39th Street. Between Cottage Grove to the east and South Parkway (now Martin Luther King Drive) to the west, their home had its own kitchen and bathroom. Sisters Norma and Barbara shared a bedroom; their brother, Robert, had his own room; and Jean slept downstairs on the couch. Rent was thirty-six dollars per month—if one had it. Sometimes, payment arrangements could be made, or neighbors chipped in to help. The Homes were a community and a respite for families during the Depression. Jean's children took free dance, music, and art lessons at the Abraham Lincoln Center. Norma tapped her pillow at night, practicing her imaginary piano. Barbara dreamed of becoming a professional ballerina. Robert wanted to be a cowboy, like his heroes on the radio. An enumerator from the Sixteenth Census of the United States marked Jean, Norma, Barbara, and Robert Galvin as "Negro" in his wide logbook. The enumerator asked Jean if she worked, to which she replied she had no income. She told the enumerator she'd been married to the same husband since she was eighteen years old.

In their new home, Maurice visited Jean late at night, while the children slept. They awoke some mornings with black licorice under their pillows. The children were told their father had snuck into their rooms and left the candy so they would know he had visited. In our interviews, I didn't have the heart to ask my great-uncle, Robert, when licorice became his favorite candy, or to ask him if it was really Jean leaving licorice, lying to her children about how much their father cared for them. I didn't dare ask what Maurice left with Jean. It felt as if I was trespassing too far into my great-uncle. The new power I have claimed over our family narrative unnerves us all. I asked my mother instead; I somehow feel safer trespassing her. My mother told me she wouldn't be surprised if Maurice left money for the family on Jean's pillow.

During Jean, Norma, Barbara, and Robert's first winter in the Ida B. Wells Homes, on December 8, 1941, President Franklin D. Roosevelt's gritty voice echoed down 39th Street. World War II had come to America. While the Depression lifted nation-wide, life in Chicago's South Side remained treacherous. Jean slept with an old police revolver—supposedly given by Maurice—under her pillow. One night, a hand felt along a first-floor windowsill and attempted to open their window. Jean shot one bullet and the hand disappeared, along with its owner. The children walked to and from school together, and were told to keep their mouths shut when they crossed Cottage Grove to avoid getting beaten up. Yet Jean's children were lucky; at night, they listened to westerns on their radio, safe under blankets. Neighbors made dandelion wine from flowers growing in sidewalk patches.

After World War II ended, conditions still worsened outside the Ida B. Wells Homes: semi-distant black neighbors occupied cardboard basement cubicles ten-families full, with no windows or toilets. Two-Gun Pete ruthlessly policed the neighborhoods, gunning down nine men by 1945. The size of the urban rat population approached that of the human population. In the year between my Grandma Barbara's fifteenth and sixteenth birthdays (from 1946 to 1947), over seven-hundred-and-fifty fires burned decrepit buildings and slums in Chicago's Black Belt.

Society called my Grandma Barbara and her siblings mulattoes, diminutives of the Spanish word *mulo*, that hybrid animal, the mule. Barbara's skin was light enough for her to introduce herself as Spanish, Irish, or anything-but-black, if she could only leave Chicago, where people knew who she was. When Barbara was eighteen years old, she met a man of Mexican heritage on a public bus. She told him she dreamed of getting out of Chicago, of traveling and dancing in ballet companies around the world. I wonder where on the bus they were sitting; I wonder what race she told him she was; I wonder when she first decided to let her light skin count for something other than black. He promised to take her to California. Barbara never wanted children. He told her he was sterile.

She quickly became pregnant.

When my mother was four or five, her father left his last name and the Los Angeles apartment his family was living in. There were four small children in Barbara's house by then. Her children grew up in rough areas of east Los Angeles. My mother and her siblings ran barefoot along the concrete banks of the Los Angeles River, getting algae and residential discharge in between their toes. Their mother, Barbara, married twice more, raising seven children while frying slices of Spam, painting shower curtains by hand, driving buses, working at the post office and later as a deputy sheriff, and finally as an elementary school teacher's assistant. When Barbara's sister, Norma, visited with her husband and children, my mother's cousins were "black because Aunt Norma had married a black man."

Barbara's mother, their Grandma Jeanie, was Menominee Indian. Yet my mother and her siblings were told they were Puerto Rican. My mother and her siblings were kept away from Chicago; they missed the births, family milestones, reunions, and deaths that typically bring families together; and my mother, as a child, was unaware of what she had lost. My Grandma Barbara was aware of the clear racial hierarchy that existed around her and her children—and anything was better than the blackness from where she had come.

Then, in 1971, at eighteen years old, my mother went to stay with her Aunt Norma in Chicago's South Side. Aunt Norma had remained in Chicago after Barbara left, embracing her black identity. My mother said Aunt Norma "had the drive of Hercules." She was one of the first black students to graduate from Mundelein College in 1953, and went on to serve as principal of a South Side school, raised six boys, and became a lawyer in her late fifties. When my mother arrived on the South Side and discovered she was black, she told me she felt like a curtain was lifted and she finally fit, racially, into her family.

Yet, I still watch my mother struggle with her identity. Culturally, my mother is not black. She was not raised within a black community; she was not segregated into schools like her black cousins in Chicago. Ethnically, my mother is part black, part white, and part Hispanic. My heart tightens when someone asks her about her ethnicity and I hear her reply: "I'm a Mutt." She means, she's a mixture of a lot of things, and she doesn't want to go into detail; she thinks her ethnicity is none of their business. For me, when she defines her race this way, it feels as diminutive as mulatto—mulo—mongrel—animal.

When the time came for my mother to choose a husband, she married a white man and moved her children into a white neighborhood. My mother still had to sort through dented cans at the Grocery Outlet and my father rationed showers for the sake of our water bills, but we were in a better place than where she had grown up. My mother wanted her children to grow up where it was safe for us to walk home from school, where we wouldn't smoke cigarettes on street corners or fall through factory roofs or accidentally burn down buildings, as she and her siblings had done. When she looked at my sister, my brother, and me, I think that my mother saw her past as her children's future. And so she, too, hid stories from us, saying we didn't need to know certain things.

But she was different than the other mothers; we were different than the other children. Our mother was the only mother who baked biscuits or cornbread. Our mother burned our grilled cheese sandwiches and scraped the black off with a knife. There was no denying our brother's brown skin tone, no hiding the curly or coarse hair-texture of my mother, sister, and brother. Our house smelled like incense and none of our furniture matched and the colors were always bright, too bright, when compared to the beige interiors of white friends' homes. And because I didn't have any explanation, because no one talked about our race, I was ashamed of my mother, and whatever it was that made her – and us – different.

Then, when I was twelve years old, a black man knocked on our front door and said he was my mother's brother. He was tall, six-foot-four or so, and we marked his height – Uncle Kevin – on our wall above Great Uncle Bob and Grandma Barbara. After the visit ended and the door shut, I asked my mother, "How do you have a black brother?"

"Jane, I'm black," she said.

What? I kept questioning her. My mother told me that Grandma Barbara had given birth to Kevin in Los Angeles, but couldn't raise him; he had to be given up for adoption. "But why was he black?" Grandma Barbara's mother was black, but Grandma had hidden her blackness; her blackness crept out in the baby's skin. I didn't understand procreation and genetics and that Grandma Barbara had slept with a black man who was much darker than her and her siblings.

"Does that make us black?" I asked my mother, referring to my siblings and me.

"Yes."

I felt limitless confusion yet also relief; I understood the something that made us different, but at the same time, I felt like I knew even less than before. I was instantly someone new. But who? I didn't always get the same answer. My great-grandmother was black; my great-grandmother was half-black, half

Native American Indian. My great-grandmother was a Black-Indian, kicked off her reservation by white men; her daughter, Grandma Barbara, was white or Puerto Rican or Spanish or Irish, but never, never black. Her blackness was hidden, a secret, kept at bay by staying in the shade and using sunscreen and rubbing creams labeled sun spot remover on her face and neck and arms.

The lies passed down from my grandmother have led to multiple family members passing as white. I have now, sixteen years after discovering my grandmother's secret, begun to question it in earnest. I have begun to read about and question the history of passing; I have begun to ask black friends about their hidden relatives, and I ask my family questions they have never felt comfortable answering. But what I am really asking is, "Am I black?"

In the past, within black communities, there was an ethos about passing: if you leave us to live as a white person, if you go somewhere else to make your life better, you better make sure you do something grand. Don't go live your life the way it would have been if you hadn't left your family, your history, your people, behind. We understand the need to pass for survival, for dreams, for an offer you couldn't resist; we won't call you out when we find our features hidden in your face or hands or the shade of your skin. (Even now, I am asked slowly, tentatively, "What ethnicity are you?") And to those that do pass: if you get out, you better make something of yourself that you couldn't as a black person. So I ask, what would Grandma Barbara's life have been, had she stayed in Chicago, with the support of her family?

By the time the Supreme Court ruled in *Loving v. Virginia* to legalize interracial marriage across America in 1967, my Grandma Barbara was long gone from Chicago and her white father had been dead one year. I think about the white man, Richard Loving, and his black wife, Mildred Jeter; I think about how much he must have loved her to fight the state of Virginia to be with her. I think about my great-grandmother, Jean, and about what happened on her wedding day in Crown Point, Indiana. I think about the anti-miscegenation laws that existed at one point in forty-two states. 1662: Virginia was first to illegalize interracial marriage. 1664: Maryland. 1705: Massachusetts. 1913-1947: thirty states illegal, eighteen legal. 1948: California legalized miscegenation. As years passed, legalization crept across the country, until 1965, when Indiana legalized interracial love, and then 1966, when the only states that had not legalized interracial marriage were seventeen states in the South. I wonder what Jean and Barbara were doing on June 12, 1967, when the Supreme Court announced its decision. I wonder if they spoke on the phone about Maurice. I want to think that maybe Grandma Barbara had it wrong about her father, that he did love her. I want to think that maybe Maurice just wasn't strong enough for the fight; I want to think that, maybe, when he died after two years of being bed-bound, it was out of guilt. I don't want to think that my great-grandfather never cared, that he thought so little of the black woman he bedded and the children she bore. I am part her, part black, but I am also part him.

But why should this even mean anything to me, when I could easily allow people to continue their initial assumptions that I am white? Why do I feel I have to audibly correct people with the statement, "I'm not all white"? I have only met my Great Grandma Jeanie once in my life, when I was five years old, and although I didn't know then what race looked like, I knew that I loved her. She came to visit us in California and, in our backyard, I sat in her lap and ran my fingers over her dark brown arms. It was summer. Her wrists were thin but strong and she had a constellation of freckles on her forearm's papery skin. I don't remember asking Great Grandma Jeanie why her skin was darker than mine, but I must have, I must have noticed our different shades. Her white hair glowed like a halo around her head and she sat up as straight as our white Barbie dolls. She let my sister and I brush her hair—something her daughter, our Grandma Barbara, never allowed. She moved as if she belonged in another time.

I didn't know that people called her black. My mother, her sisters, and their mother never talked about blackness. I wonder if I asked my mother about the darkness of Great Grandma Jeanie's skin; I must have. Why do we not remember such vital moments? I didn't see Great Grandma Jeanie's skin as black; black was for crayons and night and the plastic on videocassette tapes. No human was black. I didn't know what it meant to be black; I didn't know what the word meant. I didn't know blackness came in shades. I just knew Great Grandma Jeanie had fluffy white hair that she let my sister and me clip pink-plastic barrettes into, as we sat in the sun under our sweet-flowering ficus tree. I knew that whatever Great Grandma Jeanie was, I wanted to be like her. I am proud to be of the same blood of a woman like her. I am now proud to be my mother's daughter.

I wish I could have spoken as a woman with my great-grandmother. I wish I could have sat down on a park bench or walked on a beach or drank a glass of wine with her and asked her for all of her secrets, all of her truths. But I only met her one time. She died that fall, on October 7, 1992, when I was five years old.

After my Great Grandma Jeanie's children moved out of their apartment in the Ida B. Wells Homes, she stayed a few years before moving on herself. A new family moved in. Jean remarried, this time to a black man, and became Jean A. Hector. Apartment towers were built around the Homes, and another family moved in. Jean went back to school, in her eighties, to earn her associate degree (although I have conflicting information on her age and type of degree). The Homes' walls deteriorated; sink handles broke; profanity and graffiti covered the exterior. Before Jean died, she found out the father of her children was buried in the same cemetery where she had purchased a plot. Gangs with knives and guns and drugs controlled the projects. Jean asked to move her plot to the opposite side of the cemetery from where Maurice and his family were buried. Another family moved into the Homes. And by 2002, what had once been a desirable community had become a dangerous failure of the Chicago Housing Authority. Grandma Barbara's first home – her history – was torn down and shiny new homes were built for a new century.

When I was younger, I thought Grandma Barbara had wanted the West Coast dream life. I have come to understand that she was in pain: everything that happened to my great-grandmother and her children – their homelessness, their poverty, their segregation – was decided by race. When my Grandma Barbara looked in the mirror, she saw the reason that her father didn't love her enough to stay. I've thought, Grandma would have peeled off her skin if it meant he could love her. But she couldn't, and he couldn't. So she ran away, leaving her family and blackness behind her. And now I am back, trying desperately to regain what she erased.

On my day in the South Side, I see one white person – if I don't count myself. ■

TWO KINDS OF PEOPLE

BY RACHEL MASILAMANI

IN 1968, MY DAD WENT TO GET HIS WISCONSIN DRIVER'S LICENSE. WHEN HE TOOK THE WRITTEN PART, HE HAD TO ASK THE GUY AT THE DESK A QUESTION:

RACE:
WHITE ☐
BLACK ☐

WHAT DO I CHECK?

WELL, YOU'RE NOT WHITE.

CHECK 'BLACK'

WHAT'D YOU CHECK 'BLACK' FOR? YOU'RE NOT BLACK.

I KNOW.

WELL, WHAT'D YOU CHECK IT FOR?

GUY IN THERE SAID TO.

YOU CAN TRY AGAIN TOMORROW.

I SWITCHED SCHOOLS IN SEVENTH GRADE. STARTED GOING TO PUBLIC SCHOOL. NITA KUMAR WAS ON MY BUS.

WHERE'D YOU GET THOSE CLOTHES?

INDIA.

FUGLY!

KNOW WHAT THAT MEANS?

WHAT ARE YOU?

THERE ARE SO MANY REASONS NOT TO ANSWER THAT QUESTION.

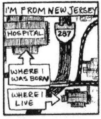

Jeni McFarland

Hair Like Ariel's

'M TEN YEARS OLD, at a salon for the first time in my life. We don't have money for this kind of thing, but my grandpa, an accountant, has a lot of clients who owe him. This salon is one of them. The woman doing my hair, Reba, is pretty, with brown feathery bangs that are stiff and styled like Ariel's hair in *The Little Mermaid*. Her powdery face is the color of a peach crayon, and her makeup settles in the lines alongside her mouth. She smells like perfume and Aqua Net, like my best friend's mom, although when she leans over to shampoo my hair she also smells like deodorant and spongy armpit flesh. She wears a purple smock. She keeps telling me, "You have so much hair," which is what my grandma says when I stay the night at her house, when she brushes my hair after bath time. "You have so much hair," and also, "You're sure that doesn't hurt?" My grandma and Reba both worry about brushing my hair too rough.

I live in West Michigan, where there's a lot of Dutch people. Most everyone I know is white, tall, lean, and Meijer-stylish. If you ain't Dutch, you ain't much, and I ain't much. Even though my family on my mom's side is Dutch a few generations back, I inherited none of the leanness or straight blonde hair. I'm about equal parts hair and head, by volume. And while I'm tall for a fourth-grader, I'm already going pudgy.

Reba has just finished rinsing the chemical straightener from my hair. I hope it will make my hair as straight as Reba's, as straight as my mom's, whose hair is also feathered, and as red as Ariel's. But as Reba towels my hair, and turns me to face the mirror, I watch my face fall at the same time as hers. "Oh," is all she says.

My hair isn't any straighter, although maybe a little less poofy. Before school the next day, I try my best to de-poof it more. I brush it down flat against my head, like Reba showed me, using my mom's round brush and curling it under at the ends. I've abandoned my comb, the red pick my dad left behind, the only thing I have that was his. Brushing like this isn't easy, because my hair is long, trailing past my shoulders. I coat it in Pink Oil, which Reba gave me, and which smells a little like the beach, or like the fruit I imagine they eat in Hawai'i. My best friend's family goes to Hawai'i every year, and she comes back tan. She has grass skirts and leis that we put on to dance in her living room. Her parents have a CD player in the living room, the first one I've ever seen, and a collection of CDs that have their own shelving on the wall. Something about my hair seems like it would go well with the leis and grass skirts, seems as though it would enjoy a flower tucked into it, the kind of big bright flower that would grow in Hawai'i.

I finish rubbing my hair with Pink Oil. I've almost used an entire sample—so much so that my hair is greasy near the scalp. By the time I get to school, though, it's all soaked in and my hair is well on its way to poof. Even though Reba cut my hair yesterday, used thinning shears on it, it still isn't shaped right: it frizzes into wings on either side of my face. My classmates still call me "Bozo the Clown." They ask me where my seltzer bottle is. I think maybe seltzer is a hair product, an expensive one that you might buy in a salon. I wonder if Reba knows about seltzer. Sometimes the girls in school ask if my hair is wiry or soft, and can they touch it?

My hair is only good right after I climb from the bathtub, when it's still dripping and flattened, weighed down by water, and trailing my back in loose curls. If only I could somehow get to school with it still wet, or maybe I could get everyone together in a pool or at the beach. I'm a good swimmer, the only sport I'm not terrible at, and they will see this, and see my long hair, and they will love me.

After school, I go to daycare at the YMCA. We play racquetball and kickball and run around in the woods out back and swim in the pool. I'm shy about putting on my swimsuit at the Y. I use the door of my locker to shield me, and try not to stare at the long smooth legs of the white girls. I already have hair down there, and I shouldn't because the other girls don't. I also already wear a bra, and have to buy my swimsuits in the misses section instead of the girls section. My swimsuit has a skirt on the bottom and padding in the top.

Sliding into the pool feels like coming home. I'm really good at dolphin-kicking, and I can hold my breath long enough to touch the bottom in the deep end. I do this often, even though it hurts my ears, and even though behind my nose and eyes it smells like burning vanilla. It's worth it for the blue-green muted sound. Under the water, I am weightless, my lungs full and burning with chlorine, my hair fanning out around me. I stay down as long as I can, then come bursting up for breath. All of us girls practice breaking out of the water and flipping our hair back like Ariel when she first surfaces with her human legs. My hair trails a huge stream of water when I Ariel-flip.

Because so many kids are crammed every day into an indoor pool, the Y super-treats the water with chlorine. It turns the blonde girls' hair green. It fades our neon swimsuits, and gives me skin rashes. And it damages my already dry, brittle hair, weakened from the chemical straightener; the breakage is so bad that, within a few weeks, my hair doesn't even reach my shoulders. It's falling out, getting thinner and thinner, and while it's dry and rough, it's also less poofy because there's less of it to poof. It's bleaching red, too, from sun and chlorine. This damage is the good kind of damage, the kind that brings me closer to normal. When I brush my hair in the morning now, using my mom's round hairbrush, it makes a ripping, snapping sound, and leaves a dusting of little broken hairlets on the bathroom counter.■

Abra Mims

Being Seen

AT NINE YEARS OLD, I heard these words about me: "Use the knife to cut her because she's not white!" I had come to play with the girl who lived down the street, only to find her with another group of kids. They were playing with an orange, plastic knife, using it to swirl patterns into the dirt. I was an unwelcome interruption and they let me know it by saying hateful things about the way I looked. I had only been there a few minutes when the order was shouted, and suddenly the serrated edge was pressing into my arm. The fear that had previously held me frozen in place now had me running home. I did not flee because I believed they could actually hurt me with a piece of plastic cutlery, I fled because they wanted to. The experience left me shaken and humiliated, but I was also angry; angry they would not let me forget the shame of what I was, and angry because they could see me.

I cried in my mom's arms that afternoon and told her some kids had been mean to me. I did not give her the details, though. My mom somehow remained unaware that my brown skin made me unlovable, and I was desperate to keep her from knowing. She was also unaware I had been lying about my race for over three years, ever since I shocked and disgusted a classmate by naively telling her the truth when she asked about my dark skin. I was terrified to learn being half black was unacceptable, so I made a silent vow to keep that part of me a secret, an act I thought would be easy to follow through since my dad, my black parent, was no longer in my life.

My dad's absence ensured that my childhood world remained mostly white. On the rare occasions there were black kids in my school, I befriended them because I genuinely liked them, not because I felt I was one of them. On the contrary, I was envious there were no obvious discrepancies in their racial make-ups. I doubted they were being asked, "What are you?" They matched their parents. One year, a kid showed up who looked just like me. He was even brought to school every day by his white mother. Instead of feeling relieved or grateful, I made sure to stay as far away from him as possible. Together, we would surely be noticed, and I wasn't willing to risk that kind of attention since my only goal was to blend in and avoid questions.

Surprisingly, some people really did not seem to notice my brownness. More often than not, though, they needed me to deconstruct it for them so they could make sense of me. I was more than happy to let others assume my mom's boyfriend—a white man with a head full of black, wavy hair—was my real dad. But people rarely, if ever, assumed this. If someone had the audacity to quiz me on my ethnicity (and they always had the audacity), I would casually exclude my dad and instead play up the suspected Apache lineage in my family. Of course, this did not explain the kink in my hair. Gradually, I came to understand that hiding really didn't work. It was clear there was a hierarchy of skin color and I would never be at the top of it. I may have worn my skin, but I did not own it; the rest of the world decided what it represented, and no matter what I claimed or refuted to be, I would always be brown.

After years of living in fear of being discovered, I decided to come out as "mixed" when I was in seventh grade. Unlike many, I do not recall my middle school years with any feelings of angst. For me, those years were a revelation. The student body of my junior high school was an impressive display of racial diversity, unlike anything I had ever encountered. My peers did not seem to care one way or another about my brown skin, probably because I was no longer an anomaly. To my bewilderment, the kids at school that looked like me weren't trying to live undercover. I began to wonder what it would feel like to have that same level of freedom; what would it feel like to just be myself? When I finally decided it was safe to stop hiding, nothing catastrophic happened. The truth did not destroy me.

Owning my blackness was liberating and empowering, but it was not without consequence. In the years since, I have been subjected to any and all opinions on what it means to be biracial. I am frequently told I look "exotic," told my race goes against the Bible, told I am really just black because there is a one-drop-of-blood rule, told I have good hair, told I don't act black, and told I have to choose one race because I can't really be both. I once had a coworker, a black woman, who made a daily habit of admonishing me for not calling myself "black." A different coworker, a white woman (who thought I was also white), once tried to convince me to complain to management over the "better treatment" our black co-workers were supposedly receiving. On multiple occasions, I have been mistaken for Latina or told I "look Jewish." I am not sure what to make of the fact that I spent so many years of my life trying to hide from the world only to ultimately feel it's a struggle to be seen.

I am a biracial woman. This is how I identify, and sometimes it feels doing so is an act of protest. In our society, where so much is still determined by race, those among us who embrace the biracial label undoubtedly make it hard for people who cannot break away from historical norms and prejudices. But this is not my problem to fix. I am not interested in perpetuating stereotypes or carrying on antiquated traditions. Admittedly, it would be easier to "choose" a race, but that is an impossible task. How could I possibly choose when it was the white hands of my mother that nurtured me and made me feel safe, but white hands, too, that wanted to take a knife to my brown skin?

I often think of that day in school when my classmate wanted to know about my skin color. I wonder what would have happened had she responded with acceptance instead of horror. And I wonder, too, how differently my childhood experiences would have been if I had grown up during a time when the U.S. president looked like me. I believe these things matter, that knowing there is space for you in the world, feeling that you belong, is vital to well-being. I did not believe these things for myself for a long time and I suffered for it. I am hopeful, however, that as the number of biracial/multiracial individuals continues to grow, we will become a more visible part of the population, and that it will become easier for us to be our whole selves, completely seen, in whatever ways we identify. ■

Via Perkins

What We Call Ourselves

I USED TO BELIEVE THAT RACE was irrelevant. During high school, I lived in a mostly white suburb of Boston, in which I attended a mostly white high school, where my friends were mostly white. Never once in my seventeen years had I experienced overt racism from anyone.

The mirror seemed to lie to me. I saw brown every time I peered into it, my black roots revealed unmistakably, but I did not look the way I felt. I felt white. I was white, after all. What other world was there than the one I knew? The one where a brown girl was safe in a secluded suburban world, so much so, that all the color drained out and she herself became white?

I was with my friends one day in the high school cafeteria, and someone playfully nabbed my water bottle. I spent every day with these kids, taking notes alongside them in class, laughing until our sides ached, and traipsing around our town as if we owned it, so I thought nothing of it. I knew it would be returned to me by the end of the period.

It did, and it arrived with two words scrawled onto the label: "Nigger Water." This seemed incomprehensible at first, as if I were reading a runic language. I had to meditate on this message, and search my soul on a level I had been too intimidated to explore before, to understand what it meant for me.

I had to learn firsthand what no history book, documentary, or personal story was able to convince me of. I was not fully embraced in my little white world, as I thought I had been. Race had always been there, in my suburb, in my high school, and in my friend group. The only difference about that day in the cafeteria was that someone made it visible.

Visibility is a blessing, because it reveals truths. I had always been black, but in that moment, I felt black for the first time. This was an incredible freedom for me. No longer tethered to my white identity, I was released to explore more about my blackness – the pain and weight of it as well as the strength and joy of it. It was necessary for me to feel black before feeling truly biracial.

Race was real, and I had two under my skin, but I still had so much to learn about both. With this basis, I enrolled into the most racially diverse state college in Massachusetts. Unlike the suburb in which I had grown up, people of color were in nearly every social circle I entered at Salem State University. Little by little, other biracial people began entering my life.

Again, I had an opportunity to learn firsthand – this time, by choice. I was uninterested in learning about race in a distanced or clinical way. My identity was still a fledgling thing, and I was collecting shoots of whiteness and blackness like wildflowers from the world around me. I was intrigued to know what my biracial peers' bouquets were like.

In the form of a senior honors thesis, I queried them individually. I left each interview with new realizations, but none were more powerful than the single factor that ran throughout them. I had feared that, perhaps, I was the only one who had taken as long a time to enter my nigrescence, or the sole person with few experiences of racism, or the oddity that had barely any non-white friends before college.

In reality, each interviewee's story was fundamentally unique. A few had always been aware of race and were constantly deciphering their blackness and whiteness. One had never faced their biraciality, and was afraid and unsure of how to do so. A couple of them were somewhere in the middle, or on a different plane entirely.

The common trend was that their stories were all different. As an isolated biracial person raised in a racially-homogeneous environment, I was relieved to discover that my experiences were not too strange or abnormal to be considered invalid. Each of us were growing and learning at different paces. Each of us had unique perspectives and insightful life lessons to share.

If I had never been branded with a racial slur in high school, I may not have had the courage to seek my biracial peers' stories in college. I may have been too ashamed of my ignorance to push through my racial discomfort and grow in my identity. Sometimes it takes the push of a false moniker, adhered by another person, to ask oneself, "If this is not me, then who am I?"

This question will become increasingly relevant in the coming years as the multiracial demographic grows. Though we make up a small percent of the American population at the moment, it would do us well to consider our collective future. What do we know about being mixed race, and what do we still have to learn? How does our existence solidify, redefine, or defy race?

A time is coming when multiracial stories will be at the forefront of American culture. We need not look further than to each other for a glimpse into that future. I have been thrilled to discover more mixed people sharing their stories every day, and I hope we continue to celebrate our perspectives and believe in our power to change race as we know it.

For some, race has always been paramount, even essential to survival. For others, race has been nearly imperceptible, only existing as passing news headlines or words on bottle labels. Whether white, black, mixed, or any other ethnic identity, our stories of coming to terms with race are individual. They take time, experience, and patience to cultivate.

The more beiged our American landscape becomes, the more opportunities there will be for those that are ignorant of race or disregard race to encounter it—even if those people are ourselves. What will we have to show the world once they are ready to see us? Once we are ready to see ourselves? ■

Eman Rimawi

But You Don't Look Like...

WHEN I THINK ABOUT WHO I AM, I get lost in thought. Lost in what it means to be "mixed." If my future kids will struggle as much as my siblings and I did. If I'll ever feel connected and accepted by all of these communities that are in my blood. Or if it will ever be "safe" to just be. The answers are never simple. But these questions are necessary.

I think about the beauty of my father's country: Palestine. And how much I felt at home when I visited in 2008. The curves of the hills in the Mount of Olives, or how you could feel the holy energies in The Holy Sepulchre church in Jerusalem. I even think back on Ramallah, where my family lives, and how they weren't allowed to travel freely in their own country, but I could, because, after all, I am American too. Even though they strip searched me and destroyed my luggage because of my ethnicity, yes, I am still an American.

When I think about my dad, I think about how Americanized he was, but still operated in a semi-Muslim and Arab way also. He didn't drink, but he loved playing lotto. He fasted every Ramadan and loved the ladies a bit too much, even while married to my mother. And I think about how devastated I was when he died unexpectedly when I was fourteen. I'm thirty-two now. And even now, I feel the sting of loss, of not being able to say goodbye, of feeling like it was my fault that he died. But the fact was that he was an unhealthy diabetic, was on his third marriage, had four kids, and had a heart attack at forty, which had nothing to do with me alone. I know he loved me and in the end, that's what matters. He loved me. He loved all of us.

My father came to America when he was nineteen; a hazel green-eyed, dark haired, olive skinned man, who spoke very little English. He was a beautiful and macho man. He's the reason I am the way I am. I am absolutely his daughter, just as my brother and sister are his too. In his mind, he was going to live the American dream, because America was where he planned on getting everything he wanted. But that wasn't his reality. He learned that the hard way, and died never getting closer to that dream. I suppose, looking back on it, the closest he got to that was through his kids.

My mother, a beautiful black and Native American woman, is the smartest person I know, but also the most heartbreaking. Because, for every reason she had to show her talents, her intelligence, and her humor, she continuously self-sabotaged her life and alienated herself from her three grown children. My mother grew up mostly in New York City, but got moved around a lot until she met my dad. She spent a lot of time in the south and all over the country. She was a smart black girl (with a touch of Blackfoot), who wanted to be a surgeon. She was smart enough to be one, but never got the chance to become one, for whatever reason.

And then she got married in May 1983. No one liked the idea of them getting married, but they did it anyway. She was seventeen and he was twenty-seven. I think back on their wedding picture. I've only seen the one: my mother looking beautiful in a simple white dress, little flowers imprinted on it. Her veil, which had little daisies, was attached to a little oval hat, coming over her smiling face. Her skin was a beautiful, chocolate brown and her lips were very red. Her smile is etched in my mind. So happy and hopeful. So innocent and bright. There was such a clear future on her face, in that picture. Even after thirty-three years later, she looks exactly the same. Her black has definitely not cracked.

My father however had a tiny smile, almost a smirk. I knew he was happy, but maybe he wasn't happy about how he got into the situation. When I had that sit down with my mom and asked her about their lives before we got there, she told me that she lied to get his attention since they met two years earlier. And while he liked her, he wasn't, from my understanding, planning on marrying her. So she called his school and his family, and told them she was pregnant and he finally contacted her. Apparently, she wasn't and just said that to get his attention. She loved him and wanted to get away from her mother. When she told me that, I was stunned. I had no idea about any of this. I guess you never know what someone, especially your parent, will say when you ask a question like that.

They had me first. I came out light and curly headed, with my father's face. I was his female version. My mom told me that my grandmother came to the hospital after I was born and asked for her baby. They all wanted to claim me. I was her first grandchild that she could actually hold and see. And I was my parents first child. I was very light skinned, which I was told everyone loved. I had a complex about my skin color for many years as a child though.

Then my brother was born a year and a half later. He was tanner than me. No one believed that we were my mom's kids. They didn't look at our features. They just looked at our skin tone. I was olive like our dad, my brother was reddish brown, like some of our relatives that looked more Blackfoot. People always thought our mother and grandmother were our babysitters. At least in Long Island and in Mississippi they did, where my grandparents lived.

For a few years, before I turned seven, we spent most of our time with my grandparents, in Mississippi and Louisiana. No one believed me when I told them they were my relatives. Especially when I told my teachers and classmates that the woman picking me up was my grandmother. Or that the reddish brown skinned boy was my brother. My sister was born when I was six. Unfortunately, my mom lost three kids in between my brother and sister. I didn't know about them until I asked her about their lives before us. It just came up in conversation. A lot of things came up in that conversation. And my sister looks like a lighter milk chocolate version of our mother.

As we got older, we'd argue with people in the street about us all being related. Like we had to prove something to them. That I wasn't adopted. That yes, this black woman, was really our biological mother and that my brother and sister had the same parents that I did. In certain neighborhoods, people thought we were Dominican since we all looked so different, but my Spanish was never good enough to even fake it. And why would I? I am who I am.

As I got older, and after our father passed, I came into myself even more, I realized that my Arabic didn't have to be perfect and that my skin didn't have to match some of my relatives or my mom or siblings either. I am who I am. And always will be. Period. If that's not good enough for some people, that's their problem, not mine.

I felt like some people put me on a pedestal for looking the way I do. I just wanted to look like the beautiful black women in my life. And no matter how much sun I got, I'd never be like them. But that's fine. Just as my brother and sister are beautiful just the way they are, my black is beautiful too.

After the last person asked me, recently, "What are you?" I decided to simply answer, "human," and be done with it. New York City is supposed to be so multicultural and open, but I've encountered some pretty hurtful comments and questions from people. Like, am I related to any terrorists? No fool, I am not. Or telling me how exotic I look. To me, plants are exotic, and I'm not a plant. The funny and sad thing is people get offended by my responses when I answer like that. Well, hell, how about my offense to the questions or comments hurled at me? I've also had some white folks trying to "compete" with my mixedness, telling me about all the different European countries that are mixed in them. Okay, great. You started the conversation, not me. And you want to tell me that you're mixed too? That's not the same thing. Not to me, at least.

I know I get some privileges from being light skinned and educated. And luckily, I recognize it and do my best not to abuse it. I know that my brother and sister get treated and looked at differently than me. It bothers me that they do. They don't deserve to get pulled over by the cops multiple times, just because they're darker than me and have a nice car, like my brother has experienced.

I've only met one other person, other than my siblings, that had the same mix we do. And I haven't met anyone else since. I know when I finally have kids, they'll probably have questions for me about my background, about what it means to me to be mixed, and maybe what it means to them to be mixed too. And that's okay. I'll tell them that their mixed heritage is beautiful, and to never let anyone tell them differently. And that no matter what, they'll always have my love and support. ■

Charles Matthew Snyder

Negotiating Worlds
Black and White

I IMAGINE MYSELF WALKING down a thin black line on a desert path. This path cuts into a valley like the one you might have seen in a place like Arizona. This valley's copper-red mountain range is sharp against the flesh blue sky. I walk this fine line between two warring worlds: to my left, white America and to my right, black America. In this valley, on either side, I see these two worlds as flickering god heads in the form of reels of news reports being played. But, these god heads are doing exactly the same thing: screaming at the top of their lungs. Mouths open, saliva strings, and teeth shredding the world around them. I choose not to hear them and eventually, this line begins to separate into two different paths with much distance in between. The line finally stops. Ahead I can see two different trails leading to two different worlds. These god heads now stop yelling. They now stare at me, waiting to see which trail I'll take. I am walking down this thin black line on a desert path, between two worlds: at my left, white America and on my right, black America. I am walking down this path, on this line, negotiating my identity between two worlds.

Inside me, there are always two warring worlds. I have always wrestled with this "white thing," versus this "black thing." I grew up black. My mother, who is a black single mother, raised my siblings and me. We always lived in black communities. That aside, my father who is white, has always had a strong affinity for black people and blackness. So, how does one negotiate identities between two worlds, especially when your community, the one you identify with the most, including society, views you otherwise? How do you navigate this kind of wilderness? You adapt, you craft a strong foundation, a base, with pillars, holding you up. Otherwise, things can be precarious and confusing when explaining roots and ethnicity. My pillars and foundation are as follows: I am a person of color who is mixed black and white. But I primarily identify myself as black. I believe being black doesn't stop at melanin; it's a state of mind, a consciousness, and self-awareness. Yet, with these affirmations of identity, it's still a choice which sometimes leaves me feeling guilty; that the people on my father's side are rendered insignificant because of their whiteness. In a negotiation there are things won, compromised or lost.

"What are you?" "You look like you got somethin' in you." "What *are* you?" "You look like my mixed cousin." "Are you mulatto?" "You don't look black." "Are you Mexican or Latino?" "If you're black then I'm black and I'm white." "You're a half breed." "You're all mixed-up." These labels are like little knives that cut away at my body, examining me, separating my body from being. I want it to be known that being a person of color is not easy. Being black is not easy. Being mixed is not easy. To this day, I believe that archaic social strata such as the color line, is a tool of division stemming from slavery that still plays a role in my life. Because I'm ambiguous looking, because I am very light brown or tan, I don't quite fit into the black experience or canon. I say, look at the all of the mixed race black people who have contributed to the community and struggle. I look to my familial roots, my ancestors for strength. I have become apathetic to these questions which dissect my experience and make it invalid or some kind of circus spectacle. By both white and black standards, I am an oddity or "other," or at times tokenized or fetishized. All of which have made some parts of me cold and weary of the asker.

In the fifth grade, my ethnicity was challenged for the first time. Up until that point, I had always thought that I was just black. A black kid, in my class, told me I, in fact, wasn't black at all, but a "funky white boy." This label may seem jocular to some, yet, it was the beginning of self-deprecation: body versus identity, for years to come. In my mother's family, on my grandfather's side I have ancestors who survived slavery in Kentucky, who escaped the south and fled north to Chicago and Detroit. On my grandmother's side, there are connections to the first black family in Fremont, Ohio and even some of the first black steps on American soil. We are still learning and discovering. In my family, we have Harlem Globetrotters who played in the

1940s and 1950s, also black Naval men, world travelers and nurses. I come from black firsts and great American contributors and trailblazers. When I am in that valley, down those lines, those moments of scrutiny and moments cutting, I reflect upon the blood, my ancestry. It keeps me strong, it keeps me grounded. On struggling with whiteness, I admit that I have never felt very comfortable around white people. I never really wanted to be or connected to whatever white community is. I never felt like I belonged to that world. Or even felt compelled to claim it as mine. Especially when growing up in black neighborhoods and viewing anything as white as enemy, evil, or a system of oppression. In fact, because I look ambiguous, it has given me the privilege to have a keen insight on how white people view black people in our country. Such as the time when I was in a play and one of the white leading actors mentioned that the south side of Vallejo (the city I grew up in, in California) was once a nice place until the "blacks and Latino's moved in." At some point, there's always a line that's crossed; something convoluted or bizarre that's said. It's almost an expectation. These uncomfortable moments around white people, many times, are manifested in a comment or an opinion about my ethnic mixture as if being viewed as the "tragic mulatto." White people feel empowered to comment on communities of people of color when they have no idea what they're talking about. It can be in the form of a joke, or a stab. However, it's usually the unsaid that speaks the loudest. "They still do not know who we are," like my mother says. To be "white" all one has to do is consider himself or herself different; commit to living behind that dark veil fortified by denial, apathy, and avoidance (white guilt and fragility). These experiences build. The mind and body can only bear so many cuts until they bleed out in aggression, angst, anger, protest, fight. There is never admittance or apology for the effects of whiteness I have had a difficult time negotiating and coping within the white world.

There are times where I look at myself in the mirror and wonder who I really am, ethnically. I see a strong black face that reminds me of my mother and my grandfather. But I also see those European roots from ancestors on my father's side. I see my father. I pull skin back and to the side, trying to open up the flesh and tendon: "Maybe, I'm not seeing something here." I hold up pictures of my grandpa or cousins, measuring my face in black likeness, wanting to look more like them. I acknowledge my struggles with being mixed, at times, are predicated on skin color. However, the scrutiny of physical characteristics has nothing to do with the mind, heart, or soul (consciousness). The physical is not tantamount to my actual identity. I acknowledge that this path is a gift I have been given. It's my plight. I too understand the burden of hypervisibility. I want people to know: I'm not for sale or for play. I am not the brunt of ethnically geared jokes. Nor am I here to validate "*downess*," be a gatekeeper, or an ambassador for blackness. My identity and my body are not a sacrificial son for masses to judge. Honestly, when I write I like to do so in the darkest corner of a café. It's in that shadow that I can observe and see people for who they really are in the light. For whom they really are and so desire to be. Rarely do people give me hope that relations between these two worlds, black and white, have healed enough to bond in solidarity to unite. Then I think to myself: maybe the outside world is only a reflection of the turmoil I feel inside. And when I heal, this world may heal too. ■

Lily Anne Welty Tamai

Mixed Race Mama

W̲E WERE AT THE NATIONAL ZOO in Washington, D.C., looking at the zebras and admiring their muscular legs and iconic black and white stripes. I was speaking to my son in Japanese, *"shima uma. mite! shima uma da yo!"* (Zebras! Look! It's a zebra!). A little girl nearby overheard us and said enthusiastically, "Mom! I just learned how to say zebra in Spanish! It's *shima uma!*"[1]

On a visit to view the exhibition, "Citizen 13660," about Mine Okubo's artwork and the Japanese American World War II incarceration at the Skirball Cultural Center in Los Angeles, I warned my son to be careful going down the stairs behind the lobby: *"ki wo tsuke ne. abunai yo."* A middle-aged Japanese American woman seated nearby asked me, "What language are you speaking?" Japanese. "Oh, that doesn't sound like Japanese. Where are you from?"

I thought the questions had ended.

By now, people who already know my background don't ask the prying, personal questions. But people who first meet me will often still conduct an interrogation clarifying my race and origins. I know what the questions will be and I know it's going to be exhausting.

I was born in the U.S. to a Japanese mother from Tokyo, and a father who is about ten kinds of white from Riverside, California. My father had lived in Japan for about five years and achieved a level of fluency in Japanese, so the language spoken in our house was Japanese. In college I realized that I spoke Japanese because of my father and his advanced language skills. His language ability allowed for Japanese to remain in our home, whereas other

---

[1]   I want to thank Akemi Johnson for the helpful feedback on earlier versions of this essay.

interracially married couples in my mother's social circle defaulted to English in their homes since that was their common language.

We lived in a working class agricultural Latino community, and many of my friend's parents spoke only Spanish. Growing up, I spoke Japanese at home, and English at school. Of course I knew what my mixed race background was, but sometimes I identified as Latina (and I still do) because I passed. I studied Spanish for years because in public I was often spoken to in Spanish before English. Plus, my mother told me to make sure I was able to speak to and greet my friend's parents (greetings are very important in Japanese), even if they only understood Spanish. I recognized my privilege: it was easier for me to study Spanish than it was to urge agricultural workers who have elementary school educations to go study English at night after they put in fifty hours a week harvesting strawberries in the California sun.

But, over the course of the last few years I noticed some changes. Maybe because I am around people who know my background, I don't feel the heavy ethnic fatigue that I have felt for much of my life. It has been a while since I've been asked the barrage of ethnic credential clarification questions which stem from my phenotype.

Them: "What are you? Where are you from? What is your ethnicity? What is your nationality? Where are you really from? Where are your parents from? Where did you grow up? How did your parents meet? Where did you learn Japanese? 日本語は上手ですね！Your Japanese is good! Why didn't you ever tell me you weren't Mexican!? Aren't you part Filipino? Is your family from Brazil? Eres Mexicana? When did you start learning English? Are you confused? Are you sure?"

Me: "Oh. Nice to meet you."

One of the most powerful pieces of writing I was introduced to as an undergraduate was Maria P. P. Root's, "The Bill of Rights for People of Mixed Heritage." I read it and reread it multiple times. For years I carried a copy with me so I could read it after getting stung with questions. I shared it with other mixed race people who I met. It stayed with me because it gave me permission to be me. It says:

I have the right

Not to justify my existence in this world.

Not to justify my ethnic legitimacy.

Not to be responsible for people's discomfort with my physical or ethnic ambiguity.

To change my identity over my lifetime – and more than once. [2]

Lately though, the ethnic fatigue has not exhausted me. The persistence and reduced frequency of questions made me think, "Yes! It's over!" For a while now, I have not been asked those really personal questions that range from my parents' intimate relationship to having to clarify my ethnic identity based on my physical features when I barely meet someone. Maybe Maria Root was right after all. Maybe at some point things simply balance out, or we age out, and people just stop asking the questions where I am supposed to willingly divulge everything about my parents' personal and sexual life choices and explain why I look this way, and why I speak the languages I do, and what my loyalties are. Maybe my identity is changing over my lifetime like she said it would.

I was wrong about this. Well, partially wrong.

When I became a mother, I decided that I wanted to teach my son Japanese. It was my first language. It is my mother tongue. There are songs and joy from childhood that exist only in Japanese for me. Being bilingual has opened up many doors personally and professionally, and this ability has given me cultural access because I can be trusted. I can perform Japaneseness. I photograph differently when speaking Japanese. My chin is lower, my smile more reserved. My hands are placed one over the other in my lap. When I speak English, in the photos my smile is bigger, my hands more relaxed.

It was never my choice to learn this language, just like it's not a choice when people are raised monolingual or if they are adopted. This is a choice made by my parents, just like my birth name, and just like my racial background. I didn't have a say in the whole mixed race thing at the start.

I wanted to give my son the gift of a second language so he wouldn't have to work so hard to learn it in school in an artificial setting. Plus, America is

---

[2] Maria Root, *Bill of Rights for People of Mixed Heritage.* I want to thank Paul Spickard for introducing me to her work.

a language graveyard. Often the second-generation is bilingual, but by the third generation the language brought over from the first generation is lost, or just a shadow of it is left to be brought out through food, culture, gifts, and ceremonial and family events as needed. I want to break this cycle of colonialism and privileging all things English. I am swimming upstream against the strong forces of English in America.

Nearly every time I am in a public place having a conversation with my curly-haired kid, strangers will almost always ask what language we are speaking. And then the steady stream of all of the familiar race questions follow:

Them: "Where are you from? Where are you really from? Where are your parents from? Where did you grow up? How did you learn Japanese? Does he get confused? You don't look Japanese (enough)."

Me: "Oh. Okay." (silence)

Then once that is sorted out and they feel better about my phenotype and my identity (you see, it's about them, not me), the conversation shifts and they congratulate me for speaking Japanese and for teaching it to my child. But in reality, it was really kind of them to say that. After all, I am struggling with all of the English words and songs seeping into my son's vocabulary even though I only speak to him in Japanese and try to create a Japanese-only environment. There are words in Japanese that I don't know like otter, colt, and lizard (I have since looked them up). However, after multiple interactions like this, I thought about this comment more and more. I wonder if they also congratulate the mother at the park playground who is from South Los Angeles or from Oaxaca living in the U.S. speaking Spanish to her children too?

I realize there is privilege that comes with being able to speak English and a second or third language. I realize that I am fortunate to be able to make these deliberate choices about language, culture, and identity for my child, the way my parents did for me.

I am still learning how to be a mixed race mother. I am at a good place in relation to figuring out my own mixed race identity (Maria Root and many others have helped me along this journey). I sought out examples and read everything I could. The difference between my parents and me is that they were monoracial people raising mixed race children. They had no idea what it was like for me being mixed race growing up phenotypically ambiguous in a Latino community. I am mixed race raising a second generation of mixed race children. We are a generation removed from a monoracial relative and I'm learning how to navigate those differences.

My son napped while I wrote this. Then he woke up to nurse. At some point he might read this. He will have his own journey to figure out his identity and prepare to answer all of the questions. Or maybe not. But for now, we have to get ready and go to the zoo. ∎

Kyla Kupferstein Torres

Whose Girl Are You?

O N THE UPPER EAST SIDE in the 1980s, it seemed like my mother was the only black person living for blocks and blocks. The next ones I knew of personally were our cousins, the Savins, who lived ten blocks away. There were plenty of black women in the neighboring apartment buildings every day when my mother was at work; they cared for the children of the white residents, as my sitter Roslyn cared for me. Nannies piled up in the lobbies of private schools and on the benches at the area playgrounds. The obvious things had drawn my mother to the neighborhood: *Around the rich white people, Leon. That's where you know someone comes when you scream. Something happens to your children and the police are there.* It was a household-er's ideal, if not a multiracial Mecca. When looking for what would become our apartment, my parents sent my father alone on the expedition first. An application with two M.D. degrees and an income more than sufficient to pay the rent sealed the deal, and my mother remained unseen until they moved in.

Our apartment had a view of the building from the opening credits of *The Jeffersons* who had "moved on up" to their piece of the Upper East Side pie. My parents weren't Tom and Helen Willis, but two doctors with a small child made a fine addition to the building, in spite of the obvious issue. And luckily, no one would mistake me for a nanny's child the way they mistook my mom for a nanny.

"Aren't you Mrs. Cohen's girl?" a middle-aged Jewish woman asked her in the lobby of my father's office building, a residential tower three blocks from, and very similar to our own.

"No, I'm not," she answered, pulling her suit jacket tighter across her chest. "Whose girl are you?*"*

When we were small, my father told my mother that he thought my brother and I could pass. He thought that people would really believe we were white by looking at us. I never actually heard my parents have this conversation but as a child I often, glumly, thought the same. I clutched my mother's hand; I wanted to be like her. But no one ever imagined she was my mother. People marveled and did double takes at her regal beauty. Not a soul ever said, "Aren't you lucky, you'll look just like her one day!" No connection was made between this gorgeous creature and the pudgy, all-too-light-skinned-child by her side. No one looked beyond our complexions to link us together. There were small hints, a little frizz to my hair, wider lips, the vaguely off shade of light of my skin. My mother still scoffed at my father's desire to fit us into the ultra-white landscape of our neighborhood. *A crazy notion, Leon. Ridiculous.*

A lot of the other mixed kids I knew had parents who were divorced, and extended families who never associated with each other. My parents were happily married, and both my black Jamaican and Jewish families lived close to us in New York City. Though there had been some tension when my parents dated and married, by the time I was born, race wasn't experienced as a problem for our extended clan. The first cousins that I saw the most regularly were mixed too. My Buba and Zayda would have my Jamaican grandparents over for Passover and Rosh Hashana. My brother and I being mixed just wasn't a *thing* to them. There were no sidelong glances, no whispered comments, no tolerating each other. At home, with my parents or my cousins or my grandparents, there was no need to wonder about who I was or to explain myself. But as a West Indian, my mother was never far from a world of profound color-consciousness. If the United States is the home of the one drop rule, the Caribbean is the land of a million shades and a million meanings. My mother had grown up brown and skinny with kinky hair in a large family of light-skinned women with "good" hair. In Jamaica, you were what you looked like, not necessarily what you came from.

My babysitter Roslyn and I sat together as I ate my breakfast one weekday morning. My mother was preparing to leave for work, and as she moved about, collecting her things she asked in an almost offhand way:

"What color is Mommy?"

"Black."

"What color is Roslyn?"

"Black."

"What color is Kyla?"

"White." It was what I and everyone could see.

"Is Kyla the same color as Roslyn?"

"No."

"Is Roslyn the same color as Mommy?"

"Yes."

"Is Kyla the same color as Mommy?"

"Yes."

Yes. Yes. Yes. Always yes.

But the answer was no, she told me simply, as if she was reminding me to say please and thank you. For months, I was inconsolable, bothering her constantly:

"Isn't there any part of you that's white?"

One day, I climbed into her lap: "Wait! I found it! Look, there's white in your eyes!" For the rest of my childhood, it felt like that was where our resemblance stopped.

By the time I'd graduated from high school, my mother had become an accomplished amateur sculptress. After a few attempts at busts, she wanted to sculpt me. I was eighteen and had lost some baby fat. I was starting to get my adult face. She came up to see me at college and took photos of my head from every angle. When I came home for the holidays she made me come to sit for her in the studio.

"See? I told you Annette! You're just making it look like yourself!" said one classmate. "How could she help it, Enid? The girl looks *just* like her!" said another.

On the way home she kept repeating, "I don't understand what they're talking about. What on earth is it they see?" But I was starting to see it. My heart burst with joy that I was matched to her. It was nice to be thought of as beautiful, but more importantly, I was thought of as hers. Passing no more.

Around the same time, I started my journey into dating. I'd been a fat kid and teenager. I hated the way that I looked and assumed that boys did too. Most of the boys in my high school were white, and for them the hot girls were the skinny blonde ones. My first kiss, one of few in high school, was from a stranger, a Colombian man one afternoon on Bleecker Street.

I let him because no one else had ever tried and it made me feel beautiful. It was exciting and scary but, even in my own sixteen-year-old estimation, pathetic. It was clear that my only path to having a boyfriend would be to lose weight. But then there was Jeanette. She was Afro-Latina, tall and thick (though in tenth grade I would have said "fat"). She had a boyfriend. He didn't go to our elite magnet school, but by all accounts he was devoted and generous and true. I couldn't comprehend how that could be. She wasn't "hot" on the high school scale that defined my life. She lived in some other world where girls like her were beautiful. I felt doubly pathetic—I'd never even been to that world, *and* I didn't look like Jeanette.

But every so often in the life of an adolescent, things change. One night in my senior year of high school, the drummer from a popular ska band lured me outside after a show for my second official kiss. This guy was beautiful, and had high school and college girls and actual women sniffing around him all the time, and he chose ME! It didn't matter that he was already hooking up with a skinny Asian girl from my own school. When he pulled away from me and smiled, then wrote his name and number on a bar napkin, I was finally okay. I was attractive.

He was black and suddenly, Black World it would be. Slowly, during my college years, I started to realize that in Black World, I *was* the skinny blonde chick. With my adult face and body coming in, I definitely couldn't pass, but light, bright, damn near white was getting plenty of attention.

After a lifetime of feeling like I'd never be pretty because I wasn't brown, I drank it all in.

But then there were the dirty looks from black women who were always suspicious of me, my shade, and my motives when it came to their men. And then there were my suspicions of the black men who found me attractive. Why were they so into a light, bright, damn near white chick, and what did it say about their own relationship to blackness and black women, a group that I was finally starting to feel a part of? But then, I liked being desired. Was I betraying my sisters? Was the attention I was getting simply a result of black men's internalized racism? Wasn't I allowed to just feel pretty and desired? Around and around I went.

But not too long after my entry to Black World, there were white men, too. That was the ultimate validation—a guy who could have the prized skinny blonde chick, choosing me. And no one seemed to think less of me choosing a white man over a black one. After all, my father was a balding Jewish guy. But there was a nagging anxiety: if one day I wound up with a white guy, as light as I was, what would our children look like? Would I become an "other" in a white family? Would I get swallowed up, erased? Or even if I wound up with a black man and had children? Would they all match and I'd be on the outside? I feared that either way, I might just disappear. My own children could easily belong to a group where I wouldn't obviously belong. Me and my mom all over again, with no one able to see our connection. It was a risk with any monoracial guy.

I longed to date a man who was my physical match. Biracial guys were few and far between and inevitably seemed to date white women. No surprise, since most of them had white mothers. Latino men of any nationality all seemed to link up so early. Every time I'd meet one he always seemed to have a girlfriend, or even a wife, no matter how young. By the time I was in my thirties, I'd given up on finding a Dominican or Puerto Rican guy, or at least I'd given up on the chance that he'd be free to be mine if I did. I resigned myself that if I was to ever have kids, that I'd be the odd one out in my family. I was becoming devoutly single, talking to my black and Middle Eastern gay friends about having kids together in some postmodern co-parenting arrangement, then race would be just one of the unusual aspects of my family.

And then I met Juan. A mutual acquaintance got us together by telling me he'd be a good prospect for consulting work, and telling Juan that I was a cute Puerto Rican chick, good for a good time. It came up quickly on our first date; we knew we'd been tricked, but were unclear as to whether the part about me was a ruse or just confusion on our matchmaker's part. On subsequent encounters we discovered our mutual passion for equity in education, live jazz, and endless conversation. I'd found a Puerto Rican man with three degrees, no ex-wife, and no kids. "You better marry him fast," my girlfriend said "or I'm going to introduce him to someone else!" So I did. I couldn't have been happier to find a home with a Boricua, someone whose actual mix was close to mine, if in a different language. His father was brown with kinky hair. His mother *could* pass, except for the accent. Though he was browner than me, we matched. There was a good chance that our future children could look like us. With Juan, I thought I was home. I added his name to my already long Jewish one, clear that our future family would be unified in name and in look. His family, as color-conscious as my own Jamaican clan, was pleased. "You just look like a beautiful Latin woman," cooed his Titi Miriam when he brought me home. And all my Jamaican family moved beyond their anti-Puerto Rican prejudice, impressed with his character and relieved that I hadn't brought home another "Africa Black" man to marry.

Shortly after our wedding, I got a job at the school I'd attended as a child. When I filled out my initial paperwork, I was surprised to find myself adding my newly acquired surname to my business cards. At work, and in most of my life, I was now Kyla Kupferstein Torres, a new name I claimed with pride; instead of the familiar "Ms. K," students in these hallways called me "Mrs. KT." I reveled in being someone new in someplace old. I loved how Officer Donaldson, the Jamaican security officer, greeted me each day with "Good morning, Mrs. Torres" sounding all the world like one of my uncles. But I began to notice that folks didn't seem to notice the Kupferstein and stuck with the Torres. Instead of "what are you?", I started to get "are you Dominican or Puerto Rican?" On my physical therapist's table, he and I got into a conversation about the Jewish high holy days. "Did you convert when you got married?" he asked. I didn't understand until I realized he'd been looking, not listening. To him, and to a lot of people, "Torres" on my insurance card plus my face logically equaled Latina.

Then came our little boy. From his very first days, he looked like us. First like my brother, with the same huge eyes. Then Juan's nose, then my hair, with a complexion right between the two of us. Now, we're a Latino every family, perfect for a primetime Goya or Telemundo commercial. There's an incomparable pleasure when people comment on the street "You just about spat him out! A real mini-mami!" I love to look at pictures of myself with this little boy who is undeniably mine. There's no mistaking. Maybe he'll be irritated one day, hearing for the millionth time how much he looks like his parents, but there's a surge of satisfaction and redemption inside me, every time I hear it.

But now the visual works for everyone on the outside, and I've disappeared. I'm passing for Latina, whether I like it or not, and there's a whole new learning curve. Sometimes, I feel like an impostor, like when a coworker leans over and whispers her not-for-public consumption thoughts to me in Spanish, and I catch every other word, hoping I've got the gist. Most of the time, I'm just Señora Torres, just *mami* in a *familia Latina*. My son is as mixed as I am, if not more so, but most days, makes me seem less so. I got exactly what I thought I was trying to avoid. I don't get asked "what are you?" much these days, at least not when I'm with my son. The questions and challenges don't come up. At least not for others.

Shortly after our son was born, I stood in church for Juan's Tio Carlos' funeral, my Star of David hanging around my neck. As the priest swung the incense and made the sign of the cross, I realized that my little guy won't have a first communion or know the Catholic liturgy like his Puerto Rican peers. He'll look the part, but maybe folks will treat him like he's not Really Latino the same way that I was never Really Black. But I hope, no matter the question, that his answer will be yes to who he is. Yes, he is mine. Yes, I am his. Yes, he can be whoever he needs to be in this ever mixing country we call home. ■

Diana Emiko Tsuchida

The Key to Curiosity

"Mixed babies are better looking. The whole world needs to mix." "You don't look Asian. You look like you're from Latin America." "Men come up to you because you're Asian."

"You definitely don't look white." "You're white and something."

"No, I mean, where are you originally from?" "What are you?"

IN ADDITION TO BEING TOLD the above phrases, if I had actually visited the list of countries that people assume I'm from I'd have the most impressive passport. The work people have put into interpreting my Japanese, Scottish and Irish heritage has made for some unique icebreakers that run the gamut from people congratulating my dad for being an "Asian stud" who managed to marry a white woman to hearing how exotic I turned out, like a risky genetic experiment.

Are these compliments? Am I supposed to receive these as positive comments, smiling gratefully that someone has just dissected my facial features within a minute of meeting me? Instead, these are more so a reflection of the lack of vocabulary we have to talk about mixed race identity. Instead, I'm now on the defense to justify the reason I look the way I do, to unpack in a few short words, my family history.

This most often happens when I'm with my mother. With blonde hair, blue eyes and the cheery disposition of a *Leave it to Beaver* episode, our contrasting facial features and my dark brown hair makes for a harder-to-understand familial connection. When I was still a baby in a stroller, my mother was asked if I was adopted from Korea. When I was in preschool, kids wouldn't believe she was actually my mom. When we walk through shops and stores now, I sometimes find myself playing a twisted game of counting how many workers speak to us separately, as if we didn't come through the door together. And most recently on a family trip to Seattle, the ticketing worker at the Space Needle assumed my mom was in tow with the elderly, white couple behind us. As I've had to continuously explain why I look ambiguous or "half white and something else," I'm sure my mother's sensitive heart has grown tired of people questioning how I'm actually her daughter. Race is something I'll usually vent about, while she tries hard to understand and meet me halfway.

My father has strong ties to being Japanese, but is culturally American through and through. While I can phenotypically pass more for being Asian of some sort (though that entirely depends on who you ask) my own father has used my mixed race identity to suggest that I need not be called upon to practice or carry on anything Japanese – language, cultural niceties, those vital things that solidify tradition. While he deeply appreciates that I identify with being Japanese and know my own history, he's told me to "stick to my English," primarily when I express the guilt I feel for not being able to converse or be even close to speaking some decent Japanese. I don't ask so that he can tell me not to feel guilty, I ask so that he can remedy the situation by giving me language cues. I'm asking for serious advice. And yet, I feel embarrassed, ashamed and nervous, as if I should have had a handle on my own language by this time.

But my father did not prioritize this as a cornerstone of my upbringing.

So here at thirty-one years old, I navigate the world through my own racial lens, an amalgamation of the community I identify with, and how I know the world perceives me to be. And while the comments I get are relatively benign instances of curiosity or mistaken assumptions, it's exhausting to count the number of times it happens, and to take inventory of the effort you've put in to explaining yourself and your family. The dissection of your face is something that burrows deep within you until you can't find it anymore. It becomes harder to summon the feelings of being judged or angry because that is too big of a burden to bear in the first place. Instead, you find ways to cheat the system and turn the question back on the asker: "Why don't you guess what I am?"

As I identify primarily with being Asian American, the work you put into being embraced by that community is harder than you ever want to admit. But because you're ambiguous, a potential outsider that once again must verbalize the claim you have to that community, you work hard to uphold the ties that bind you – a shared history, cultural understanding, family anecdote. Looking like you belong grants you privileges, a ticket in to the tapestry of a community. Yet there are times you discover that even a good friend sees you as non-passable and, a completely white person in contrast to their darker skin. When we always seek acceptance in that tight knit community you call home, these things jar you out of your bubble of just existing, living. The people who you feel are least likely to distance themselves from you are in fact, doing just that.

Which brings to mind this duplicity: We're often pegged as the poster child for incredible racial progress yet seen as the manifestation of the loss of culture and community. How can these two things possibly coexist? More so, we are not the saviors of the next generation or the embodiment of racial peace on earth. We are also not the tragic symbols of taboo love, a mark of one parent's – usually the mother's – promiscuity and failure to maintain the family's racial lineage. We are not an exotic racial experiment nor carrying "unpure" heritage in our blood.

This is all to say that there is no cut and dry answer for how to deal with us. No one will write a handbook telling you the correct questions to ask when you're curious about someone's racial background.

So perhaps the key to your curiosity is to silence it. ■

Jenny Turner

Black and White Thinking

I WAS THE THIRD OF FOUR CHILDREN raised by a black father and a white mother in Philadelphia during the 1960s and 1970s. Back then, there were no support groups for interracial families or mixed race children, not that we would have joined anyway. We led a relatively isolated life, other than going to school. My older sister went to the local public school at first, but my parents soon moved her to a city-wide magnet school. I still remember the stories of my sister bringing home leaflets about the "tragic mulatto," who will never fit in anywhere, provided to her by her teacher, an African American woman, of all people. The final straw was when a classmate set fire to one of my sister's pigtails. The rest of us never attended the neighborhood school.

I certainly remember my discomfort when being asked "What are you, anyway?" Looking back, I wish I had responded with a wounded look, "I'm a little girl"—maybe that would have given some of the questioners a clue about how dehumanizing a question they were posing. I usually feigned confusion, which led to "No, no, what race are you?" Sometimes I wish I had dared respond, "Human, what race are you?" with a puzzled look. But I knew better. I had quickly learned that most people asking that question were not interested in how I viewed myself, but were collecting information so that they could make their own judgments.

The guidance that my parents provided was that we are part black and part white—it is what it is—and there is nothing wrong with that. My mom, who had arrived in the U.S. from France only fifteen years earlier, said that anywhere else in the world, we would be viewed as what we were—even in South Africa, where that status would entitle us to a specific government-sanctioned level of discrimination. But here in the land of the free, American society had the "one-drop rule," which seemed to be vigorously enforced by both whites and blacks, despite its origins in support of white supremacy. The argument that being able to check multiple boxes for race on a government form will eviscerate support for African American communities seems disingenuous to me—surely people who check more than one box can be counted in different groups for different purposes. It seems like the same, all or nothing, black and white thinking that has left us polarized on so many issues. Life is far too complicated for that approach to work.

My actual response to "What are you?" was to explain that I was half black and half white. That led to jokes about "which half?" or sometimes about zebras. The response from both black and white questioners was often, "Oh, so you're black." "Well, as I just said, I'm part black and part white." "No, you're black." The general reaction seemed to be that if I didn't declare myself black (with perhaps a muted apology for the existence of my white mother), I was rejecting any black part of me. So I adjusted my response to "my dad's black and my mom's white," figuring that at least they wouldn't argue with me about that and could then draw their own conclusions.

I don't think I was uncomfortable with being mixed race, biracial, half and half (despite the instructional leaflet my sister was given, no "tragic mulatto" here)—I was uncomfortable with having to explain myself and argue with people about my own identity. Even as a kid, I understood that what I am is not okay with a lot of people. My parents' advice: that's their problem, not yours. Be you.

Nothing is more personal than one's identity (of which race is just a part). Perhaps those people who felt obliged to define my race for me would nowadays be telling a transgender woman, "Oh, so you're a dude." We've clearly made some progress since my youth. I have to say, I don't get asked, "What are you" as much any more. Part of it is that people will say things to a child that they would not say to an adult, part of it is that most people in my community already know or assume my background, part of it is that over time American society has become more comfortable with racial/ethnic mixing, and part of it is that I now live in California, which I immediately noticed was way more relaxed about interracial mixing when I arrived here from the East Coast years ago.

When I was growing up, the census and other forms that required you to check a box for your race did not allow people to check multiple boxes.

Our strategy was not to check any box then. Sometimes there was an option to check a box labeled "other." Usually, we skipped that question. So, when I arrived at college, my resident advisor took one look at me and rushed over a minority peer counselor to help me adjust. I still remember my Asian immigrant roommate wondering how come no one was offering to help her settle in. All my life, I had gone to integrated schools, and now here I was at a university where all of the black students self-segregated and sat at a long table together in the dining hall. Many of them glared at me as I stood in line with my roommate – how dare I not toe the line! I remember just being appalled – why would you work hard enough to get into a top-tier university and then voluntarily isolate yourself from most of the community? This flew in the face of everything I believed in – it seemed to me that segregation, voluntary or not, negated my very right to exist.

Looking back, I see that many of those students took my behavior as a rejection of the black student community, which was not what I intended. Sadly, it did not seem like there was a middle ground; you either joined the group or you were ostracized. There's that all or nothing thinking again. In hindsight, I see that the offer of a peer counselor was well intentioned, not necessarily based on an assumption that I was not equipped to function in an integrated setting. It was several years until I had any black friends in college, and even then, they were those who were able to step out of the all-black group and interact with other people.

A few years ago, another biracial graduate from my school wrote an article about the evolution of her thinking on race, parts of which absolutely infuriated me. She described the early welcome for minority students before freshman year, before "the snowstorm" when all the white students arrived. (Yes, I find that term offensive.) She identifies as "black, though my dad is white" (no, I don't find that offensive) and was unhappy to be stuck in the "small, sad group of biracial kids" (you betcha, I find that offensive) instead of the happy group of black kids for some of the activities. I, being racially incognito until I arrived, was not invited to the bonding sessions before school started. (Interestingly, she also wrote about not wanting to be called an "incognegro" by the black student community – a term for black kids deemed not black enough – perhaps I was being called that when I was there.) In her article, she also described her years-long estrangement from a biracial friend because the friend did not declare herself or her mixed race kids as black. I wanted to ask her, "Who put you in charge of designating other people's identity?" She defined her own identity (black, but my dad is white). I would never presume to try to tell her otherwise. That is completely her call. The bottom line is that my identity is defined by me, not by anyone else, and is based on reality, not on how other people view me.

I'm really proud of all of my heritage and am happy to share the information with others. But in sharing that information, I am not looking for help in defining my identity, and neither are kids today. It's hard enough figuring out your identity as you grow up without being regularly questioned about it. Parents can be a trusted source of guidance. But in the end, your identity is all about *you*. Whatever identity feels right to you is what matters, not input from acquaintances, classmates, or strangers.■

Maya Washington

The Mixed Question

DURING MY FRESHMEN YEAR at the University of Southern California, I applied and was accepted to live in a co-ed freshman dorm community for students interested in African American history called Somerville Place, named after John and Vada Somerville, the first African American graduates of USC's School of Dentistry. Reading between the coded lines of the glossy housing brochure, it was quite evident that this was a "black" themed floor. It was open to all students, but based on how it was described, it was clear that this space would attract black students. The building also housed a less coded Chicano Floor, and a Quiet Floor for students who wanted to be in community with others who shared their interests or preferences.

Coming all the way from Minnesota, I knew that living in a community with other black students would be important at a predominantly white institution. I was raised in an all-white suburb just outside of Minneapolis and chose USC for the great weather and the promise of diversity. While the student population was mostly white at the time, about 40 percent of the student body was non-white and comprised of every ethnicity imaginable. I applied to live on Somerville Place looking forward to the prospect of having a roommate who didn't ask why I don't wash my hair every day or why my hair is curly when it's wet and straight when I blow it dry. Greater than my fear of annoying grooming questions, I was really concerned that being away from my black-identified family, in a mostly white environment, would be really difficult if I didn't have a safe black space to come home to at the end of a long day of classes.

My mother and her fifty-eight-year-old cousin, Benny, helped me move in and get situated. When we got to my room, the standard issue twin bed on the right was covered with a few boxes and clothes, suggesting that my roommate had already started the process of moving in, but she was nowhere to be found. I was a little nervous, wondering who was going to be sleeping next to me. Will we get along? I wondered as we started unpacking my things. At least I knew that if we had any issues, they wouldn't be about race. I pulled out my frilly pink everything (bed spread, sheets and pillow cases) and a few family photos that I arranged on the desk. After a couple of hours, we took a break and went to Sizzler.

When we returned from dinner, a cute honey-brown girl named Jennifer and her boyfriend Stewart were in the room hanging out. We exchanged pleasantries and said our goodbyes to our loved ones and began the awkward but hopeful process of getting to know each other. It wasn't hard for either of us. Everything about her was familiar to me. She could have been one of my cousins, or a sister. We were the same height, give or take an inch or two – just enough over the five foot mark to make it count. We wore our hair long in either flat-ironed or wash-and-go natural curls, and had similar skin tones.

Jennifer was inquisitive and chatty. She gave off a sophisticated "popular girl" vibe with her winning smile and easy conversation. She jumped right in as she hung up her clothes, "Yeah, so Stewart saw that you'd put your family portrait up on the desk. He was like, 'Cool, your roommate's mom is Lena Horne.' "

"Um, no, my mom's not Lena Horne," I blush, knowing that my mom looks exactly like Lena Horne, but at the same time thinking that the odds of anyone's mom being an icon as big as Lena Horne living in this dorm seemed really slim. I imagined her boyfriend wasn't the sharpest tack in the box, and maybe she wasn't either if he had managed to convince her that such a thing was probable.

"She's not? She looks like her, sweet girl. I have to tell Stewart," she laughs, pulling an endless tangle of belts, purses, and shoes out of a box.

As our conversation continued, I quickly discover that neither she nor Stewart were simple-minded. They were just Hollywood. As she surrendered the details of her seventeen-year-old life, it became clear that Jennifer and I were as much alike as we were different. We both started our careers in entertainment as child actors and dancers. Only, she did this in Hollywood and not Minneapolis. She had a recording contract with a major record label and worked on her album, and performed with her sister and cousin on the weekends. Her Jewish dad was a professor at USC and her black mother was a TV writer. My black parents worked in corporate America. She was worldly and stylish. I was nerdy, sheltered, and from Minnesota. My bedding was pink and I hung little pictures of Angels on my bulletin board. Her bedding was black and her bulletin board was covered in fashion ads for makeup and designer clothes. I quickly came to understand why her logic would allow my mother to be Lena Horne – because of Hollywood.

We met the other floormates, sixteen boys and sixteen girls from all walks of life and black experiences. Less than 25 percent of us were from outside the state of California so I struggled to fit in a bit. I was a Minnesota walleye out of water for sure. Still, it was comforting to know that whatever growing pains we went through with one another wouldn't likely be about race. The other girls on the floor pretty much covered the gamut of brown and tan skin tones, and a variety of hair textures. On the surface, I didn't even encounter the nuances of colorism which can be extremely painful for everyone involved. It was refreshing the way that we could talk about issues that affected the black community into the wee hours of the night, and often traveled in a pack as a sort of built in brother and sisterhood developed in that space.

One night, a few floormates and I were discussing the importance of race remaining part of college admissions decisions. I became increasingly passionate about the issue. Jelani, a hippyish kid from Florida with a wild afro in the early stages of becoming locs, laughed at my passion for the issue, "You mixed girls are always so militant."

I immediately tensed into a death stare. "I'm not mixed!" I charged, fuming.

"You're not? I thought you were mixed," he shrugged confused as to why I was so upset.

I wasn't even sure why I was angry. Defensive. Offended. Whatever that very real emotion I was feeling was – it totally threw me off. I was the only black girl in first grade. My sisters and I had integrated in an entire school district. It was as if my blackness was being called into question. And it was. And it hurt. Unlike Minnesota, California boasts the most interesting combinations of black one might possibly find anywhere else on the globe. Perhaps the Caribbean islands come close: black and Jewish, black and Asian, black and South Asian, black and Pacific Islander, black and Persian, black and French, black and Latinx, and a number of other unique combinations.

The more I thought about it, I actually did look more like the biracial kids on the floor than I'd really considered. I'd never even contemplated their mixedness or my own. Every person on that floor, biracial or not, represented the literal genetic gumball machine that is my biological family. On both sides, our genetics have cranked out every skin tone, texture, shape, and sized expression of "black" known to humanity. My response to Jelani's accusation that I was mixed, was the first time I considered that people saw me differently than how I saw myself. This was the first time the mixed question came up, and it's never gone away.

There was only one other time at that point in my life where something similar occurred, only it happened to my mother. On a church trip to Israel a few years prior, my mother had difficulty explaining to a man (who'd just offered her camels and a lovely life if she allowed him to marry me) that she was a black American. He repeatedly asked where she was from.

His skin was darker than hers, and he didn't speak English well, so the exchange went on for a while. She continued to insist, "African American. Black. Negro…" and he continued to remain confused. We were waved back onto our tour bus and a couple of white-haired white ladies on board saw the commotion and asked her what happened.

"I was trying to tell him black, black, but he just didn't understand," my mom explained. The lady laughed, shifting in her seat, "Ha, he thought you were black?"

"I AM black." My mom stabbed back with the same death stare I gave Jelani.

Reflecting on that incident back in Israel from my dorm room in California, I considered why I got so mad after Jelani's comment. I'd never had to defend my genetic blackness before. Sure, I'd been told I talked like a white girl before, but no one went so far as to suggest that I wasn't 100 percent black. Even though my mother is Creole, I never felt the need to identify as "other" because my mother asserted her black identity above all else.

For her, growing up in rural Texas during Jim Crow, the world was divided between white and colored. She lived in a small Creole enclave where her parents and grandparents migrated from Louisiana in the 1940s. This was a time when Creoles (descendants of African, French, Spanish, and Native American unions in colonial Louisiana) were called "gumbo eaters" and "crawfish heads" by the kids at the all-black segregated school. A time when my grandmother forbid the children to speak French outside the house, or at all, for fear that they'd be mistreated in the community. While it is true that there are historic instances of fair-skinned, multiracial blacks passing for white, my mother owned her blackness as a way of denouncing the denial that others who look like her have sometimes chosen. "I'd rather identify with that which people find most unacceptable than to claim whiteness of any kind," she offered reluctantly when I started sharing my experiences with this "mixed question" I'd begun to encounter.

As my young adulthood and career in entertainment pressed forward, I was confronted with my multicultural background with every interview and casting session, "What are you mixed with? Is that your real hair?" My agents would often submit me for roles and jobs looking for "ethnically ambiguous" talent. Sometimes I would book them. In a matter of years, I went from being African American in the Minneapolis/St. Paul market, to being without a concrete race in the eyes of Hollywood. It's a phenomenon that I still haven't gotten used to.

The auditions were either not a cultural fit or didn't represent my experience as a black woman – or at least how I perceived my experience. Being labeled "ethnically ambiguous" meant that I was unable to claim 100 percent of my blackness, simply because it just wasn't what stared back at the casting directors when they looked at my headshot.

I picked up conversational Spanish in high school and college, and worked as a bilingual theater presenter at the California Science Center as a work-study job. It was a repertoire style educational department where we performed mini-plays about everything from HIV/AIDS to Crime Scene Investigation and Telecommunications. I was too naïve to think it was weird that I was doing bilingual theater. I was just happy to be working as an actor in Los Angeles with my closest friend and acting school classmate, Efren, who was Mexican. We had a lot of fun working with a really wacky group of actors and directors. One Saturday, we made a special appearance on a Spanish language children's program on a local Los Angeles television channel promoting our live show about Alexander Graham Bell. It was a completely Spanish speaking set. I started chatting with an older gentleman who worked as a stage-hand while we waited for our segment. He asked me repeatedly in Spanish where I was from. My answer was always "Minnesota." He asked where my parents were from, I said, "Texas." Then he asked about my grandparents, I said, "Louisiana." It was clear that we just weren't getting to the answer he was looking for. I finally said, *"Soy negra."*

He rolls his eyes, still unsatisfied, *"Soy negro también, pero ¿de dónde eres?"* His skin was darker than mine.

Before I could muster a response, I was called to the set for our segment. This was the beginning of a series of disappointed Latinx people approaching me in Los Angeles and pretty much everywhere else expecting me to speak great Spanish, and being sent on Latin market auditions I had no business attending. Through genealogical research, we've confirmed that we have Hispanic heritage (Spain) but the Afro-Latinx people that see familiarity in my physical appearance are often disappointed when I explain that my people are from Louisiana. I've developed a certain unexplained anxiety and shame around the issue that probably makes them think I'm refusing to own a Latin American identity. This also extends to Ethiopians and Eritreans, Cambodians, Filipinos and mixed race Pacific Islanders who suspect I'm denying who I am when approached in languages that I don't understand. My ethnically ambiguous first name, "Maya," seems to only make things more confusing or intriguing for people.

My blackness is one of my favorite things about myself. I'm proud of the resilience and courage of my African ancestors who were enslaved in the American colonies. My Creoleness seems to be a way of putting all of these experiences in a contextual framework that fits. It also allows me to honor the lives of the Native women who found themselves with mixed race children, away from their tribes and communities. It even allows me to honor the European women who were part of this lineage. And it's okay. It's beautiful, actually. Embracing all aspects of my heritage is a way of acknowledging my uniquely American-ness. Knowing that my DNA has been on the North American continent for centuries and centuries is awe-inspiring when I take the time to actually really think about it. I don't feel the shame I once felt, nor do I feel a need to defend or quantify my genetic blackness at this point in my life.

About ten years ago, I started adding "African American of Creole descent" to the "other" box on my casting profiles, after just about every box for "Ethnic Appearance" is checked. The only thing I'm never mistaken for is white in the casting world. Still, the idea of being ethnically ambiguous has just never felt like a fit, even though that's how others see me. Rather than "pass" for other ethnicities (a reality for many actors who fit into the "Ethnically Ambiguous" box) I've started writing and directing my own plays and films. I have an ownership and level of creative expression that wouldn't be possible otherwise. I can create and inhabit worlds that make sense to me, rather than attempt to fit into spaces that don't understand the nuances of ethnicity and racial heritage in the United States, or that rely on useless tropes and stereotypes that no longer reflect our new America.

Owning and embracing my multicultural heritage has required me to acknowledge my cousins and in-laws who are part white, Mexican, Tongan, Native American and a host of other "others." For the most part, my mother's family identifies as black. The non-black spouses have sort of folded into our black/Creole cultural family. Previously, I didn't see them as having an ethnic identity—something I now realize is as much a faux pas as white people who say that they don't see color. For whatever reason, we just never made a big deal about it when someone married a non-black person. Our ancestors had been doing that for centuries after all. That included my oldest sister Lisa. Her husband, Will, is a very blond and blue-eyed German with some Native American ancestry. Their children, my eleven and thirteen-year-old nieces, identify as biracial and look just like my mom and have a classic "Creole" appearance.

Unlike my nieces, I didn't have to address the mixed question in my childhood. In hindsight, I realize that people may have just assumed my mother was white or non-black and we just didn't know it. My nieces are being raised in the same community that my sisters and I were raised in. Only now, there are more people of color, and a handful of biracial families in the neighborhood. I find myself wanting my nieces to settle into identifying as Creole, hoping it makes sense to them the way it does to me. Plus, there is a movement within the Creole community to preserve our history and to be acknowledged within the framework of blackness as fierce as Beyoncé in full formation. At the same time, I know first-hand the annoying and sometimes hurtful questions they will be asked throughout their lives. My greatest hope is that they'll find ways and words to express themselves that truly reflect all the heritages that make them who they are with a sense of pride, or at least a deep sense of okayness.■

Shiane Wilcoxen

I & I

'M JUST BABYSITTING SUE'S NIGGER BABY." I was six years old, on punishment, standing in the corner of my white grandmother's kitchen when she said those words to her friend Marty on the other end of the phone. I recall this Marty woman was Hispanic and a coworker of my grandmother.

I didn't quite understand what "nigger" meant then. But, for some reason, it stuck with me for years to come. When I brought it up to my grandmother on her deathbed twenty-four years later, she apologized. She apologized for everything. Even the fact that she knew my mother's first husband (a black man) had molested me and she did nothing to stop it.

At eight years old my mother married a second time, this time to a Hispanic man. He remains my step-father to this day. I love my stepdad. He raised me and my two younger sisters and older brother as his own. He never pushed us to be adopted by him, never asked us to change our name, or even call him "Dad." He just wanted to be respected and for us to behave.

Up until I was about fifteen years old, in my heart, I too was Hispanic. You couldn't tell me any different. I was honoring my stepfather and his heritage. He was the only father I've ever really known. It wasn't until my junior year in high school that I finally embraced being biracial, or even a black girl for that matter. The movie *Poetic Justice* had just come out, and I fell in love with box braids. I saved up money and went to a black salon and got my hair braided. When I went to school the following day all heads turned. Most, if not everyone, students and faculty alike thought I was Mexican or Puerto Rican up until that point. I was so naïve and really didn't understand what all of the fuss was about, until a black girl came up to me and told me that Mexicans weren't allowed to have weaves and braids.

A majority of my friends were Hispanic or white. I had a few black girl-friends, but we had grown apart since grade school. More often than not, black girls hated me, spat on me, and punched me, pushed me down. I was constantly taunted for being "Light skinned with good hair." They picked on me because all the black boys chased after me and tried to be my boyfriend.

Growing up I had never known my black family. I only knew my white family and my Hispanic stepfamily. From all accounts, I was told my father was a good-for-nothing who had abandoned me and my mother when I was three months old. My mother was nineteen when she had me and he was about twenty-eight if I remember correctly. She already had a two-year-old by the time she had me. But his dad was a white man, so I guess it was okay in my white family. But when my mother brought home a black baby all hell broke loose. Most of my childhood was spent in and out of foster care and being sent to live with different white relatives. I can't count how many grade schools I went to. At one point, the courts sent me to go live with my mom's first husband and his new wife. Because I was a little girl I didn't know that what he was doing to me was wrong, so I never told anyone. It was normal in my life I guess. I hate to say it, but it's quite possible the reason I barely dated black men growing up. I mostly dated white or Hispanic guys.

When I finally started coming into my own during my last two years of high school, and made a declaration that I was a black girl, a lot changed for me. My friendships and sisterhoods with black women strengthened. I no longer felt like I needed to be someone else just to fit in. I started checking off "African American" or "Black" to self-identify. I stopped dressing in a manner that identified with my Hispanic peers. My clique even changed. I became more comfortable as I accepted myself more and more, the same way black peers started to accept me. It was like, this hidden gem was in there somewhere just waiting for the validation to come out and shine. Thank goodness for Janet Jackson, box braids and that movie. It was just a hairstyle, but it was monumental in my growth as a black girl. For those last two years in high school, that was my signature look. Even throughout my early twenties, I still had an inner struggle to appease my mother and continue to say I was mixed, just to get her off my back. She liked to remind me all of the time how she gave birth to me and that I came from a white woman's womb. She always threatened to "beat the black" out of me whenever she didn't get her way with me, or when I disobeyed her. She was always trying to take away the one thing I was proud of. She often called me "nigger" to see what I would do, but I always let it roll off of me, because I didn't want to end up in a physical fight with her.

My identity crisis caused me considerable emotional pain over the years. Realizing and embracing that I am a black girl helped me to heal from a terrible childhood. I had my son at twenty-five, and his father is Hispanic. My child is beautiful. I would get upset sometimes that I mixed him up even more, and feared he would soon have his own identity crisis, but thankfully, he has identified as Hispanic, and I let him be who he feels he is. I don't pressure him to feel any other way. Once I got over the obstacles of my treacherous childhood, and the agony I suffered, I moved on to becoming comfortable with my sexuality. I came out of the closet at thirty years old; first to my husband, then to my family, and then to the world. Now, as a thirty-nine-year-old woman, mother of one son, I still declare that I am indeed a black woman, and I only date black women. I tried dating white women twice, and the cultural differences were too much to bear. I am proud of who I am. I am not likely to say I am mixed or biracial. I am not a mulatto. I abhor the term Redbone. I am a black woman. In fact, I am a gay-black-Jewish-Buddhist-woman who is also an author, chef, and humanitarian. I stand proud of who I have become and live my life openly. I advocate for my black sisters and brothers, and all people of color, especially queer people of color. It's hard to stand in my shoes everyday as a gay black woman who so often finds herself either met with disdain or outright hate. Nevertheless, I will always advocate for my black sisters and brothers, I know no other way to live. I don't feel a tiny bit bad that identifying as a black woman lessens my one foot in the door of my white existence. ■

Same Roads

THE STREETLIGHTS AND HEADLIGHTS blink on as Dad and I cruise up the 101 to my mom's bank's softball game. We listen to NPR for a few minutes before I turn to him. "Dad, what's your favorite childhood memory?"

He pauses and scratches his stubble. "Well, that was a long time ago."

We laugh together and shift to more recent memories. Even though I know the story of how he and my mom met in the Chase training program, I ask to hear it at least once a year. Even though I know this story of how this black man from a working class Los Angeles family married a white woman from a social climbing suburban East Coast family by heart, I like to hear it again. I am comforted by their eighties romance of Earth, Wind & Fire and Meatloaf.

"I was just sitting on the subway," he says, "and your mom cornered me."

I roll my eyes out the rolled up window. "Come on, Dad."

I picture my mother in a trench coat pointing at my dad, sitting innocently with a briefcase in his lap.

He nods and scrunches his nose the same way my Nana does, the same way I do. "She came up to me and said, 'You work at Chase, don't you?'"

I ask how it was to work together, if they had to keep it secret.

"People didn't really know. We were in different departments," he thinks out loud. "Working there was really tough for your mom, you know."

I didn't know.

"Well, your grandfather was a big deal at Chase – knew lots of important people. So there were some people there who loved your mom for being his daughter, but some who gave her a lot of shit, and were a lot harder on her for it. They figured she hadn't earned being there. I think she felt like she always had to prove herself."

We pass the exit to the fabric store, and I listen to the winds in the eucalyptus trees lining the freeway. "From what I can tell," he says, "your grandmother was used to getting her own way. Just because she was so beautiful." My great aunt once told me that it was a close contest of who was more gorgeous: my dad's mom or my mom's mom.

We turn with the freeway. "Nora's stubborn like your mom. That's why she's so hard on her. Well, that and other things." He pauses for the smile I know is on his face. He's easy with references to this: "You know how your grandmother is."

My grandmother is bipolar. My grandmother, in her mania, vocalizes her disapproval of my father. Then, though, after comments about his weight or unemployment, he doesn't laugh.

He looks over his shoulder twice to change lanes before continuing. "You know, it's funny. I remember that first time I was going to meet your grandparents. When I walked in, Nora exclaimed, "Annie! You didn't tell me he was a Mexican!"" We laugh over this moment that I've heard only a handful of times. We maybe laugh, too, over our shared ambiguously brown bodies. I don't yet know that my dad's Swedish grandfather changed his last name after he was disowned for marrying a Sioux woman.

"They didn't talk to her for a long time," he tells me. "It was hard on your mom. You know she's your grandpa's favorite. It wasn't until your sister was born that he really came around."

"But," I interrupt, "I thought everyone came to the wedding."

"Yeah, but they didn't decide until about a week before."

"Yeah!" I reply, relieved for the story I remember.

After the game, my dad suggests I ride home with Mom. We get into the car, and she turns off the audio book that she has been listening to. It is one she received from the library by accident: a Republican manifesto that lists all of President Obama's faults, legitimate and illegitimate. She jokes that it is an education on her family.

This is when I decide it's a good time to tell her the story I got from my father.

I have momentarily forgotten that, while it is okay for my mom to make jokes about her family, it is only sometimes okay for my dad to do the same.

I feel her face change without looking at her. She scratches her short, auburn hair and moves her hand to her chin, the way she does to get a picture of something. "I don't know what your father's talking about. Nora didn't always get what she wanted."

"Oh." I slump in my seat and try to think of something to say.

She speaks first. Her voice is tempered, with a quiver below the surface. "My family wouldn't talk to me," she says. "They offered to send me to cooking school. Or to France."

"Had they talked about doing that before? Or was it just because it was Dad?"

"No. It was all new. They really didn't want me to marry your father."

"Oh." I'm jarred by this redefinition of my family, by abandonment becoming part of the word. "But, they came to the wedding, didn't they?"

"Yeah, but, they stopped talking to me right after they went home. It was strained the whole time they were there. Even Sally. And she was in my wedding party. I had to move everyone around and tell my friend Betsy that she wasn't my maid of honor anymore." I turn to look at her through the passing shadows, and her blue eyes remain focused on the road ahead, dry.

I don't have to ask many questions on the drive home. Mom just keeps going. "You know, he never told me about Chicago." She doesn't hesitate before she says it. She has turned this thought over for years, waited to speak it. "One day, I came home from work, and he told me that he was going to start an iron foundry out there. He would be gone for weeks at a time." We pass the exit to JoAnn's Fabrics, where she took me to buy yarn when she taught me how to knit. I remember us sitting on my bed using the same bag of needles she had used when she was carrying my sister and then me. She walked me through the steps, unraveling and purling, re-teaching herself as she taught me for the first time.

"I was really scared," she says. "It was right around the riots, but we didn't know." I nod, trying to remember the LA of 1992, as the bluish-grey sky peeks through the now black eucalyptus trees. Even now, she keeps her gas tank at half full in case she needs to quickly get us out of the city. Her voice hardens when she tells stories of driving home to an empty house, with my sister and me in the backseat, passing through intersections where all four corners were aflame. "So, there I was. Suddenly a single parent with you two girls." She changes lanes to exit the freeway. "You probably don't remember him being gone, do you?"

I think of my father in our entryway, lit from behind. I'm small as I press into his body, barely up to his knees, as he puts on his hat and picks up his suitcase. I hold my mom and sister or they hold me. I can't remember which, but I'm crying then and now. "I do."

We exit at Beverly, a different route than the one I had come by, but a street that, together, we've driven hundreds of times. "Sometimes you have to do things for your family," she says. "Even though you know that it's not what's best for you. You just have to make sacrifices. A lot of people told me I should leave your father. All of my girlfriends." I try hard to stay focused on the empty hill before us, quickly filling with fog.

I have often thought about my parents' marriage. How it feels after dinner guests leave and how my sister and I have defended one parent to the other. I have more than once thought they stayed together to prove to everyone else that they could do it. I have more than once tried to not think about which parent to live with if they ever divorced.

At the last stop, I stare at the red light twinkling through the tears on my eyelashes. "You think it's fun," she says, "to ask these questions about the beginning. But there's a lot you don't know."

The tires hum beneath us, trying to lull us into how we were before. As we pull into the driveway and she turns the key towards her, I watch the headlights flicker out. She gets out, and I wipe my face and think about how we started the drive. "Mom, what's your favorite childhood memory?"

"Well, that was a long time ago." ◼

AFTERWORD

■ ■ ■

Heidi W. Durrow

The Fluidity of Racial Identity

I AM A PROFESSIONAL MULATTO.

When research centers release reports that show that the mixed race population is the country's fastest growing demographic, or when a story like the Rachel Dolezal case breaks out, media folks call me for comment.

I am now an expert on a topic that I was expected to be silent about when I was growing up and the American conversation about race had no place for a discussion of mixed race identity or experience.

I am the daughter of a white Danish immigrant and an African American Air Force man. My parents married in a small brick Lutheran church in Denmark because it was still illegal for whites and blacks to marry in South Carolina in 1965.

For the next fifteen years, our family of five – my parents and two brothers and I – was stationed mostly overseas. We never talked about race in our family, but we weren't color blind. We understood that my father had deep chocolate brown skin and my mother had creamy-colored white skin and that my brothers and I were a brown somewhere in between. But the color of our skin had no meaning. We were just another American family abroad.

When we moved back to the states in 1980, we felt like immigrants in our own homeland. We knew the language and customs, but we were immigrants to America's ideas of race. "What are you?" our classmates would ask my brothers and me.

The "Question" is one that is all too familiar for the writers of this anthology regardless of their age, cultural mix, or geography. Their answers to the "Question," however, are as varied as their heritage: "human," Blasian, biracial, half and half, mixed.

For me, the answer to the Question was too complicated for people to understand: We were black and Danish; children of two languages and a Danish home culture that was sometimes just a result of our mother's singular quirks. Our comfort foods were peanut butter and jelly sandwiches, hamburgers and grilled cheese, but also *frikadeller, aebleskiver* and *leverpostej*. We believed in Santa Claus and *nisser*, and Danish elves, in equal measure. It was simple to us: we were Afro-Vikings.

We soon learned that in America, we weren't American. We were black. We learned to say we were black when asked. And we were silent about the cultural complexity of our everyday lives.

But slowly the country's ideas about mixed race identity and experience started to change.

Time magazine famously proclaimed on a 1993 cover that the "ethnically ambiguous" were fast becoming the new face of America. In 1995, Lise Funderberg published her ground-breaking book of interviews with biracial Americans, *Black White Other: Biracial Americans Talk About Race and Identity*. In 1998, award-winning author Danzy Senna published her seminal tongue-in-cheek essay, "The Mulatto Millennium" in which she proclaimed:

> Strange to wake up and realize you're in style [and that] mulattos had taken over. They were everywhere. Playing golf, running the airwaves, opening restaurants, modeling clothes…The radio played a steady stream of Lenny Kravitz, Sade, and Mariah Carey. I thought I'd died and gone to Berkeley. But then I realized that, according to the racial zodiac, it's the official Year of the Mulatto…hybridity is in.

Then the U.S. Census changed too. For the first time in 2000, people could check more than one box to identify their race on the Census form. In the 2010 U.S. Census, 9 million people—or 2.9 percent of the population—chose more than one race, a change of about 32 percent since 2000. (There's still no Afro-Viking box. But I digress.)

When Obama ran for the presidency in 2007 he showcased his multiracial and multicultural family. He proudly claimed his white mother from Kansas and his black father from Kenya. (What a sea change from the heated response to Tiger Woods famously calling himself Calibanasian.)

Obama introduced a portrait of a family that America hadn't acknowledged before.

In his pivotal March 2008 speech on race—which was prompted by mounting criticism of his connection to Rev. Jeremiah Wright, Obama said:

> I can no more disown [Reverend Wright] than I can disown the black community. I can no more disown him than I can my white grandmother—a woman who helped raise me, a woman who sacrificed again and again for me, a woman who loves me as much as she loves anything in this world, but a woman who once confessed her fear of black men who passed by her on the street, and who on more than one occasion has uttered racial or ethnic stereotypes that made me cringe. These people are a part of me and they are a part of America, this country that I love.

He was playing our song!

When Obama won the election in 2008, we started to believe that maybe this wasn't just a multiracial moment but the beginning of a multiracial movement.

Finally America was recognizing that the mixed race and multiracial experience was the American experience. Mixed race identity was at the center of what would bring us together as a nation.

The demographic numbers showed the progress too. In 2008, 14.6 percent of all new marriages were interethnic or interracial marriages according to a Pew Research Center study. Today, multiracial children make up the country's fastest-growing demographic making up almost 50 percent of the multiracial population at 4.2 million.

And with the beginning of the social media age, we could finally connect with each other too. Just search "mixed race" or "biracial" on Facebook or Twitter and you can instantly find other voices and people who understand your experience, and have dealt with the same kind of marginalization or pain.

No longer was being mixed necessarily "one of life's unsolvable mysteries" in the words of essayist Carlos Adams who was born pre-*Loving* and "never heard anyone who spoke truth to my existence."

Like my story, many of these writers' stories follow a familiar pattern: a realization that their mixed blood marked them as different or other; a discussion of a sometimes daily struggle to deal with the difference between their lived experience and how they were perceived racially or culturally; and finally a turning point that helped them give voice to the complexity of their experiences—some for the first time in this anthology.

Although these stories follow a familiar pattern, there is a diversity of experiences represented in this collection that powerfully demonstrates that the mixed experience cannot be reflected in a single story. Being mixed has not just many labels but many different meanings. We learn what it means to claim a multigenerationally mixed identity from Herbert Harris who reflects: "I grew up in a family where race was...a continuum of tones, colors, and textures... What enabled [my mixed race ancestors] to succeed was the capacity to live with the paradoxes of identity, and to turn paradox into a creative force." We learn from Kyla Kupferstein that as painful as it was to not look like anyone else in your family growing up, it's possible to mourn the loss of feeling different as an adult. Kupferstein who discovers the joy of finally having a reflection in her son writes: "I don't get asked 'what are you?' much these days, at least not when I'm with my son...My son is as mixed as I am...but most days makes me seem less so." And we learn what it means to be mixed but look monoracial from Jackson Bliss who for too long felt "incomplete in a country that couldn't see my wholeness and couldn't honor my racial hyphenation either." Yes, many of these stories are centered on alienation and longing, but not on tragedy. And ultimately, the strength of this collection rests on the ways in which these narratives defy the trope of the "tragic mulatto."

It is just as important to note, however, that these stories can also serve as a necessary balm for people who have felt invisible. As I read these essays, I felt a kind of comfort. The stories these mixed race writers share sound almost like confessions, but confessions from people who profess to be whole on the other side of their struggles. Playwright Velina Hasu Houston writes: "My mixed race and multicultural identity and my meditation of them emanate from living the truth of my identity...I like to address everything that I am without apology or fanfare." As I read these stories, I thought again and again: I am not alone.

Finally, the essays in this collection—written before the November 2016 election—largely reflect the idea that we, as a nation, have been on a trajectory toward a better understanding and acceptance of multiracial and mixed race identity and experience. But we are now on the eve of saying farewell to our first biracial African American president and must usher in the administration of a president who ran his campaign largely on a message of misogyny, racism, and religious intolerance. The election of Trump is as momentous an event as the *Loving* decision or the ability to check all that apply on the U.S. Census in the story about how mixed race and multiracial identity experience will unfold.

In this way, this collection serves as an invaluable snapshot of a before and after for the multiracial community. And it forces us to look to the future and ask: Is it time to realize that our multiracial moment is over and our multiracial movement never coalesced?

Our stories of the mixed race and multiracial experience provides evidence that contradicts the lie that America is not divided by race. So now—perhaps more than ever—we need to vocally complicate society's ideas about race. But how? For the past decade I have highlighted the issues and stories of the mixed race and multiracial experience through a weekly podcast, my fiction and non-fiction writing, and an annual cultural arts festival that has become the largest nationwide gathering of mixed race people and families. And for the first time, I have questioned whether it is the right time to address ideas of "mixedness" given the assault on the rights of minorities by the new administration's proposals. And yet, as I think back on my youth, I realize being silent is not an option. Charles Matthew Snyder says it best in his essay when he writes: "Maybe the outside world is only a reflection of the turmoil I feel inside. When I heal, this world may heal too."

America will be beige by the year 2043. Period. Our storytellers must help lead the way, and help the nation heal.∎

I should not have to prove my ethnicity to anyone. I know who I am.

— Christina Aguilera

APPENDIX 1

■ ■ ■

Glossary

AFRICAN AMERICAN: A racial classification specifier that was advanced in the 1980s to give Americans of African descent a title equivalent to Euro-Americans. While the term peaked in popularity during the 1990s and 2000s, today it is often perceived as carrying a self-conscious political correctness that is unnecessary in an informal context, yet is rarely considered offensive. Nevertheless, many blacks do not embrace the term "African American" because it denotes a connection to a country far removed from their American ancestry. Interestingly and according to a recent study in the *Journal of Experimental Social Psychology,*[1] it found that among white Americans, the term "black" elicits a more negative association than "African American." Immigrants from some African, Caribbean, Central American, and South American nations and their descendants may or may not identify with this term because land and resources were not stolen from them in this space, and their ancestors were not brought to America as slaves.

AMERASIAN: Originally referred to children of American Asian national origin, usually fathered by white Americans. The term has been used broadly with children fathered by American servicemen in Asia. (Root 1996).

BIRACIAL: A term that began showing up regularly in scientific papers in the 1970s, often referring to communities with both black and white members. But because of the specificity of "bi," meaning two, some argued that "biracial" was too limited a term. Biracial now refers to someone who has parents from two different races.

---

[1] Erika V. Hall, Katherine W. Phillips, Sarah S.M. Townsend, "A rose by any other name? The consequences of subtyping 'African Americans' from 'Blacks'" Journal of Experimental Social Psychology 56 (2015), 183-190.

BLACK: A racial classification specifier of Americans with total or partial ancestry from Africa. "Black" replaced the derogatory terminology applied to African Americans such as "Negro" or "nigger" because it was turned into a positive designation during the Black Power movement.

BLACK-JAPANESE/BLACKANESE (also "Afrasian," Afroasian, and "Blasian"): Characterizes people of mixed African (black) and Asian ancestry. The term also can refer to modern descendants of aboriginal Asian ethnic groups such as the Negritos.

CAUCASIAN: In the U.S., the root term Caucasian has also often been used in a different, societal context as a synonym for "white" or "of European ancestry." In biological anthropology, Caucasoid has been used as an umbrella term for phenotypically similar groups from these different regions, with a focus on skeletal anatomy, and especially cranial morphology, over skin tone. Ancient and modern "Caucasoid" populations were thus held to have ranged in complexion from white to dark brown. (See White).

COLOR BLINDNESS: A sociological term that is a powerful and appealing liberal discourse in which white people insist they do not notice a person's skin color. What it is, in fact, is the refusal to recognize that race is the baggage people of color carry with them, and that racism is part of their everyday lives. Many Americans view color blindness as helpful to people of color by asserting that race does not matter. (Tarca, 2005) But in America, most underrepresented minorities will explain that race does matter, as it affects opportunities, perceptions, income, and so much more. When race-related problems arise, colorblindness tends to individualize conflicts and shortcomings, rather than examining the larger picture with cultural differences, stereotypes, and values placed into context. Instead of resulting from an enlightened (albeit well-meaning) position, color blindness comes from a lack of awareness of racial privilege conferred by whiteness. (Tarca, 2005) White people can guiltlessly subscribe to color blindness because they are usually unaware of how race affects people of color and American society as a whole.

COLORISM: The privileging of light skin over dark, colorism is a societal ill felt in many countries around the world, including Latin America, East and Southeast Asia, the Caribbean and Africa. Here in the U.S., because we are such a diverse population with citizens hailing from all corners of the earth, our brand of colorism is both homegrown and imported. Colorism is not only practiced by white people, it is also a form of racism that exists within communities of color. Dozens of research studies have shown that skin tone and other racial features play powerful roles in who gets ahead and who does not. These factors regularly determine who gets hired, who gets convicted, who gets married, and who gets elected. (Vedantam, 2010) Light skin is so coveted that whitening creams continue to be best-sellers in the U.S., Asia and other nations. It is a global phenomenon currently worth about $10 billion and is expected soon to reach $23 billion. Mexican-American women in Arizona, California and Texas have reportedly suffered mercury poisoning after turning to whitening creams to bleach their skin. In India, popular skin-bleaching lines target both women and men with dark skin. The practice of whitening is prevalent in places where slavery and racism have deep roots, like Africa and the Caribbean, and it also thrives in places bedeviled by other troubling melanin legacies, including Asia, the Middle East, and Latin America. That skin-bleaching cosmetics have persisted for decades signals the enduring legacy of colorism. Yet the uncomfortable truth around the world is that darker skin is a problem and – not in and of itself, but as a matter of racism's legacy of racism – our collective ideas of what is considered beautiful and even good. In order to understand why some people bleach, why lighter is considered preferable and more desirable, we need to understand why so many humans are uncomfortable in the skin they're in.

CREOLE: The term "Creole" has many meanings throughout different parts of the world. In the sixteenth century the term was used in parts of the United States to describe native born persons who were descendants of French, Spanish and the Portuguese who were settlers in Latin America, the West Indies and the Southern United States. In Louisiana, they were French speaking white descendants of early French and Spanish settlers. These Creoles settled between Baton Rouge, Louisiana and the Gulf Coast, and small communities in eastern Missouri and Southern Alabama. They were considered elite members of society and they celebrated their French culture and lived according to the mannerisms and traditions of European society. The French and Spanish born in Nouvelle Orleans were then considered Creoles while those born in the Old World were simply called French or Spanish. The French Creoles were skeptical of the New Americans who were migrating from Kentucky and other parts of the U.S. Louisiana was unlike any place in America at the time because of its racial makeup. The New Americans were appalled at the way of life in Creole society. They were disturbed by the dominance of the French language, the number of free people of color, and the way slaves were allowed to practice African traditions. French men often took African and Native American women as mistresses or common law wives, and sometimes married them. The off-spring from their mistresses became a new class of creoles known as *gens de couleur,* or free people of color. This class of people would soon expand when refugees from

Haiti and other French speaking colonies would migrate to New Orleans, effectively creating a new middle class between the white French Creoles and the slaves. White French Creoles spoke French while black Creoles spoke Louisiana Creole, which is a mixture of English, French, African or Spanish. In time, the term Creole came to represent children of black or racially mixed parents as well as children of French and Spanish descent with no racial mixing. Persons of French and Spanish descent in New Orleans and St. Louis began referring to themselves as Creoles after the Louisiana Purchase to set themselves apart from the Anglo-Americans who moved into the area. Prior to the Civil War, a three-caste system existed: white, black, and Creoles of color. After the Civil War and Reconstruction, however, the Creoles of color – who had been part of the free black population before the war – were merged into a two-caste system, black and white. The identification of a Creole was, and is, largely one of self-choice. Creole culture is a blend of many cultures with a rich heritage that has cultural and culinary influence beyond its Louisiana origins. Many young Creoles of color today live under pressure to identify themselves as African Americans, while there are some young white Creoles who do not want be considered mixed race. As of 2010, about two million Louisiana Creole live in the United States. (Not to be confused with Cajuns who are of French or French Canadian (from Acadia in Nova Scotia) ancestry, and settled mainly in the countryside of southern and south-central Louisiana. While they have some similarities in their cuisine and language influences and are both rooted in Louisiana since colonial times, they are unique in their heritage and culture.)

CULTURE: Refers to the cumulative deposit of knowledge, experience, beliefs, values, attitudes, meanings, hierarchies, religion, notions of time, roles, concepts of the universe, and material objects and possessions acquired by a group of people in the course of generations through individual and group striving. Culture guides people how to perceive, feel, think, act, and discern what is acceptable or unacceptable, important or unimportant, and right or wrong.

DIASPORA: A Greek term that means "to scatter," diaspora was used exclusively to describe the dispersion of the Jewish people following their expulsion from the Holy Land. Today it is used to describe a community of people who live outside their shared country of origin or ancestry, but maintain active connections with it. Whether one is aware of his or her heritage, nearly every American is part of at least one diaspora. Many of us come from mixed heritages, and, therefore, claim multiple diaspora communities.

DISCRIMINATION: The practice of unfairly treating a person or group of people differently based on specific characteristics such as race, nationality, religion, ethnic affiliation, age, sexual orientation, marital or family status, and physical or mental disability. Discrimination usually leads to the denial of cultural, economic, educational, political or social rights of members of a specific non-dominant group.

DIVERSITY: A term used to describe a variation between people using a range of factors such as ethnicity, national origin, gender, ability, age, physical characteristics, religion, values, sexual orientation, disability, socio-economic class, or life experiences. In many cases, the term diversity also implies an appreciation of these differences.

ETHNICITY: A shared cultural heritage that includes beliefs, behaviors and traditions held in common by a group of people bound by linguistic, historical, geographical, religious or racial homogeneity.

ETHNOCENTRISM: The tendency to view others using one's own group and customs as the standard for judgment, and seeing one's group and customs as the best.

EURASIAN: A term that refers to persons of European and Asian parentage.

GULLAH/GEECHEE: Descendants of African slaves from Central and West Africa who originally settled on the coastal plains of Georgia (initially by the Ogeechee River, hence the name), North Carolina's Cape Fear area, South Carolina, Florida, and the Sea Islands, a chain of over 100 tidal and barrier islands located alongside the coast of these states. After eighteenth century European-American settlement of Georgia and Florida, planters imported enslaved Africans as laborers. Many were used to work the cotton, rice and indigo plantations on the Sea Islands, which generated much of the wealth of the colony and states. The slaves developed the notable and distinct Gullah/Geechee Creole culture and language, which has survived to contemporary times. Today, many of the islands are now known for resort, recreational, and residential development, and the Gullah area is confined to the Georgia and South Carolina Lowcountry (also known as the Gullah Geechee Corridor). The Gullah people are known for preserving most of their African linguistic and cultural heritage more than any other African American community in the U.S. The language is an English-based creole language that contains many African loanwords and significant influences from African languages in grammar and sentence structure. The Georgia communities are distinguished by identifying as either "Freshwater Geechee" or "Saltwater Geechee," depending on whether they live on the mainland or the Sea Islands, while Gullah has come to be the accepted name of the islanders in South Carolina.

HALF-BREED/HALF-HALF: A term used to refer to the offspring of parents of different racial origin, initially used to describe the offspring of a Native American Indian and a white person of European descent. Half-breed is the English version of the French word *métis*. Considered derogatory terms, half-breed and half-half are also used as a neutral descriptive term.

HAPA: A Hawaiian pidgin word used to describe mixed race people, primarily though not exclusively, those who are half white and half Asian. It's short for *hapa-lua*, the Hawaiian word that literally means "half," and it originated as a derogatory term toward mixed race children of plantation guest workers from the Philippines, Korea, China and Japan, and the women they married in Hawaii in the early part of the twentieth century. In recent years, hapa has become a term mixed race people in Hawaii are proud to embrace, and the term has found pathways into the mainland.

HYPODESCENT: In societies that regard some races of people as dominant or superior and others as subordinate or inferior, hypodescent is the automatic assignment of children of a mixed union or mating between members of different socioeconomic groups or ethnic groups to the subordinate group. The opposite practice is hyperdescent, in which children are assigned to the race that is considered dominant or superior.

INTERRACIAL: Activities between or involving different races such as an interracial marriage.

JIM CROW: Named after the plantation song, "Jump Jim Crow" (a song-and-dance caricature of blacks performed by white actor Thomas D. Rice in blackface, which first surfaced in 1832), Jim Crow refers to a series of racist laws and measures against African Americans and other people of color that enforced racial segregation primarily in the South at the end of Reconstruction in 1877. It was codified on local and state levels and most famously with the U.S. Supreme Court in *Plessy v. Ferguson* (1896), in which the Court ruled that "separate but equal" facilities were constitutional. It was the rise of the civil rights movement in the late 1950s combined with a series of significant landmark cases brought before the Supreme Court (*Korematsu v. United States* (1944); *Brown v. Board of Education of Topeka* (1954); *Loving v. Virginia* (1967)), which helped eradicate Jim Crow. While de jure segregation was not brought to an end until the passage of the Civil Rights Act of 1964 and the

Voting Rights Act of 1965, many laws (often Black Codes) remained on the books in primarily Southern states as late as the 1990s. Inasmuch as Jim Crow was a milieu that permeated culture and ideology historically, the struggle against American racism continues, and in that regard, the effects of Jim Crow remain relevant today.

LOVING V. VIRGINIA, 388 U.S. 1 (1967): A landmark civil rights decision of the U.S. Supreme Court, which invalidated laws prohibiting interracial marriage. The case was brought by Mildred Loving, a black woman, and Richard Loving, a white man, who had been sentenced to a year in prison in Virginia for marrying each other. Their marriage violated the state's anti-miscegenation statute, the Racial Integrity Act of 1924, which prohibited marriage between people classified as "white" and people classified as "colored." The Court's unanimous decision determined that this prohibition was unconstitutional, overruling *Pace v. Alabama* (1883) and ending all race-based legal restrictions on marriage in the United States. The decision was followed by an increase in interracial marriages in the U.S., and is remembered annually on Loving Day, June 12. In 2013, it was cited as precedent in U.S. federal court decisions holding restrictions on same-sex marriage in the U.S. unconstitutional, including in the 2015 U.S. Supreme Court decision *Obergefell v. Hodges.*

MELTING POT: A term used to refer to an American monocultural society in which there is a conscious attempt to assimilate diverse peoples into a homogeneous culture, rather than to participate as equals in the society while maintaining various cultural or ethnic identities used to describe the assimilation of immigrants to the United States. The exact term "melting pot" came into general usage in 1908, after the premiere of the play, *The Melting Pot,* by Israel Zangwill. This term is often challenged, however, by those who assert that cultural differences within a society are valuable and should be preserved.

MESTIZO: A Spanish-origin word, designates racial mixing of someone with Indian and Spanish ancestry. Not commonly used by young multicultural people today, it now has a broader meaning, referring to people Latino and European ancestry. Because of the shared Spanish ancestry, this term is also used by older Filipinos and Filipino Americans to refer to multi-generationally mixed or biracial Filipinos. (Root 1996: x)

MICROAGGRESSION: A comment or action that subtly and often unconsciously or unintentionally expresses a prejudiced attitude toward a member of a marginalized group (such as a racial minority). The power of microaggression lies in its invisibility to the perpetrator, who typically finds it difficult to believe that he or she possesses biased attitudes. The term was coined by psychiatrist and Harvard University professor Chester M. Pierce in 1970 to describe insults and dismissals he regularly witnessed non-black Americans inflict on African Americans. Eventually, the term came to encompass the casual degradation of any socially marginalized group, such as the poor or the disabled. Psychologist Derald Wing Sue defines microaggressions as "brief, everyday exchanges that send denigrating messages to certain individuals because of their group membership."[2]

MISCEGENATION: A term coined in 1863 term that refers to a marriage, cohabitation, or sexual relationship between persons of different races. Miscegenation is also termed as mixed marriage or interracial marriage. This was formerly considered as illegal in some jurisdictions in the U.S. Similar laws were also enforced in Nazi Germany as part of the Nuremberg laws, and in South Africa as part of the system of apartheid. In 1967, the U.S. Supreme Court held in *Lovings v. State of Virginia* that laws banning interracial marriages are unconstitutional. The last remaining state-law ban on interracial marriages was a provision in the Alabama constitution, which the legislature voted to repeal the ban, which became effective in 2000. Contemporary usage of the term is less frequent, except to refer to historical laws banning the practice.

MIXED BLOOD: Historically, there has been controversy over interracial couples, which still exists in some contexts, such as fears of "racial impurity" when people have children of mixed blood.

MIXED RACE: Denotes or relates to a person whose parents belong to different racial or ethnic groups. Despite the stigma sometimes associated with a mixed race heritage, and the fact that some mixed race people identify with just one ethnic group, the term itself is usually considered not only acceptable, it appears to be the most popular term used by young people of mixed race to describe themselves because it is inclusive of any and all mixed folks today.

MONORACIAL: Refers to people who claim a single racial heritage. It is also a system of racial classification that only recognizes one racial designation per person. (Root 1996: x)

MULATTO: The etymology of the term mulatto comes from the Spanish and Portuguese word "mulatto," (which is itself derived from "mula" (from old

---

[2] Sue, Derard Wing (2010). Microaggressions and Marginality: Manifestation, Dynamics, and Impact. Wiley. pp. 229–233

Galician-Portuguese), or from Latin "mulus," meaning "mule"), the infertile off-spring of a horse and a donkey. Countering the racist idea of a racially mixed couple of black and white ethnicity, the term mulatto was applied to their offspring (a hybrid considered less than human – the dysgenic consequences of race mixing), a comparison considered derogatory and deeply offensive. During the colonial and early federal period in the Southern colonies and states, mulatto was used to identify persons of any mixed ethnicity, including Native American, African and European. Beginning in 1790, the federal census included "mulatto" as an official census racial category. By 1930, after several southern states had adopted one-drop rule as law (Virginia's 1924 Racial Integrity Law comes to mind), Southern Congressmen pressed the U.S. Census Bureau to drop the mulatto category so that all persons had to be classified as either "black" or "white." The one-drop rule, which was influenced by the popularity of racism, eugenics and ideas of racial purity, remained in place until the 1960s, when federal legislation ended Jim Crow and legally sanctioned state segregation. In the meantime, multiracial people wanted to acknowledge their full heritage and won a victory of sorts in 1997, when the Office of Management and Budget (OMB) changed the federal regulation of racial categories to permit multiple responses. This resulted in a change to the 2000 U.S. Census, which allowed participants to select more than one of the six available categories. Since then, people have been allowed to identify as having more than one type of ethnic ancestry. Today, the term mulatto is now considered archaic, and the more acceptable terms to identify oneself with multiple ethnicities include "mixed-race," "multiracial," and "biracial."

MULTICULTURALISM: Multiculturalism is a political philosophy that involves ide-ologies and policies which vary widely, ranging from the advocacy of equal respect to the various cultures in a society, to policies of promoting the maintenance of cultural diversity, to policies in which people of various ethnic and religious groups are addressed by the authorities as defined by the group to which they belong. A philosophy that became a significant force in American society in the 1970s and 1980s, to encourage people to appreciate ethnic diversity and learn about and respect diverse ethnic backgrounds.

MULTIRACIAL: Refers to people who are of two or more racial heritages. It is the most inclusive term to refer to people across all racial mixes. Thus it also includes biracial people. (Root 1996: xi)

MUSTEE/MUSTEFINO: The term mustee was used to refer to a person with one-eighth African ancestry, while mustefino refers to a person with one-sixteenth

African ancestry.

OBERGEFELL V. HODGES 135 S.CT. 2071 (2015): A legal case in which the U.S. Supreme Court ruled (5-4) on June 26, 2015, that state bans on same-sex marriage and on recognizing same-sex marriages duly performed in other jurisdictions are unconstitutional under the due process and equal protection clauses of the Fourteenth Amendment to the U.S. Constitution. Countering many of the arguments put forth by same-sex marriage opponents and mirroring similar language in the 1967 decision in *Loving v. Virginia,* which abolished bans on inter-racial marriages, the Court framed the issues accordingly in Obergefell. The *Obergefell v. Hodges* decision came on the second anniversary of the United States v. Windsor ruling that struck down Section 3 of the Defense of Marriage Act (DOMA), which denied federal recognition to same-sex marriages. It also came on the twelfth anniversary of *Lawrence v. Texas,* which struck down sodomy laws in thirteen states.

ONE-DROP RULE: The one-drop rule is a social and legal principle of racial classification in the U.S. that asserts any person with even one ancestor of sub-Saharan-African ancestry is black. This concept evolved over the course of the nineteenth century and became codified into law in the twentieth century. It was associated with the principle of "invisible blackness" and is an example of hypodescent, the automatic reassignment of children of a mixed union between different socioeconomic or ethnic groups to the group with the lower status. Today, while these laws have been eradicated and no longer exist, sociologically, the concept remains somewhat pervasive, embraced mostly by African Americans who like to cite this slavery-based "rule" that anybody with a single drop of black blood should solely identify as being black, or rejected as not being black enough.

OCTOROON: A person having one-eighth black blood, the offspring of a quadroon (one quarter black) and a white parent; that is, someone with family heritage of one biracial grandparent, in other words, one African great-grandparent and seven Caucasian great-grandparents.

PEOPLE OF COLOR: The term is an attempt to describe people with a more positive term other than "non-white" or "minority" because it frames them in the context of the dominant group. Identifying as a person of color in solidarity with other people of color acknowledges similar or shared oppressions by white people, a willingness to work together against racism and perhaps, a deeper commitment to allyship.

PREJUDICE: A pre-judgment or unjustifiable, and usually negative, attitude of one type of individual or groups toward another group and its members. Such negative attitudes are typically based on unsupported generalizations (or stereotypes) that deny the right of individual members of certain groups to be recognized and treated as individuals with individual characteristics.

QUADROON: A person having one-quarter black blood, the offspring of a mulatto (half black) and a white parent; in other words, one African/Aboriginal grandparent and three white or European grandparents.

QUINTOON: A person having one-sixteenth black blood, the offspring of an octoroon (one-eighth black) and a white parent.

RACE: Race is a socially meaningful category of people who share biologically transmitted traits that are obvious and considered important, such as facial features, stature and hair texture. But for most cultures, skin color seems to be the most important trait when it comes to race. Although humans are sometimes divided into races, the morphological variation between races is not indicative of major differences in DNA, which has led some scientists to describe all humans as belonging to the same race—the human race. Race is associated with biology, whereas ethnicity is associated with culture.

RACIALIZATION: In sociology, racialization or ethnicization is the processes of ascribing ethnic or racial identities to a relationship, social practice, or group that did not identify itself as such. It is the act or process of imbuing a person with a consciousness of race distinctions or of giving a racial character to something or making it serve racist ends. While it is often born out of domination, the racialized and ethnicized group often gradually identifies with and even embraces the ascribed identity and thus becomes a self-ascribed race or ethnicity. These processes have been common across the history of imperialism, nationalism, and racial and ethnic hierarchies.

RACISM: Oppression against individuals or groups based on their actual or perceived racial identity. The use of race to establish and justify a social hierarchy and system of power that privileges, preferences or advances certain individuals or groups of people usually at the expense of others. Racism is perpetuated through both interpersonal and institutional practices.

SEGREGATION: A system that keeps different groups separate from each other, either through physical dividers or using social pressures and laws. Segregation may also be a mutually voluntary arrangement but more frequently it is enforced by the majority group and its institutions. Exclusive neighborhoods and gated communities that are predominantly white are examples of economic segregation and demonstrate how whiteness and middle- to upper-class ideologies are mutually reinforcing.

TRAGIC MULATTO: The tragic mulatto is an archetypical mixed-race person (a "mulatto"), who is assumed to be sad, or even suicidal, because they fail to completely fit in the white world or the black world.

TRANSCULTURAL: A person, or state of mind that is highly influenced by many cultures and ethnicities. People of this nature often speak more than one language, have lived in different countries, listen to various types of music, date outside of their race, and so on.

TRANSRACIAL: A person who is born of one race, who makes the decision to become or represent themselves as another race. This is often done by persons who are mixed or biracial and can hence pass for multiple races.

WHITE PRIVILEGE: It implies that being born with white skin in America affords people certain unearned privileges in life that people of another skin color simple are not afforded. There are many different types of privilege, not just skin color privilege, which impacts the way people can move through the world or are discriminated against. It is not something you earned, it is something you are born into that afford you opportunities others may not have.

WHITE SUPREMACY: White supremacy – the belief in the superiority of the white race, especially in matters of intelligence and culture – achieved the height of its popularity during the period of European colonial expansion to the Western Hemisphere, Africa, and Asia stretching from the late 1800s to the first half of the twentieth-century. White supremacists have based their ideas on a variety of theories and supposedly proven facts; the most prominent of these include the claims of pseudo-scientific racist academic research that attempted to correlate inferiority and pathological behavior with categories of racial phenotypes, especially head size in the case of eugenics. There is a direct correlation between the rise of imperialism and colonialism, and the expansion of white supremacist ideology justifying the changing international order, which increasingly saw Europeans assuming political control over peoples of darker skin color through military force and ideological means, such as religion and education. It is important to note that the range of those considered "white" expanded considerably in the twentieth century. For example, in the United States, not all ethnic groups with white skin were initially considered white. It was not until well into the twentieth century that the Irish and Italians, for example, were considered white. By the end of that century, the United States federal government had also expanded its definition of whites to include Arabs.

WHITE: Not a true skin color, it is a racial classification specifier used for people of European ancestry. The contemporary usage of "white people" as a group contrasts with the terms "black," "colored," or "non-white," which originates in the seventeenth century. Today it is used as a racial classifier in multiracial societies, such as the United States (White American), the United Kingdom (White British), Brazil (White Brazilian), and South Africa (White South African). Various social constructs of whiteness have been significant to national identity, public policy, religion, population statistics, racial segregation, affirmative action, white privilege, eugenics, racial marginalization and racial quotas. ■

APPENDIX 2

■ ■ ■

Suggested Reading

Abrams, Sil Lai. Black Lotus: A Woman's Search for Racial Identity. New York: Gallery Books/Karen Hunter Publishing, 2016.

Bailey, Cornelia Walker and Bledsoe, Christena. God, Dr. Buzzard, and the Bolito Man: A Saltwater Geechee Talks About Life on Sapelo Island, Georgia. New York: Anchor, 2001.

Beltran, Mary C. and Camilla Fojas. Mixed Race Hollywood. New York: New York University, 2008.

Betts, Tara. Arc & Hue. New Jersey: Aquarius Press, 2009.

Botts, Tina Fernandes. Philosophy and the Mixed Race Experience. Lanham, MD: Lexington Books, 2016.

Bow, Leslie. Partly Colored: Asian Americans and Racial Anomaly in the Segregated South. New York: New York University Press, 2010.

Broyard, Bliss. One Drop: My Father's Hidden Life – A Story of Race and Family Secrets. New York: Back Bay Books, 2008.

Carter, Greg. The United States of the United Races: A Utopian History of Racial Mixing. New York: New York University Press, 2013.

Cashin, Sheryll, Loving: Interracial Intimacy in America and the Threat to White Supremacy. Boston: Beacon, 2017.

Chang, Sharon H. Raising Mixed Race: Multiracial Asian Children in a Post-Racial World New Critical Viewpoints on Society. U.K.: Routledge, 2015.

Cross, June. Secret Daughter: A Mixed race Daughter and the Mother Who Gave Her Away. New York: Penguin Books, 2007.

Durrow, Heidi W. The Girl Who Fell from the Sky. New York: Algonquin Books, 2011.

Elam, Michele. The Souls of Mixed Folk: Race, Politics, and Aesthetics in the New Millennium. Palo Alto, CA: Stanford University Press, 2011.

Forbes, Jack D. Black Africans and Native Americans: colour, race and caste in the evolution of red-black peoples. Oxford: Basil Blackwell, 1988.

Fulbeck, Kip. Part Asian, 100% Hapa. San Francisco: Chronicle Books, 2006.

Funderburg, Lise. Black, White, Other: Biracial Americans Talk About Race and Identity. New York: Harper Perennial, 1995.

Garrod, Andrew, Robert Kilkenny and Christina Gómez. Mixed: Multiracial College Students Tell Their Life Stories. New York: Cornell University Press, 2013.

Guevarra, Rudy P. Becoming Mexipino: Multiethnic Identities and Communities in San Diego. New Jersey: Rutgers University Press, 2012.

Ho, Jennifer. Racial Ambiguity in Asian American Culture. New Jersey: Rutgers University Press, 2015.

Hofmann, Kevin D. Growing up Black in White. Toledo, OH: The Vine Appointment Publishing Company, 2010.

Jackson, Michelle Gordon. Light, Bright and Damn Near White: Black Leaders Created. The One-Drop Rule. Royal Oak, MI: Jackson Scribe Publishing Company, 2014.

Jolivette, Andrew. Louisiana Creoles: Cultural Recovery and Mixed race Native American Identity. Lanham, MD: Lexington Books, 2007.

Kein, Sybil. Creole: The History and Legacy of Louisiana's Free People of Color. Louisiana: LSU Press, 2000.

Khanna, Nikki. Biracial in America: Forming and Performing Racial Identity. Lanham, MD: Lexington Books, 2011.

Kina, Laura and Wei Ming Dariotis. War Baby/Love Child: Mixed Race Asian American Art. Seattle: University of Washington Press, 2013.

McBride, James. The Color of Water: A Black Man's Tribute to His White Mother. New York: Riverhead Books, 2006.

Murphy-Shigematsu, Stephen. When Half Is Whole: Multiethnic Asian American Identities. Palo Alto, CA: Stanford University Press, 2012.

Ng, Celeste. Everything I Never Told You. New York: Penguin, 2015.

Obama, Barack. Dreams from My Father: A Story of Race and Inheritance. New York: Broadway Books, 2004.

O'Hearn, Claudine Chiawei. Half and Half: Writers on Growing Up Biracial and Bicultural. New York: Pantheon, 1998.

Ozeki, Ruth. My Year of Meats. New York: Penguin, 1998.

Pascoe, Peggy. What Comes Naturally: Miscegenation Law and the Making of Race in America. U.K: Oxford University Press, 2010.

Pollitzer, William. The Gullah People and Their African Heritage. University of Georgia Press, 2005.

Prasad, Chandra. Mixed: An Anthology of Short Fiction on the Multiracial Experience. New York: W. W. Norton & Company, 2006.

Rockquemore, Kerry Ann. Beyond Black: Biracial Identity in America. Lanham, MD: Rowman & Littlefield Publishers, 2007.

Root, Maria P. P. The multi-racial experience: racial borders as the new frontier. Thousand Oaks, CA: Sage Publications, 1996.

Root, Maria P. P. Racially Mixed People in America. Thousand Oaks, CA: SAGE Publications, 1992.

Rowell, Victoria. The Women Who Raised Me: A Memoir. New York: William Morrow, 2008.

Sheffer, Jolie. The Romance of Race: Incest, Miscegenation, and Multiculturalism in the United States (1880-1930). New Jersey: Rutgers University Press, 2012.

Spickard, Paul. Race in Mind: Critical Essays. Indiana: University of Notre Dame Press, 2015.

Spickard, Paul. Mixed Blood: Intermarriage & Ethnic: Intermarriage and Ethnic Identity in Twentieth Century America. Madison: University of Wisconsin Press, 1991.

Tharps, Lori L. Same Family, Different Colors: Confronting Colorism in America's Diverse Families. Boston: Beacon Press, 2016.

Trethewey, Natasha. Bellocq's Ophelia. Minneapolis: Graywolf Press, 2002.

Walker, Rebecca. Black, White & Jewish: Autobiography of a Shifting Self. New York: Riverhead Books, 2002.

Washington-Williams, Essie Mae. Dear Senator: A Memoir. The Daughter of Strom Thurmond. New York: Harper Perennial, 2006.

Williams-Leon, Teresa and Nakashima, Cynthia L. The Sum of Our Parts: Mixed-Heritage Asian Americans. Philadelphia: Temple University Press, 2001.

Williamson, Joel. New People: Miscegenation and Mulattoes in the United States. Louisiana: LSU Press, 1995.

Worrall, Brandy Lien. Completely Mixed Up: Mixed Heritage Asian North American Writing and Art. Vancouver, B.C.: Rabbit Fool Press, 2015.

Zack, Naomi, editor. American Mixed Race: The Culture of Microdiversity. Lanham, MD: Rowman & Littlefield Publishers, 1995. ∎

ABOUT THE CONTRIBUTORS

■ ■ ■

CARLOS ADAMS began his college career at the age of thirty six. He attended Whatcom Community College where he was the recipient of the Laidlaw Award for Outstanding Graduate. He transferred to Fairhaven College of Interdisciplinary Studies at Western Washington University, and majored in American Cultural Studies. Adams received the Outstanding Graduate Award from the American Cultural Studies Program, and was selected to speak at his graduation ceremony. Adams went on to receive his graduate degrees at Washington State University majoring in American Studies. After graduation, he taught at several colleges and universities, and currently teaches American Minority and Ethnic Studies as an adjunct instructor at Pierce and Green River Colleges in Washington State.

DEDRIA HUMPHRIES BARKER is a member of the Squaw Valley Community of Writers. Her work has appeared in Redbook magazine, The Detroit News, *ABSO-LUTE VISIONS: An Anthology of Speculative Fiction, Literary Mama,* and Sundry: A Journal of the Arts. She has been published by the Society for the Study of Midwestern Literature and the Ohio and Michigan historical societies. A native of Detroit, she earned an MA in English from Wayne State University, moved to the state capital and became a professor of English at Lansing Community College. TWITTER: @dedria_hb.

CARLY BATES is from Phoenix, Arizona. She received a BA of music from Arizona State University in 2016. "French Vanilla" is from a larger performance piece entitled "Negotiations," in which Bates and her collaborators, Raji Ganesan and Allyson Yoder, explore identity, heritage, and disbelonging. She currently works with Essential Theater, a local playback theatre company, and is the editor of the *Mixed Roots Stories Commons.* http://mixedrootsstories.com.

JACKSON BLISS is a hapa writer of fiction and creative nonfiction. He has a MFA in fiction from the University of Notre Dame where he was a Fiction Fellow, and winner of the 2007 Sparks Prize. He earned his PhD in literature and creative writing from University of Southern California where he worked with TC Boyle, Aimee Bender, and Viet Thanh Nguyen as a College Merit Award Fellow, FLAS fellow in Japanese, and two-time ACE/Nikaido Fellow. Jackson was the first 2013 runner-up for the Poets & Writer's California Exchange Award in fiction. His short stories and essays have appeared or are forthcoming in several publications including *Antioch Review, Guernica, Kenyon Review, Fiction, Boston Review, Tin House ZYZZYVA, Arts & Letters, Notre Dame Review, 2012-2013 Anthology of APIA Literature, African American Review, Kartika Review,* and the *Huffington Post UK.* Jackson teaches creative writing, literature, and rhetoric at the University of California Irvine and CSUN. www.jacksonbliss.com.

F. DOUGLAS BROWN is the author of *Zero to Three* (University of Georgia Press 2014), recipient of the 2013 Cave Canem Poetry Prize. He also co-authored with poet Geffrey Davis, *Begotten* (November 2016), a forthcoming chapbook of poetry from Upper Rubber Boot Books as part of their Floodgate Poetry series. Brown teaches English at Loyola High School of Los Angeles, and is both a Cave Canem and Kundiman fellow. His poems have appeared in the *Academy of American Poets, The Virginia Quarterly (VQR), Bat City Review, The Chicago Quarterly Review (CQR), The Southern Humanities Review, The Sugar House Review, Cura Magazine,* and *Muzzle Magazine.* www.fdouglasbrown.com.

ALISON CARR was born in San Francisco, California and raised in rural Maine. She studied at Tufts University, and received her MSW from the University of Michigan. She is a school social worker, and currently resides in Brooklyn, New York.

FREDRICK D. KAKINAMI CLOYD was born in Ōme, Japan to an African American father and Japanese mother. He received his MA in cultural anthropology and social transformation, and has published in *Oakland Word, National Japanese American Historical Society Journal,* and *Discover Nikkei,* an online journal. His poem "For Kiyoko, Epitaph/Chikai" was published in *Kartika Review* (Spring 2012), and was exhibited in "Generation Nexus: Peace in the Postwar Era" exhibit for the grand opening of the Historical Learning Center for the National Japanese American Historical Society in San Francisco in 2013. His first book: *Dream of the Water Children: Memory and Mourning in the Black Pacific* (2Leaf Press) is due for release in 2017. http://dreamwaterchildren.net

SANTANA DEMPSEY, who was adopted along with her biological sister at the age of six, is a professional actress and transracial adoption advocate. She graduated cum laude from the University of Missouri, Columbia with a BA in theatre, and is best known for her one-woman show "The Other Box," which was a finalist for the Hispanic Playwrights Residency Lab at INTAR Theatre in New York City. Since then, she has performed in that play in New York City and Los Angeles. Her first literary work, "Thanks Mom and Dad," published in *Woman Speak Magazine.* Dempsey currently resides in Los Angeles, California and is working on an interdisciplinary art project called, *Somewhere In Between.* www.santanadempsey.com. FACEBOOK: @ Santana-Dempsey-316054305249659, INSTAGRAM: @santanadempsey, TWITTER: @SantanaDempsey

TIMEKA DREW received a BA with honors from Indiana University, Bloomington where she studied religious studies after spending three years in the prestigious Honors Program at The Catholic University of America in Washington D.C. She worked for the *Mobile Press-Register's* family of publications, serving as editor of its parenting magazine, *Bay Family* and was a regular contributor to the weekly lifestyle publication, *Zalea,* and the weekly arts and culture newspaper, *Current.* She is currently the National Director of the Liberty Tree Foundation.

NAOMI RAQUEL ENRIGHT was born to an American father and an Ecuadorian mother in La Paz, Bolivia, and raised in New York City. She has a longstanding interest in issues of identity and culture, and is currently a diversity practitioner in a New York City independent school. She holds a BA in anthropology from Kenyon College and previously taught Spanish. Enright currently resides in Brooklyn, New York.

MONA LISA CHAVEZ-ESQUEDA is currently a PhD candidate at the University of Utah, College of Social Work. She is a school social worker at a local elementary school, and a psychotherapist in a private practice.

ANIKA FAJARDO was born in Colombia and raised in Minnesota. She has earned awards from the Jerome Foundation, the Minnesota State Arts Board, and the Loft Literary Center. Her writing has been published in journals such as *Los Angeles Review of Books, Hippocampus Magazine,* and *Dos Passos Review,* and in several anthologies including *Brief Encounters: A Collection of Contemporary Nonfiction* (WW Norton, 2015), and *Sky Blue Water: Great Stories for Young Readers* (University of Minnesota Press, 2016). She lives in Minneapolis where she serves on the board of the Loft Literary Center.

LIBERTY FERDA earned an MFA in creative nonfiction from the University of Pittsburgh. She currently writes on race and adoption for "The Lost Daughters" website (www.thelostdaughters.com), and is a regular contributor to magazines and newspapers in the Pittsburgh region. Some of her other publications include contributions to *Other Tongues: Mixed Race Women Speak Out* (Inanna Publications, 2010) and *Psalms for Mother Emanuel: an Elegy from Pittsburgh to Charleston* (The Pittsburgh Foundation, 2016), a poetry chapbook addressing the racially-charged shooting at Mother Emanuel church in 2015.

CHELSEA LEMON FETZER holds an MFA in fiction from Syracuse University. Her fiction and poetry have appeared in journals such as *Callaloo, Tin House, Mississippi Review,* and *Minnesota Review.* A selection of her poetry received the honor of finalist for the 2015 Venture Award, and her debut chapbook is in the works. Fetzer is the founder of the nonprofit organization, The Create Collective, Inc., and has also led writing workshops through PEN American Center's "Readers & Writers" program, the Black Writers Conference at Medgar Evers College, the New York Writers Coalition, and LitMore. She currently lives in Baltimore where she serves on the board of CityLit Project.

WAYNE MARTIN FREEMAN is originally from Chino, California. He holds a BA in anthropology from the University of California Riverside, and a MA in communication from the University of Colorado Boulder. He is currently a PhD student in the department of Ethnic Studies at the University of Colorado Boulder.

FRANCES FROST has published two novels, *Mourning Calm* (InvisionBooks, 2016), and *Life in Spades* (InvisionBooks, 2013). An author and independent publisher, Frost is a graduate of Wake Forest University and the University of Delaware. Born in Seoul, South Korea and raised in San Antonio, Texas and Baltimore, Maryland, she currently resides in Silver Spring, Maryland. www.francesfrost.com.

WENDY A. GAUDIN is an American historian, an essayist, poet, university educator, and the proud descendant of Louisiana Creoles who migrated to California. She earned her PhD in American History from New York University, with prior degrees from the California State University and the Louisiana State University. Her essay, "Beauty," won the *North American Review's* 2016 Torch Memorial Prize for creative nonfiction. Her most recent publication, "The Women Who Loved Beauty," was featured in the spring 2017 issue of *Puerto Del Sol.* Gaudin currently teaches at Xavier University of Louisiana.

HERBERT HARRIS is a native of Washington, D.C., where he attended George-town University. He subsequently obtained an MD and PhD from the University of Pittsburgh, School of Medicine, and completed his residency training in psychiatry at Yale University. While attending Yale, Harris organized a conference on race and identity, and edited *Racial Identity: Psychological Development and Creative Expression* (Routledge, 1995), which was based on the conference. His career has included both research and clinical practice, and he has held several research positions in govern-ment and industry. He is currently in private practice in Chapel Hill, North Carolina.

RENA M. HEINRICH, raised in Anchorage, Alaska, is a theater director and actor who has been directing and performing professionally for over twenty years. She is a PhD candidate in Theater Studies at the University of California, Santa Barbara, specializing in the shifting identities of mixed race figures in American drama. Hein-rich is also the co-creator and co-host of "Hapa Happy Hour," a podcast dedicated to exploring and celebrating the mixed race experience.

VELINA HASU HOUSTON is an internationally celebrated writer with over twenty commissions in theatre and opera. Her work has been produced nationwide and globally to critical acclaim at prestigious institutions, notably the Manhattan Theatre Club, Los Angeles Opera, The Pasadena Playhouse, and the Old Globe Theatre. Honored by the Kennedy Center, Smithsonian Institute, Rockefeller Foundation, Japan Foundation, Wallace Foundation, Doris Duke Charitable Foundation, and others. Houston founded graduate playwriting studies at the School of Dramatic Arts, University of Southern California, where she is Distinguished Professor of Dramatic Writing, Resident Playwright, Director of Dramatic Writing, and Asso-ciate Dean of Faculty. A Fulbright scholar, she served on the U.S. Department of State's Japan-U.S. Friendship Commission for six years, and writes critically about representations of mixed race in cinema and theatre. She currently resides in Los Angeles, California. A published poet and essayist, she adapted her signature play, *Tea,* into a novel of the same title, due in 2017 from Showa Press. https://matchabook.wordpress.com, http://www.velinahasuhouston.com, TWITTER: @gyokurogirl, INSTAGRAM: @gyokurogirl, SNAPCHAT: @matsuyamamama.

MARK S. JAMES is an assistant professor of English at Molloy College in Rockville Centre, New York, and teaches American literature, African American literature, and American studies. He is a former Fulbright Scholar to Ukraine, and his published work has appeared in *Icons of African American Literature, The Black Literary World* (Greenwood, 2011), and www.mixedracestudies.org.

ALLYSON JEFFREDO is the 2016 recipient of The Loft Spoken Word Immersion Fellowship. She published her first chapbook of poetry, *Songs After Memory Fractures* (Finishing Line Press, 2016), and has published her work in *The Fem, Cider Press Review, Slipstream Press* and others. She received her MFA in creative writing from California State University San Bernardino, and currently teaches writing to elementary and college students of the Inland Empire (Southern California).

NADINE M. KNIGHT grew up in Baltimore, Maryland. She received her PhD in English and American language and literature from Harvard University, and is currently an associate professor of English, and is affiliated with Africana Studies at College of the Holy Cross in Worcester, Massachusetts. Her primary scholarly interests are in African American literature and American Civil War studies. Knight's articles have appeared in *MELUS: Multiethnic Literature of the United States, College Literature,* and *New Voices in Classical Reception Studies.* http://www.holycross.edu/academics/programs/english/faculty/nadine-m-knight

JEWEL LOVE is originally from Oakland, California. During his senior year of high school he began to learn about social justice issues and race relations in America, which helped him become a more self-actualized human being. He received his MA in clinical psychology from Antioch University, and his BA in Black Studies from UC Santa Barbara. He is a marriage and family therapist intern in private practice, in Oakland, California.

DEVORAH MAJOR is an award winning poet and fiction writer, creative non-fiction writer, performer, and editor. She served as San Francisco's third Poet Laureate (2002-2006); is a senior adjunct professor in the Diversity Studies and Writing and Literature departments at California College of the Arts; and poet-in-residence of the San Francisco's Fine Arts Museums. She has published five poetry collections, two novels, and two biographies for young people. Her latest poetry collection is *and then we became* (City Lights Books, 2016), and her poetry collection *street smarts* (Curbstone Press, 1996) received the PEN Oakland Josephine Miles Literary Excellence Award. Her novel, *An Open Weave* (Seal Press, 1997), won the ALA Black Caucus First Novel Award. In June 2015, major premiered her poetry play "Classic Black: Voices of 19th Century African Americans in San Francisco" at the San Francisco International Arts Festival, and was commissioned by the Oakland East Bay Symphony in 2004 to collaborate with composer Guillermo Galindo to create and perform in "Trade Routes," a symphony with spoken word and chorus that premiered in 2005. major-harden has read and performed nationally and internationally. www.devorahmajor.com. FACEBOOK: @devorah.major, INSTA-GRAM: @devmajor, TWITTER: @devorahmajor.

JANE MARCHANT is a writer, photographer, and activist from Berkeley, California. She has lived in treehouses in Southern Turkey, slept under the stars in the Australian Outback, and visited every nature park in the Hashemite Kingdom of Jordan. She is currently writing a research-based memoir on her family's history of racial passing, for which she has received funding from the John Anson Kittredge Fund. Marchant's writing and photography have appeared in *Guernica/A Magazine of Art & Politics, The Columbia Science Review,* and the Buzzfeed Community. She holds a BA in creative writing from Columbia University, where she is pursuing her MFA in nonfiction writing. www.janerebeccamarchant.com.

RACHEL MASILAMANI is a Pittsburgh-based comics creator who has been quietly amassing a unique and significant body of work since the dawn of the century. She was awarded a Xeric Grant for the first issue of her series, RPM Comics, and has published her work in small run self-published comics and anthologies like the *Indiana Review, Graphic Classics* and *Aster(ix).* She is currently working on a new graphic novel, *Nonpartum,* which is being published in installments on *Mutha Magazine.* http://www.rpmcomics.com. http://muthamagazine.com/author/rachel-masilamani/

JENI MCFARLAND holds an MFA in fiction from the University of Houston, where she served as a fiction editor for *Gulf Coast* magazine. She is a 2016 Kimbilio Fellow, with work appearing in *Crack the Spine, Forge,* and *Spry,* which nominated her for the *storySouth* Million Writers Award. She is also a finalist for the 2015 Gertrude Stein Award in Fiction from the *Doctor T. J. Eckleberg Review.* She currently resides in Concord, California. TWITTER: @jeni_mcfarland.

ABRA MIMS is a native Texan who currently resides in Boston, Massachusetts. Her work has appeared on the website, "Knot So Subtle," and she was a cast member of the 2016 "Boston Listen to Your Mother" show. www.brownmomwhitebaby.com.

VIA PERKINS is a multidisciplinary artist from the Boston area, and earned her BA in music from Salem State University in 2013. As a writer and researcher of mixed race identity, she presented honors thesis *Burgeoning Biraciality* at the UMass Amherst Undergraduate Research Conference, and served as a panelist for the Mixed Remixed Festival in Los Angeles. Perkins currently works as a journalist for the *Local Town Pages.* LINKEDIN: @viaperkins.

EMAN RIMAWI, a black, Native American and Palestinian woman, is a spoken-word artist, educator, and youth organizer for dozens of nonprofit organizations in New York City including The Audre Lorde Project, FUREE, Casa Atabex Ache, and The Jed Foundation. She teaches creative writing, community organizing, history, and political science workshops to youth in New York City. As a recent amputee who lost both of her legs, she founded AMPed Up (http://ampedupclothing.com/), a clothing line for and by amputees. Rimawi is currently developing graphic novels and children's books where differently-abled people are the main characters, as well as facilitating workshops to support businesses who employ differently-abled people to better support and interact with their staff. www.emanrimawi.com. FACEBOOK: @emanrimawiandtheworld.

CHARLES MATTHEW SNYDER, raised in the San Francisco Bay Area and Vallejo, California, studied at California State University Dominguez Hills in Carson. In 2015, Snyder joined the VONA (Voices of Our Nation) community as a Poetry Fellow. Since then, his poetry has appeared in *Abernathy Magazine* and his essay, "That Blue Gold: Reflections on American Privilege," in *Los Morenas de España*. Snyder is working on his first collection of poetry. www.charliesnyderpoet.com. FACEBOOK: @SnyderActorWriter.

LILY ANNE WELTY TAMAI grew up in the agricultural community of Oxnard, California, speaking Japanese and English in a mixed-race household. Tamai has a PhD in History from the University of California Santa Barbara. She conducted doctoral research in Japan and in Okinawa as a Fulbright Graduate Research Fellow and was also a Ford Foundation Fellow. She published a chapter in *Global Mixed Race* (NYU Press 2014), as well as journal articles in *Pan Japan, and Southern California Quarterly*. Her forthcoming book is titled, *Military Industrial Intimacy: Mixed Race American Japanese, Eugenics and Transnational Identities*. Tamai is the former curator of history at the Japanese American National Museum in Los Angeles. She is currently a lecturer at UCLA in the Asian American Studies Department. She also serves on the U.S. Census Bureau National Advisory Committee on Racial, Ethnic, and Other Populations.

KYLA KUPFERSTEIN TORRES is a writer and educator. She lives in New York City with her husband and son.

DIANA EMIKO TSUCHIDA was born and raised in San Jose, California. She has written on the perceptions and representations of mixed race Asian American women, and conducted interviews with some of the most influential Asian American women in the culinary world. Her work has appeared in the *Village Voice, Those People,* and the Center for Asian American Media. Tsuchida is the creator of "Tessaku," a historical project that collects interviews with Japanese Americans who experienced the internment camps. She received her MA in Ethnic Studies from San Francisco State University, and is currently a freelance digital media consultant and copywriter. http://dianaemiko.com. TWITTER: @emikosworld, INSTAGRAM: @dianaemiko.

JENNY TURNER has an MS in biology from University of California, San Diego and an ScB in biology from Brown University in Providence, Rhode Island. She works as a medical editor and desktop publisher in the San Diego area.

MAYA WASHINGTON is a poet, actor, filmmaker, and arts educator. She holds a BA from the University of Southern California, and an MFA from Hamline University. Her work has appeared in literary journals and anthologies including *Prairie Schooner, Gulf Coast,* and *The Playwright's Center Monologues for Women* (Heinemann Drama, 2005). She edited *White Space Poetry Anthology* (2014), featuring the work of deaf and hearing artists (www.whitespacepoetryproject.com) as a companion to her award-winning film, *White Space* (2011). She is currently in post-production on the football documentary, *Through the Banks of the Red Cedar* about her father, Vikings and Michigan State football legend Gene Washington. She has received funding from the Jerome Foundation, Minnesota State Arts Board, Minnesota Film and Television and others. Her film work has allowed her projects to have a global reach, most recently in Toronto, Budapest, Hong Kong, Berlin, and Rome. www.mayawashington.org, and www.themayawashington.com. FACEBOOK: @ imayawashington, INSTAGRAM: imayawashington, TWITTER: @imayawashington.

SHIANE WILCOXEN, a native of Chicago currently residing in St. Louis, is a private chef and event planner, poet and writer. A graduate of the Robert Morris University-School of Culinary Arts in Chicago in 2006, she began teaching cake decorating and basic culinary skills to at-risk youth at park districts and youth centers throughout "Chicagoland." In 2010, Wilcoxen founded Team 101 Chicago, an LGBTQ youth based organization. She will release her first book of poetry and short stories, and her novel, *Kissing Skies*, in 2017.

JESSICA WILLIAMS holds degrees from Washington University in St. Louis and Georgetown University. She currently works in communications in Los Angeles, where she was born. Her writing can be found at DefunctTeenMag.com. This is her first publication. INSTAGRAM and TWITTER: @jwilljuice.∎

ABOUT CATHY J. SCHLUND-VIALS

■ ■ ■

CATHY J. SCHLUND-VIALS is a mixed race Cambodian and white American born in Thailand and adopted by an American Air Force father and a Japanese mother. It is this personal history that has shaped her as a scholar whose work is marked by immigration, migration and diaspora that repeatedly examines moments of dislocation, rupture, and movement. She holds a Joint Appointment as professor in the Department of English and the Asian and Asian American Studies Institute in the College of Liberal Arts and Sciences at the University of Connecticut, and has served as director of the Asian and Asian American Studies Institute at UConn since 2010. She currently serves as the President of the National Association for Asian American Studies.

Schlund-Vials' work on visual culture, popular culture, human rights, and Asian American studies has appeared in a number of collections and journals. She is the author of *Modeling Citizenship: Jewish and Asian American Writing* (Temple University Press, 2011), and *War, Genocide, and Justice: Cambodian American Memory Work* (2012). She has also co-edited and edited a number of collection, including *Disability, Human Rights, and the Limits of Humanitarianism* (2014), *Keywords for Asian American Studies* (2015), and *Interrogating the Perpetrator: Violation, Culpability, and Human Rights* (2016). Her latest book is *Asian America: A Primary Source Reader* (Yale University Press, 2017), co-edited with K. Scott Wong and Jason O. Chang, and she is currently working on a number of publishing projects with Fordham University Press, and University of Georgia Press. ■

ABOUT SEAN FREDERICK FORBES

■ ■ ■

PHOTO: Samuel LaHoz

SEAN FREDERICK FORBES is a mixed race professor, poet, and editor of Afro Latino descent. He currently serves as series editor of 2Leaf Press' 2LP EXPLORATIONS IN DIVERSITY, and is the co-editor of the series' first book, *WHAT DOES IT MEAN TO BE WHITE IN AMERICA? Breaking the White Code of Silence, A Collection of Personal Narratives* (2016), and series editor of *BLACK LIVES HAVE ALWAYS MATTERED, Black Lives Have Always Mattered, A Collection of Essays, Poems, and Personal Narratives.* The author of the poetry collection, *Providencia: A Book of Poems* (2013), Forbes' work has appeared in various journals including *Chagrin River Review, Crab Orchard Review, Long River Review, Midwest Quarterly,* and *Sargasso: A Journal of Caribbean Literature, Language and Culture.*

Forbes studied English and Africana Studies at Queens College (CUNY), where he was an Andrew W. Mellon Fellow, and received his MA and PhD in English from the University of Connecticut. In 2009, he received a Woodrow Wilson Mellon Mays University Fellows Travel and Research Grant for travel to Providencia, Colombia. Forbes served as associate director of Humanities House, a living and learning community, at the University of Connecticut during the 2013-2014 academic year. Forbes is the poetry and nonfiction reader for the journal *WESTVIEW* published by Southwestern Oklahoma State University. He also leads professional learning and growth workshops for elementary and secondary school teachers who seek to advance creative writing to the language arts curriculum. www.seanfrederickforbes.com. ■

ABOUT TARA BETTS

■ ■ ■

PHOTO: Tony Smith/DesignSmith

TARA BETTS is a mixed race award-winning poet, author and scholar of African American and white French descent. Betts is the author of *Break the Habit* (2016), *Arc and Hue* (2009) and the libretto, *The Greatest: An Homage to Muhammad Ali* (2010). She holds a Ph.D. in English from Binghamton University, and an MFA in creative writing from New England College. She was a lecturer in creative writing at Rutgers University in New Brunswick, New Jersey and is currently a professor at University of Illinois-Chicago. A Cave Canem graduate, she held residencies from the Ragdale Foundation, Centrum and Caldera, and was awarded an Illinois Arts Council Artist fellowship.

Her work has appeared in numerous journals and anthologies, including *POETRY, Ninth Letter, Crab Orchard Review, Essence, Nylon, American Poetry Review, Gathering Ground, Bum Rush the Page, Villanelles,* both *Spoken Word Revolution* anthologies, *The Break Beat Poets, Octavia's Brood: Science Fiction Stories from Social Justice Movements,* and *GHOST FISHING: An Eco-Justice Poetry Anthology.* She also appeared on HBO's "Def Poetry Jam" and the Black Family Channel series "SPOKEN" with Jessica Care Moore. www.tarabetts.net.■

ABOUT HEIDI W. DURROW

■■■

PHOTO: Timothi Jane Graham

HEIDI W. DURROW is mixed race of Danish and African American descent. She is *The New York Times* best-selling author of The Girl Who Fell From the Sky (2010), which received writer Barbara Kingsolver's PEN/Bellwether Prize for Socially Engaged Fiction, and is a book club favorite. *The Girl Who Fell From the Sky* has been hailed as one of the Best Novels of 2010 by the *Washington Post,* a Top 10 Book of 2010 by *The Oregonian,* and named a Top 10 Debut of 2010 by *Booklist. Ebony Magazine* named Durrow as one of its Power 100 Leaders, and in 2011 Durrow was nominated for an NAACP Image Award for Outstanding Literary Debut.

Durrow is a graduate of Stanford University, Columbia's Graduate School of Journalism, and Yale Law School. She has worked as a corporate attorney and a Life Skills trainer for professional athletes of the National Football League and the National Basketball Association. She is the founder and executive director of the Mixed Remixed Festival, a film, book and performance festival celebrating stories of the mixed race experience. She is an award-winning podcaster who currently hosts a weekly show called, "The Mixed Experience." Her writing has appeared in *The New York Times,* National Public Radio, and *Essence Magazine.* Durrow is an occasional contributor to National Public Radio and blogs for the *Huffington Post.* www.heidiwdurrow.com. ■

COVER ARTIST

■ ■ ■

LAURA KINA is a mixed race Asian American artist and Professor of Art, Media, & Design, and Director of Critical Ethnic Studies at DePaul University. She is cofounder of the Critical Mixed Race Studies Association and conference, and coeditor of *War Baby/Love Child: Mixed Race Asian American Art* (University of Washington Press, 2013) and *Queering Contemporary Asian American Art* (University of Washington Press, 2017).

Drawing inspiration from popular culture, art history, textile design, historic photographs and family photos, Kina's works focus on the fluidity of cultural difference and the slipperiness of identity. Asian American history and mixed race representations are subjects that run through her work. Colorful pattern fields combined with figurative elements and subtle narratives characterize her paintings. The work featured on the cover of *The Beiging of America* are from her "Loving Series." Her website is at www.laurakina.com.

Top Left: Laura Kina (artist). *Loving Series: Erik Glenn.* Charcoal on paper. 42.5 x 34 in. (2006)

Top Right: Laura Kina (artist). *Loving Series: Self-Portrait.* Charcoal on paper. 42.5 x 34 in. (2006)

Bottom Left: Laura Kina (artist). *Loving Series: Shoshanna Weinberger.* Charcoal on paper. 42.5 x 34 in. (2006)

Bottom Right: Laura Kina (artist). *Loving Series: Greg Grucel.* Charcoal on paper. 42.5 x 34 in. (2006)

OTHER BOOKS BY 2LEAF PRESS

■ ■ ■

2Leaf Press challenges the status quo by publishing alternative fiction, non-fiction, poetry and bilingual works by activists, academics, poets and authors dedicated to diversity and social justice with scholarship that is accessible to the general public. 2Leaf Press produces high quality and beautifully produced hardcover, paperback and ebook formats through our series: 2LP Translations, 2LP Classics, Nuyorican World Series, 2LP Explorations in Diversity and 2LP Current Affairs, Culture & Politics.

NOVELS
The Morning Side of the Hill
A Novella by Ezra E. Fitz, with an Introduction by Ernesto Quiñonez

LITERARY NONFICTION
Our Nuyorican Thing, The Birth of a Self-Made Identity
by Samuel Carrion Diaz, with an Introduction by Urayoán Noel
Bilingual: English/Spanish
(NUYORICAN WORLD SERIES)

YOUNG ADULT
Puerto Rican Folktales/Cuentos folclóricos puertorriqueños
by Lisa Sánchez González
Bilingual: English/Spanish, Available in Hard Cover only
(NUYORICAN WORLD SERIES)

ANTHOLOGIES
Nothing to be Gained Here: Less Than Ideal Art and Ideas for a Less Than Ideal World
by Vagabond
(NUYORICAN WORLD SERIES)

Black Lives Have Always Mattered
A Collection of Essays, Poems, and Personal Narratives
Edited by Abiodun Oyewole
(2LP EXPLORATIONS IN DIVERSITY)

The Beiging of America:
Personal Narratives about Being Mixed Race in the 21st Century
Edited by Cathy J. Schlund-Vials and Tara Betts, with a Foreword by Michelle Elam and an Afterword by Heidi Durrow
(2LP EXPLORATIONS IN DIVERSITY)

What Does it Mean to be White in America?
Breaking the White Code of Silence, A Collection of Personal Narratives
Edited by Gabrielle David and Sean Frederick Forbes
Introduction by Debby Irving and Afterword by Tara Betts
(2LP EXPLORATIONS IN DIVERSITY)

WHEREABOUTS: Stepping Out of Place,
An Outside in Literary & Travel Magazine Anthology
Edited by Brandi Dawn Henderson

PLAYS
Rivers of Women, The Play
by Shirley Bradley LeFlore, with photographs by Michael J. Bracey
(Available in Paperback only)

MUSIC/ARTWORK
Die Jim Crow-The EP
Edited by Fury Young, Artwork by Marc. B. Springer

AUTOBIOGRAPHIES/MEMOIRS
The Fourth Moment: Journeys from the Known to the Unknown, A Memoir
by CJ. Garrison, Introduction by Sarah Willis

Dream of the Water Children:
Memory and Mourning in the Black Pacific
by Fredrick D. Kakinami Cloyd
Foreword by Velina Hasu Houston, Introduction by Gerald Horne

POETRY
Written Eye: Visuals/Verse
by A. Robert Lee

A Country Without Borders: Poems and Stories of Kashmir
by Lalita Pandit Hogan, with an Introduction by Frederick Luis Aldama

Tartessos and Other Cities, Poems by Claire Millikin
by Claire Millikin, with an Introduction by Fred Marchant

Off Course: Roundabouts & Deviations
by A. Robert Lee

The Death of the Goddess, A Poem in Twelve Cantos
by Patrick Colm Hogan, with an Introduction by Rachel Fell McDermott

Branches of the Tree of Life
The Collected Poems of Abiodun Oyewole 1969-2013
by Abiodun Oyewole, edited by Gabrielle David
with an Introduction by Betty J. Dopson

After Houses, Poetry for the Homeless
by Claire Millikin, with an Introduction by Tara Betts

Birds on the Kiswar Tree
by Odi Gonzales, Translated by Lynn Levin
Bilingual: English/Spanish
(2LP TRANSLATIONS)

Boricua Passport
by J.L. Torres
(NUYORICAN WORLD SERIES)

Incessant Beauty, A Bilingual Anthology
by Ana Rossetti, Edited and Translated by Carmela Ferradáns
Bilingual: English/Spanish
(2LP TRANSLATIONS)

The Last of the Po'Ricans y Otros Afro-artifacts
Poems by Not4Prophet, Graphics by Vagabond
with an Introduction by Tony Medina
(NUYORICAN WORLD SERIES)

Providencia, A Book of Poems
by Sean Frederick Forbes, with an Introduction by V. Penelope Pelizzon

Broke Baroque
by Tony Medina, with an Introduction by Ishmael Reed

Brassbones & Rainbows, The Collected Works of Shirley Bradley LeFlore
by Shirley Bradley LeFlore, Preface by Amina Baraka,
with an Introduction by Gabrielle David

Imaginarium: Sightings, Galleries, Sightlines
by A. Robert Lee

Hey Yo! Yo Soy!, 40 Years of Nuyorican Street Poetry,
The Collected Works of Jesús Papoleto Meléndez
Edited by Gabrielle David and Kevin E. Tobar Pesántez
Translations by Adam Wier, Carolina Fung Feng, Marjorie González
Foreword by Samuel Diaz and Carmen M. Pietri-Diaz,
Introduction by Sandra Maria Esteves, Afterword by Jaime "Shaggy" Flores
Bilingual: English/Spanish
(NUYORICAN WORLD SERIES)

2Leaf Press is an imprint owned and operated by the Intercultural Alliance of Artists & Scholars, Inc. (IAAS), a NY-based nonprofit organization that publishes and promotes multicultural literature.

NEW YORK
www.2leafpress.org

Made in the USA
Coppell, TX
10 January 2021

47965700R00155